HUGH MILLER: OUTRAGE AND ORDER

HUGH MILLER
OUTRAGE AND ORDER
A Biography And Selected Writings

By George Rosie
With An Introduction By Neal Ascherson

Dedicated to the memory
of Harriet Simpson Tait Rosie

MAINSTREAM
PUBLISHING

Introduction © Neal Ascherson
Biography © George Rosie

This edition published by
MAINSTREAM PUBLISHING COMPANY (EDINBURGH) LTD.
25a South West Thistle Street Lane
Edinburgh EH2 1EW

The publisher acknowledges the financial assistance of the Scottish
Arts Council in the publication of this volume.

ISBN 0 906391 17 2

Typeset by Spectrum Printing Company, Edinburgh.
Printed by Billing & Sons Ltd., Guildford, London and Worcester

EDITORIAL NOTE

The work of Hugh Miller has been surprisingly, and perhaps shamefully, neglected. Since the beginning of the twentieth century very little has been written about the Cromarty stonemason who became one of Victorian Britain's most successful scientific popularisers and newspaper editors, and none of Miller's books— which were hugely successful in the latter half of the nineteenth century—are now in print. So the idea behind this book is to do something at least to repair the omission, and hopefully spark off some interest in the remarkable work of a remarkable man.

To an extent, therefore, the book is a sampler of Hugh Miller's writing; a brief biography setting the scene for a hopefully representative sample of Miller's huge output of essays and journalism. The biography is necessarily brief, too short, in fact, to do justice to Miller's dazzling, heroic, and often tragic life and career. A full-scale modern biography of Hugh Miller remains to be written.

All the essays and extracts in the collection have been edited; most lightly, a few quite heavily. Almost all Miller's writings appeared in the twice-weekly newspaper *The Witness* (of which he was the editor) and much of it contains references and names which meant much in the 1840s and 1850s, but would mean very little in the 1980s. Most of these have been taken out. Also, Miller's *Witness* had a Victorian fondness for gigantic paragraphs, and these have been broken up to something closer to modern useage.

In tinkering with Hugh Miller's writing I have been made aware that I am dealing with work that was subtle and intricate. In this respect I would like to thank my wife Liz for the editing work she did, and for her timely (and tactful) warning that I was over-editing and cutting too much. After her admonitions I tried to treat the essays with the light touch they deserve, and if my hand has been heavier than it should have been, I apologise in advance.

Thanks also to Neal Ascherson for his foreword and his enthusiasm for the idea of the book; to Sara Stevenson of the National Portrait Gallery of Scotland for help with the Hill Adamson photographs; to the staff of the country-life section of the National Museum of Antiquities; and to the ever-helpful custodians of the manuscripts in the National Library of Scotland.

George Rosie.
Edinburgh, 1981.

CONTENTS

INTRODUCTION
by
Neal Ascherson

"A PICTURESQUE figure indeed he must have seemed, as he passed moodily and ponderingly along the streets of Edinburgh . . . In figure, he was tall, though his chest weakness and stooping habits had bent him, so throwing his huge head forward with its reddish hair and whiskers, and giving him in his gait a sort of clumsy slouch. From under heavy brows came the flashing of his blue-grey eyes; the nose looked small between the mass atop and the square broad jaw below . . . "

So in his imagination W.M. Mackenzie saw Hugh Miller as he trundled along Princes Street, clutching his grey shepherd's plaid about him. The year might have been 1854 or 1855. Miller was at the height of his fame, and tourists pointed at his troll-like form in recognition. He was the editor of *The Witness*. He, next to Thomas Chalmers himself, had been the leading actor in the Disruption which tore apart the Church of Scotland ten years before. He was a self-taught palaeontologist whose work on Devonian fish fossils and attempts to reconcile the geological evidence with the doctrine of divine creation were famous throughout the English-speaking world. His numerous books and memoirs were to be found in most literate households in Scotland, and in North America as well. He was acquainted with great scientists like Agassiz and with pioneers like Octavius Hill, the Edinburgh photographer, whose calotypes of Miller dressed in the stonemason's clothes he had worn as a boy were to make his over-powerful features familiar to thousands a century later—thousands who had never heard of the once-mighty sage who sat for the picture.

This was a great Victorian indeed, but specifically a Scottish Victorian. Mathew Arnold may have thought himself tormented by doubt, a little black dog tagging along some distance behind him, but behind Hugh Miller came gigantic, bloody phantoms of irrational terror, shapes from that seventeenth century of fanaticism and witchcraft in which the Scottish consciousness finally crystallized. The great, squat man moving along the Edinburgh street already hid what Robert Chambers called "a jarring nerve in the brain". A few years later, he wrote a screaming, incoherent farewell note and shot himself through the chest. Three years after that, Darwin published

The Origin of Species which gradually but irretrievably washed away the fundamental principles of Miller's thought as if they were sandcastles on a beach.

Why he went mad and killed himself in that large, expensive house down at Portobello we do not really know. George Rosie speculates here that tertiary syphilis may have been responsible. The symptoms make this plausible, and Miller's frantic religiosity, even his effusiveness about his own marriage, suggest that there may be a Mr Hyde behind the scene. But there were enough intellectual tensions building up within Hugh Miller to blow him apart without physical disease. He was determined to have God as the prime mover in a scientific history of the earth. Prepared to argue, as with great ingenuity he did, that the Mosaic chronology of the Creation must be discarded and that each "day" in the Genesis account must be expanded to a geological epoch lasting thousands or millions of years; he could not admit that some principle other than a Creator's will brought about the slow succession of fossil forms.

Miller at first resisted Agassiz when the great man came to Scotland in 1840 to journey into the Highlands with a correspondent from *The Scotsman* and proclaim that this landscape had been created by glaciers (the greatest of all *Scotsman* scoops was Maclaren's exclusive series announcing to the world that there had been an Ice Age). He resisted all his life, with growing anxiety, the doctrines of "development" which were to find their most effective expression through Darwin; development, Miller wrote, "cashiers the Creator as such, and substitutes instead a mere animal manufacturing piece of clock-work which bears the name of natural law." Miller implied that each age of creation was static and quite distinct from the next, like a lantern-slide displayed for a moment, then snatched aside and replaced by another; far from believing in a positive natural selection, he thought in terms of a "degeneration of species" in which the earliest forms of each type were the most "noble" but which brought about the steady deterioration of the type—a prefiguration among lower creatures of the Fall of Man in the last age.

In this sense, Hugh Miller was a tragic intellectual hero. He volunteered to cover God's retreat, to hold off as long as he was able the encroaching armies of scientific materialism. Miller was the last man in Scotland who, until even his Atlas-muscles failed, held together the ancient sky in which science, philosophy and theology were stars in a single vault. But this Titan was also a journalist. He felt able and entitled to comment on every kind of question and event in Scotland and abroad, and he did so in the pages of *The Witness* and elsewhere. Here too there were contradictions; his sense of justice (Afghanistan, the Clearances) struggled with his instinct for order and submission; he was much less of a social and political radical than the more militant and fanatical elements who took over the Free Church after the Disruption, men at once less liberal than Miller and much more aware of the evils of inequality and physical poverty than he—even though he had begun his own life as an apprentice quarryman wandering the country in search of work.

In rediscovering, editing and publishing some of Hugh Miller's journalism, George Rosie has taken the decisive step in restoring this tormented, gifted figure to his proper stature in Scottish nineteenth-century history. And these extracts will provide some literary surprises for those who have never read him; Miller toiled for hours to achieve these gleaming, apparently effortless strokes of phrase, and he was perhaps the most consciously dramatic of all scientific writers in his own time. His books—*The Old Red Sandstone, My Schools and Schoolmasters* and the others—lived on in edition after edition for many decades after his death. But these articles, Miller reacting to his own day, for the first time allow us today to understand the grasp he had on the minds and the consciences of his contemporaries.

Part One
Hugh Miller: A Biography

HUGH MILLER: A BIOGRAPHY
by
George Rosie

LAST things first; some time in the early hours of Christmas Eve, 1856, Hugh Miller woke in the grip of a terrible dream, utterly oppressed by a sense of malevolence. He got out of bed, pulled on a heavy seaman's sweater, went into his study, found a piece of folio paper, and in the centre scribbled a brief note to his wife Lydia. "My brain burns," Miller wrote, "I *must* have *walked;* and a fearful dream rises upon me. I cannot bear the horrible thought. God and Father of the Lord Jesus Christ, have mercy upon me. Dearest Lydia, dear children, farewell. My brain burns as the recollection grows. My dear, dear wife farewell. Hugh Miller."

Miller then picked up the six-shot revolver he kept at his bedside, lifted his sweater, pressed the revolver against the left side of his chest, and pulled the trigger. He was killed more or less instantly as the bullet ripped into his left lung, grazed his heart, severed the pulmonary artery at the root, and lodged itself in one of his ribs. The revolver fell from Miller's hands, and he collapsed in the doorway between the two rooms. He was found in the morning by one of his servants, lying on his left side in a pool of blood.

Two days later four doctors (one of them Miller's close friend, and another his family doctor) carried out a post-mortem examination on his body, and swore "on soul and conscience" that Miller had been killed by the "pistol shot through the left side of his chest; and this, we are satisfied, was inflicted by his own hand." The four doctors concluded that, "From the diseased appearances found in the brain, taken in connection with the history of the case, we have no doubt that the act was suicidal under the impulse of insanity."

Hugh Miller's anguished suicide at the age of fifty-four at his home, Shrub Mount, in Portobello near Edinburgh, brought to a sudden halt one of the most remarkable careers to grace Victorian Britain. From a distinctly unpromising start as a stone-mason working the sandstone quarries and building sites of the northern Highlands, Miller grew into one of the most formidable—and influential—intellectuals in Scotland. He became a remarkable, wide-ranging essayist, a crusading newspaper editor, a tireless Presbyterian warrior, a brilliant and original geologist and palaeontologist, and one of the best popularisers of science in the mid-nineteenth century.

Miller's literary talent was enthused over by Charles Dickens and John Ruskin; his scientific expertise was highly-rated by Thomas Huxley, Charles Lyell, Louis Agassiz, Roderick Murchison and Richard Owen; his powers as a Protestant polemicist won the admiration of the great Presbyterian divine Thomas Chalmers; and as a moralist and philosopher Miller had no greater admirer than Thomas Carlyle who found his work suffused with "a peaceful radical heat that is beautiful to see" and who thought Miller's suicide was "the world's great loss".

At the same time, Miller was an enigmatic and often baffling man. He was, for instance, a romantic Scottish nationalist who deeply approved of the Union with England, a trained and highly-skilled bank officer who penned fanciful stories and sentimental verse, a fierce Presbyterian who was in favour of Catholic emancipation, a devout Christian who argued for secular education. Miller was a radically-inclined journalist who savaged the gentry, but who despised the Chartists and the Socialists, a man of the people who saved some of his bleakest words for the unruly Scottish working class. Miller was a hard-working scientist with a powerful undertow of mysticism in his make-up, a level-headed researcher who saw ghosts and phantoms. Even Miller's physique was a paradox; he was a big, burly, well set-up man, proud of his physical strength, whose lungs were rotting from silicosis, and whose brain was diseased, either from cerebral syphilis or tumour.

Before he collapsed in a miasma of dream and wicked fancy, for most of his adult life Hugh Miller fought a stubborn, sometimes brutal, and often very moving, rearguard defence of his God against the "Infidels" of science, with their potent theories of "development" and "evolution". Where other Churchmen—and particularly those of the Anglo-Catholic faction of the Church of England—retreated into blind faith and an illogical (and to Miller contemptible) anti-scientism, Miller met the enemy head on. In a long series of books, articles, essays and lectures, Miller hurled at the Infidels their own weapons of hard fact, carefully-assembled evidence, and well-constructed scientific theory. It was a heroic fight which lasted almost twenty years, and which Miller never abandoned until the night he put a bullet in his chest.

In his way, Hugh Miller was a near-perfect metaphor for the half-Lowland, half-Highland corner of Scotland that produced him. He was the product of two cultures. His father (also Hugh Miller) was a cat-footed Lowland seaman, with a taste for hard work and hard cash; his mother was an intelligent and imaginative Gaelic girl, with a strong talent for weaving tales, and a powerful sense of history. Although Miller liked to regard himself as very much his father's son, a level-headed, Saxon kind of Scot, his personality seems to have contained a good deal of his mother.

Interestingly, in one of his early essays (in the *Inverness Courier*) Miller reflected on the differences between Celtic and Saxon Scots, and the analysis —which is a bit hackneyed—contains within it a fair description of his own, complex, disposition. "Both are shrewd," Miller wrote, "but each in his own way. The Highlander is characterised by shrewdness of *observation,* the Lowlander by that of *inference;* the Highlander is delighted by the external beauty of things, the Lowlander into diving into their secret causes; the Highlander feels keenly, and gives free vent to his feelings, the Lowlander, on the contrary, cautiously conceals every emotion, unless it be very potent indeed; the Highlander is a descriptive poet, the Lowlander is a metaphysician."

Hugh Miller was both. His talent as a "descriptive" poet, combined with his passion for "diving into secret causes", produced some scientific writing which was at once original and stunningly beautiful. The same combination of talents made him one of the most feared journalists in Scotland, with a talent to conjure up the telling phrase that nailed the truth to the wall, and a massive intelligence which saw right to the heart of the problem. Miller's ability to describe some of the most important events of his time (both national and international) together with his power to search out their *significance* produced some of the best journalism of the nineteenth century.

His life was both highly successful and flawed with tragedy. He lost his hard-working father when he was only five years old, his two sisters when he was a teenager, and his well-loved grandfather a year later. His first child, the light of his life, died before she was two years old, just when Miller's career was beginning to show some success. The Old Red Sandstone of the Black Isle, from which Miller extracted some of his most original geology and brilliant writing, and which made his reputation as an intellectual, also threw up the dust that rotted his lungs, and undermined his health and mind. The "impulse of insanity" under which he committed suicide on Christmas Eve 1856, lends a kind of bleak symmetry to his life.

THE WITCH, THE SEA AND THE STONES

The town of Cromarty into which Hugh Miller was born on October 1802 was not the sluggish, part-derelict backwater it is now. At the turn of the nineteenth century Cromarty was in its heyday, on the finest deepwater harbour in Europe, a thriving place with a good port and more than its share of handsome, well-constructed public buildings. Thanks to the drive and hard cash of two far-sighted eighteenth-century businessmen—George Ross and William Forsyth —Cromarty had been transformed from a huddle of tide-besieged fishermen's cottages into the focal point for the Eastern Highlands. As well as being a busy commercial port and ship-building centre Cromarty made nails, shovels and agricultural implements, wove hemp and flax, brewed beer, made lace, cured herring, white fish and pork and shipped out cattle, timber and wheat.

The relatively enormous upsurge of economic activity sucked into the town hundreds of people from the Gaelic-speaking areas on the other side of the Cromarty Firth and it was from that side of the water that Miller's mother, Harriet Wright, came. She was the granddaughter of one Donald "Roy" Ross, a belligerent old Gael, reputedly gifted with second sight, who was converted from being a typical semi-pagan Highlander into one of the fiercest Presbyterians north of Inverness. Harriet Miller was only eighteen when her child Hugh was born; she was a tall, thin, young woman, with a reputation for being fey, and a brilliant spinner of tales and legends.

Miller's father, on the other hand, was a steady, middle-aged man of forty-four, born and bred in Cromarty (the Lowland side of the Firth) and, according to his son, one of the most resourceful shipmasters to sail out of the little port. In his trading sloop, with its distinctive square topsails and white stripes running down the hull, Hugh Miller senior sailed the coast of Scotland, picking up cargoes where he could, collecting kelp from the Hebrides, selling it to the glassmakers in Edinburgh, and returning to Cromarty with ship-loads of consumer durables and luxuries.

Hugh Miller senior came from an unbroken line of Easter Ross seamen, and his grandfather was one John Feddes, a small-time buccaneer of the late seventeenth and early eighteenth century, who (like many British shipmasters) bolstered his income by raiding Spanish ships off the coast of South America. In fact it was John

Feddes the pirate who built in 1711 the two-storey cottage in which Hugh Miller was born (and which still stands, guarded by the National Trust for Scotland). According to local history, John Feddes was an awkward, ungainly young man who had set his sights on the best-looking young woman in the village, one Jean Gallie. When she married someone else, Feddes left Cromarty in despair and, according to his great grandson, "wreaked his disappointment on the poor Spaniards". When he returned, flush with his Spanish gold, he found Jean Gallie both a widow and penniless. Feddes snapped her up, built the cottage for her (their initials are still carved over the fireplace lintel) and "here they lived for about fifty years, exceedingly well pleased with each other to the last".

When young Hugh Miller was born in 1802, the midwife who delivered him predicted from the odd configuration and size of his skull that the baby was destined to be the Cromarty idiot. She was wrong, and the first few years of Miller's life were happy enough. Business was brisk for his father's sloop and the family were never short of cash and the little luxuries it could buy. "I have my golden memories," Miller recalled later in his stunning autobiography *My Schools and Schoolmasters,* "of splendid toys that he used to bring home with him—among the rest a magnificent four-wheeled wagon of painted tin, drawn by four wooden horses and a string; and of getting it into a quiet corner and there breaking up every wheel and horse and the vehicle itself, into their original bits, until not two of the pieces were left sticking together."

The stuff of Miller's "golden memories" came to an end in November 1807 when his father's ship, trying to make its way out of Peterhead in a storm, foundered somewhere off the Buchan coast and was lost with all hands. That calamity was spiked into Miller's memory by an event he never forgot. With no reason to worry about his father (Harriet had just received a letter from Peterhead), the five-year-old Hugh was asked to go and close the cottage door. "Day had not wholly disappeared," he recalls, "but it was posting on to night, and a grey haze spread a neutral tint of dimness over every more distant object, but left the nearer ones comparatively distinct when I saw at the open door, less than a yard from my breast, as plainly as I ever saw anything, a dissevered hand and arm stretched towards me. Hand and arm were apparently those of a female; they bore a livid and sodden appearance; and directly fronting me, where the body ought to have been, there was only blank transparent space, through which I could see the dim forms of the objects beyond. I was fearfully startled and ran shrieking to my mother telling her what I had seen."

The period which followed his father's death Miller recalls as "a dreary season" in which the cottage was racked by the girl-widow's weeping and the crying of his two infant sisters. The five-year-old Hugh sat in dumb misery, or wandered the headland around Cromarty, looking in vain for the two square top-sails and white stripes of his father's sloop. The grinding misery of that time probably did a lot to reinforce the melancholy, superstitious side of Miller's nature. Certainly his wife Lydia thought so. "Add to everything," Lydia Miller wrote to her husband's nineteenth century biographer, "that much of his mother's sewing was making garments for the dead. Fancy that little low room in the winter evenings, its atmosphere at all times murky from the dark earthen floor, the small windows, the fire in the hearth, which though furnished with a regular chimney, allowed much smoke to escape before it found passage. Fancy little Hugh sitting on a low stool by that hearth fire, his mother engaged at a large chest which served her for a table on which there is a single candle. Her work is dressing the shroud and winding sheet, the dead irons click incessantly, and her conversation as she passes to and fro to heat her irons at the fire, is of the departed, and of mysterious warnings and spectres."

The child, she said, had been "surrounded and permeated with the atmosphere" and then was put to bed in the same room "where he can still see the work proceed and hear the monotonous click-click of those irons till his eyes close and the world of dreams mingles with that of reality". Lydia had no doubt that the misery and terror of those days made Hugh Miller prey to "the inability to distinguish between waking and sleeping visions" which may have killed him fifty years later. "The peculiarity of his mother's character told against him," she claimed firmly. "There was plenty of affection but no counter-balancing grain of sense of a kind which would qualify these tremendous doses of the supernatural."*

*This account of Miller's early life and conditioning comes from *The Life and Letters of Hugh Miller* by Peter Bayne, a long, two-volume biography published in 1871. It was written with the very close cooperation—and possible supervision—of Miller's widow, Lydia. But in the National Library of Scotland there is an unpublished manuscript written by Miller's nephew Hugh Miller Williamson, which provides a sour counterpoint to the pious and often cloying Bayne/Lydia account. For example, young Williamson suggests that Lydia and Miller's mother detested one another, and Lydia took her revenge via Bayne, by drawing the old lady as "a mental weakling, fearfully superstitious, and indeed fit only to stir a cauldron . . . "

Certainly, from Miller's own account, the fanciful "night-side" of his nature made itself felt early. The boy was intrigued by the stories about his great-grandfather John Feddes, and the first letters he learned to trace were JF and JG, the initials of the old buccaneer and his wife. "One day when playing all alone at the stair foot—for the inmates of the house had gone out—something extraordinary caught my eye on the landing place above; and looking up, there stood John Feddes—for I somehow instinctively divined that it was none other than he—in the form of a large, tall, very old man attired in a light blue great coat. He seemed to be steadfastly regarding me with apparent complacency; but I was sadly frightened; and for years after, when passing through the dingy ill-lighted room out of which I inferred he had come, I used to feel not at all sure that I might not tilt against old John in the dark."

Fortunately for Hugh Miller there were other adults in his life than his young mother. When his father died, his two uncles, James and Alexander (Sandy) Wright, took the young Hugh under their wings. James, the elder of the two, was an intelligent and inquisitive man, a harnessmaker to trade, an amateur antiquarian, and steeped in the history and legend of the Eastern Highlands. Sandy (Hugh's favourite) was a cartwright, deeply religious, but a bright, lively man with a profound interest in everything that went on around him. Sandy Wright had been a seaman in the British navy, fought with Nelson and Admiral Duncan at Camperdown, and had manned the naval batteries that were dragged ashore during the siege of Alexandria. According to Miller his uncle Sandy's curiosity was so intense, that he wandered along the beach at Alexandria picking up pebbles, fossils and bits of vegetation, while the French grapeshot and musket-balls whistled round his ears.

At the local "dames" school and then at the Cromarty "parish" school, young Miller was introduced to the mysteries and delights of literature. "I actually found out for myself," he recalls, "that the art of reading is the art of finding stories in books, and from that moment reading became one of the most delightful of my amusements." With the aid of a "box of birch-bark about nine inches square" young Miller began his library, drifting from scripture tales for children, through *Jack and the Beanstalk* and *Blue Beard and the Pirates,* to children's versions of Homer, the *Pilgrim's Progress, Robinson Crusoe, Gulliver's Travels,* the accounts of the voyages of Anson, Drake, Raleigh and Dampier, to obscure treatises by Flavel. When he was nine, Miller became "thoroughly a Scot" after his uncle James gave him a copy of Blind Harry's life of the Scots hero-patriot William Wallace. "I was intoxicated with the fiery narratives of the blind minstrel," Miller wrote, "with his fierce breathing of hot, intolerant patriotism, and his stories of astonishing prowess; and glorying in being a Scot, and the countryman of Wallace and Graham, I longed for a war with the Southrons that the wrongs and sufferings of these noble heroes might yet be avenged."

But there was more to young Miller's life than books. Cromarty was a school of hard knocks and vivid experience. The town was booming, peopled with nail-workers and carters, brewers and the crews of naval frigates and trading sloops. Every year the entire *caravanseri* of the herring fishery descended on Cromarty, bringing fishing boats from all over Scotland and "bevies of young women employed as gutters, and horribly incarnadined with blood and viscera, squatting around the heaps, knife in hand." Miller and his friends darted in and out of this "exciting scene that combined the bustle of the workshop with the confusion of the crowded fair", thumbing rides on the herring yawls, raiding the apple-orchards of the gentry and stoning the Gaelic boatmen from the other side of the Cromarty Firth who refused to pay their annual tribute of twenty peats to the Cromarty parish school.

And as the parish school lay cheek-by-jowl with Cromarty's "killing house" where around a hundred pigs a day were despatched to meet the demands of the town's saltpork trade, the murmur within the classroom was often drowned out "by the roar of death outside". As a treat, some of the parish school boys were allowed to watch, or even join in the slaughter, and returned to regale their class-mates with tales of hero-pigs that took three axe-blows to die, and in the process almost tore the slaughterman's thumb off. Young Miller had little taste for the slaughter, and even less for the parish school's annual cock-fight. This bizarre institution (which was quite common in Scottish schools) demanded that every boy pay the schoolmaster two pence for every bird he threw into the classroom cock-pit. "That day of the Festival," Miller recalled with distaste, "from morning till night, used to be spent in fighting the battle. For weeks after it had passed, the school floor would continue to retain its deeply stained blotches of blood, and the boys would be full of exciting narrative regarding the glories of gallant birds which had continued to fight until both their eyes had been picked out." It was not, he observed ruefully, "every grammar school in which such lessons are taught".

"But there were," he said, "several other branches of my education going on at this time outside the pale of the school, in which, though I succeeded in amusing myself, I was no trifler". One such "branch" was on the beaches and rocks around Cromarty, wandering among the granites, gneisses, quartz-rocks, clay-slates and mica-schists of the shore. It was round about this time that Miller discovered the hammer, "an uncouth sort of implement with a handle of strong black oak, and a short compact head, square on one face and oblong on the other". He found it among the lumber of his mother's cottage, and she told him that it belonged to old John Feddes, his buccaneering great-grandfather. Armed with the old pirate's hammer, Miller took to wandering the beaches, "breaking into all manner of stones with great perseverance and success".

And what he found entranced him. Sheer delight! He was dazzled by the worlds of colour, texture and pattern he found locked up in the drab-looking stones. He found crystals of garnet in the mica-schist that were identical to the ones in his mother's brooch. He traced grains of granite "in which the quartz is white as milk, and the feldspar red as blood". He located huge blocks of green hornbeam, cubes of rich galena, and occasional chunks of glittering iron pyrites which contained, he thought, "large promise of gold". On one occasion he found "in a large-grained granite a few sheets of beautiful black mica that, when split exceedingly thin, made admirable coloured eye-glasses, that converted the landscape around into richly-toned drawings of sepia". The boy spent long hours wandering around Cromarty, peering delightedly at the world through spectacles made of stone.

Another "branch" of Miller's education was supervised by his favourite uncle, Sandy Wright, who took him foraging along the seashore when the tide was low. "There are professors of Natural History," Miller pronounced later, "that know less of living nature than was known by Uncle Sandy; and I deemed it no small matter to have all the various productions of the sea with which he was acquainted pointed out to me in these walks, and to be in possession of his many curious anecdotes regarding them." Miller never forgot what Sandy Wright taught him. How to winkle out lobsters and crabs from their hiding places, where to locate the lump fish, how to clean its spawn and eat it like caviar, where to find the vividly-coloured seamouse, the ink-producing cuttle fish, and the more exotic shellfish, like Patella Pellucida "with its lustrous rays of vivid blue on its dark epidermis that resemble the sparks of firework breaking against a cloud". And what Sandy Wright lacked in scientific facts, he more than compensated for by teaching young Miller "the habit of observation", how to make deductions from the evidence of his own eyes.

In fact, Miller's curiosity led him into some sticky corners. On one occasion, determined to explore a system of caves near Cromarty, known as the "Doocot" (Dove Cot) cave, he and his friend John Swanson got cut off by the tide and risked their necks trying to scale the cliffs. Eventually they gave up and lay huddled together for warmth in the cave mouth as "the rising wind began to howl mournfully among the cliffs, and the sea, hitherto silent, to beat heavily against the shore, and to boom, like distress guns, from the recesses of the two deepsea caves".

Here Miller's over-active imagination took over, and reduced the nasty experience to a nightmare. A few yards from where they lay, the corpse of a drowned seaman had been washed up a month previously, and Miller had seen the body. "The hands and feet miserably contracted and corrugated into deep folds at every joint . . . and where the head should have been there existed only a sad mass of rubbish". Every time Miller closed his eyes to sleep he saw nothing but the dead seaman "stalking up the beach from the spot where he had lain, with his stiff white fingers, that stuck out like eagles toes, and his pale, broken pulp of a head, and attempt striking me".

The two boys were rescued from their predicament by a boat load of Cromarty fisherman who had come searching for them. And Miller managed to extract some artistic capital from the experience. He described his predicament "in some enormously bad verse" which amazed the author by becoming popular enough to be read "at tea parties by the *elite* of the town. Poor old Miss Rond, who kept the town boarding-school, got the piece nicely dressed up, somewhat on the principle upon which MacPherson translated Ossian; and at our first school examination—proud and happy day for the author— it was recited with vast applause by one of her prettiest young ladies, before the assembled taste and fashion of Cromarty."

A powerful influence on young Hugh Miller was his cousin George, a Gaelic-speaking stonemason, who lived with his family at Lairg in Sutherland. Although the Munro household was only thirty miles to the northwest, it was well into the Gaelic-speaking

Highlands. The entire Munro family (parents, three sons, plus some
of their livestock) lived in a "low, long, dingy edifice of turf, four or
five rooms in length, but only one in height". The main room in the
Munro household had "in the old Highland style, its fire full in the
middle of the floor, without back or sides; so that, like a bonfire in
the open air, all the inmates could sit round it in a wide circle—the
women invariably ranged on one side; and the men on the other".

It was in this smoke-wreathed atmosphere that Miller was
introduced to the remnants of Gaelic culture. Like many young
Highlanders of the time (in fact like much of Europe) Miller's cousin
William Munro was much taken with the Ossianic legends and used
to gather round the fire with a circle of neighbours "and repeat the
wild Fingalian legends". Miller was intrigued but not impressed,
finding the stories "very wild legends indeed".

But he was genuinely struck by the piety of the Munro household
and the way his uncle "took the book" for Gaelic family worship.
"The entire scene was a deeply impressive one," he recalled much
later, "and when I saw in witnessing the celebration of high mass in a
Popish cathedral many years after, the alter suddenly enveloped in a
dim picturesque obscurity, amid which the curling smoke of the
incense ascended, and heard the musically modulated prayer
sounding in the distance from within the screen, my thoughts
reverted to the rude Highland cottage where, amid solemnities not
theatric, the red umbry light of the fire fell with undulating glimmer
upon dark walls, and bare black rafters, and kneeling forms, and a
pale expanse of dense smoke that, filling the upper portion of the
roof, overhung the floor like a ceiling, and there arose amid the
gloom the sounds of prayer truly God-directed, and poured out from
the depths of the heart; and I felt that the stoled priest of the
cathedral was merely an artist, although a skilful one, but that in the
'priest and father' of the cottage there was the truth and reality from
which the artist drew".

But the countryside around the Munro cottage did offer young
Miller a new and very different geology and history from the Old Red
Sandstone around Cromarty. And for three successive autumn
holidays, Miller ranged the hills about Lairg and Loch Shin,
exploring the ruins of the Pictish brochs that then peppered the
district, shivering with "fearful joy" while walking through the adder-
infested bracken, learning the herbs and plants with which "the old
Highlanders used to attach occult virtues such as procuring love or

exciting hatred".

And, by now, thoroughly interested in mineralogy (the predecessor of geology) he fell to among the Sutherland rocks. He found huge boulders of gneiss veined "by threads and seams of a white quartz abounding in drusy cavities, thickly lined along their sides with sprig crystals. Never had I seen such lovely crystals on the shores of Cromarty or anywhere else. They were clear and transparent as the purest spring water, furnished each with six sides, and sharpened a-top into six facets. Borrowing one of cousin George's hammers, I soon filled a little box with these gems which even my mother and aunt were content to admire, as what of old used, they said, to be called Bristol diamonds and set in silver brooches and sleeve buttons."

On Miller's third (and last) visit to the Munro family, he found things greatly changed. His cousin William, an enthusiastic businessman, had sunk his money into some unwise speculation in the south, lost the lot and was "tiding over the difficulties of a time of settlement six hundred miles from the scene of disaster". Meanwhile, Miller's favourite cousin George (the literary-inclined stonemason) had found a wife, and built himself a cottage on a hill overlooking Lairg where "he was happy in it, far above the average lot of humanity, with his young wife". George Munro had taken with him his share of the family library, and stocked the cottage with drawing instruments, a paint box and the tools of his trade, "and I was generously made free of them all—books, instruments, colour box, and hammers".

George Munro, the serious-minded young Gaelic stone-mason, was a powerful influence on Miller (and is evidence that a streak of talent ran in the maternal side of Miller's family). As well as being a skilled mason, Munro could draw, paint, enjoyed mathematical problems, had a good grasp of architecture, and while he was an apprentice in Glasgow, became a very handy boxer. Although Munro's life in Lairg seemed idyllic to young Miller, Munro soon wearied of it, became superintendent of a sawmill, then a slater, translated Bunyan's *Visions* into Gaelic, studied botany, tried to become a school teacher, decamped to the south of Scotland, supervised the building of a bridge over the Firth of Forth, became a civil engineer, investigated and reported on a copper mine at Airdrie, studied surveying (and built his own theodolite) and ended his days comfortably off in the town of Stirling.

"Of all my cousins," Miller wrote later, "cousin George was the one whose pursuits most nearly resembled my own and in whose society I most delighted to share." And not only was young Miller impressed by his cousin's relish for architectural designs or "rendering some piece of Gaelic verse into English or some piece of English prose into Gaelic", he was struck by the fact that cousin George had the entire winter to follow his own interests. In the north of Scotland, the combination of short days and foul weather virtually closed down the building industry between November and March, "a circumstance which I carefully noted at this time in its bearing on the amusements of my cousin, and which afterwards weighed not a little with me when I came to make a choice of a profession for myself".

But once again Miller's boyhood idyll was ruptured by tragedy, and once again the young widow Miller was plunged into grief. In the summer of 1816 Miller's two young sisters—Jean aged eleven and Catherine aged nine—contracted a fever and "sank under it within a few days of one another". The death of her two daughters, following on the death of her husband, devastated Harriet Miller who "for weeks and months wept for her children, like Rachel of old, and refused to be comforted because they were not". Miller himself, by that time a fractious youth of almost fifteen, was not his mother's favourite and overheard the distraught young widow revile God for not taking her son and leaving one of her daughters. "It was bitter for me to think, and yet I could not think otherwise, that she had cause of sorrow both for those whom she had lost, and for him who had survived".

The tragedy was compounded within the year when Miller's grandfather also died, apparently of a broken heart. "As is perhaps not uncommon in such cases," he wrote, "his warmer affections strode across the generation of grown-up men and women—his sons and daughters—and luxuriated among the children, their descendents. The boys, his grandsons, were too wild for him; but the two little girls—gentle and affectionate—had seized his whole heart; and now they were gone, it seemed as if he had nothing in the world left to care for".

Miller's school days petered out in a flurry of truancy, petty crime and general tedium when he was transferred from the parish school to the new "subscription school" (so called because the teacher was paid by "subscriptions" raised by the townspeople). From his own account, Miller was growing fast and running wild, totally dissatisfied with his school work, and picking quarrels and fights with his schoolmates. On one occasion he pulled a knife on another boy, "a stout and somewhat desperate mulatto", and struck him in the thigh. "I had certainly reached a dangerous stage," Miller reflected," but it was mainly myself that was in jeopardy".

His bitterest enemy of the time seems to have been the subscription school-master. The difficult, devious and probably sullen Miller was clearly driving the man to distraction, and Miller's school days ended with a set-to with the young school teacher. Miller refused to pronounce the word "awful" in the way the master demanded, and was promptly lashed round the ears with the leather belt. Miller objected, the master tried to beat him down, and there followed a roaring school-room brawl between the school teacher and the boy, in which Miller came off a sorry loser which "filled me with aches and bruises for a full month thereafter". It was, he knew, a sorry end to a school career which had begun with some promise. But Miller recognised that he had become "a wild insubordinate boy, and the only school in which I could properly be taught was the world-wide school in which Toil and Hardship are the severe but noble teachers".

THE APPRENTICE STONEMASON

For months after his spectacular exit from the subscription school, Miller was the despair of his relatives, and especially his mother, who re-married at the end of 1819. Miller slouched around Cromarty, hung about doing nothing in particular, messing about in the woods, in the caves, around the rocks, spending his time with foresters, labourers and fishermen, and dreaming up ploys with his dwindling band of schoolmates. Interestingly though, his literary ambition remained and he started, and largely wrote, *The Village Observer* which ran for three issues at the beginning of 1820, and in which Miller and his adolescent friends Struck Out Fearlessly against the government, deplored the Peterloo massacre, worried about the Reformers, and denounced the Radicals in no uncertain terms.

But there were, he knew, sterner days ahead. "The necessity of ever toiling from morning to night and from one week's end to another, and all for a little coarse food and homely raiment, seemed to be a dire one; and fain I would have avoided it. But there was no escape; and so I determined on being a mason". His mother, both his uncles (and especially his Uncle James), were outraged. Notwithstanding his school performance, they knew Hugh Miller to be an intelligent and able youth. They had long nursed ambitions to see him ensconced in one of the "learned professions" and were grieved at the idea of him wasting himself in the stone-quarries and building sites of Easter Ross. They begged, cajoled, even threatened him, but it was no good. Young Miller was adamant that he wanted to be a mason, James and Sandy relented and in February 1820 he was apprenticed for three years to an elderly uncle, David Williamson, "who usually kept an apprentice or two and employed a few journeymen". And so, "with a suit of strong moleskin clothes and a pair of heavy hob-nailed shoes, I waited only for the breaking of the winter frosts, to begin work in the Cromarty quarries".

The delight which Miller found in the quarries of Easter Ross in his first days as an apprentice is vividly described in the *Old Red Sandstone* but along with it came a stiff dose of misery. Although seventeen, young Miller was still seven inches short of his adult height, and slightly built. The sheer grinding effort of cutting and hauling blocks of sandstone took its toll on the youth "and I used to suffer much from wandering pains in the joints, and an oppressive feeling in the chest as if crushed by some great weight. I became subject too, to frequent fits of extreme depression of spirits, which took almost the form of walking sleep—results, I believe, of excessive fatigue—and during which my absence of mind was so extreme, that I lacked the ability of protecting myself against accident, in cases the most simple and ordinary".

But Miller learned—and grew—quickly. Within months his sinews stiffened, his palms calloused, and his arms and back grew stronger, and he began to pick up the expertise needed to make a good journeyman mason. He also learned the heady joys of dram-drinking, and just as quickly, the mind-befuddling effects. After two large glasses of *usquebeath* (whisky) drunk after the laying of a foundation stone, Miller went home to his books and found "the letters dancing before my eyes, and that I could no longer master the sense". The experience stayed with him and though never an abstainer, he took some pride in the fact that he could work for a year "in which I did not consume more than half-a-dozen glasses of ardent spirits, or partake of half-a-dozen draughts of fermented liquor".

Although the town of Cromarty had more than its share of economic activity, the masons of the district had to find work around the district. One of the best sources was Cononside, one of the better-heeled areas on the other side of the Cromarty Firth, where the gentry were in a flurry of improving their estate houses. In the spring of 1821 David Williamson and his apprentice set off to the west to help build "a jointure house for the lady of a Ross-shire proprietor, lately dead".

On his first night in Cononside, Miller woke about midnight to see a light dancing in a ruined churchyard and to hear "a continuous screaming of the most unearthly sound". Miller's active imagination immediately conjured up a ghost, but he learned the unearthly voice belonged to one Isabel MacKenzie (known as "Mad Bell"), a deranged middle-aged woman in her fifties who was normally kept chained in her damp-floored hovel until she escaped and terrifed the neighbourhood with her wild ways. In fact Mad Bell became the strangest of Miller's many strange acquaintances. She had long periods of clarity, and recognised in Hugh Miller a very unusual apprentice. "What makes you work as a mason?" she demanded of him. "All your fellows are real masons, but you are merely in the disguise of a mason; and I have come to consult you about the deep matters of the soul". This was no hollow boast. Mad Bell was well versed in—among other documents—Flavel's *Treatise on the Soul of Man* and Miller soon found himself locked in theological conversation with the deranged woman "who with all her sad brokenness of mind, was one of the most intellectual women I ever knew".

Mad Bell was also a rich storehouse of local legends and myths, "and many an ancedote she could tell of the old chieftains forgotten on the land which had once been their own, and of the Highland poets whose songs had been sung for the last time". She was the first to relate to Miller the "raid of the Ghillie-Christ", a now notorious (and possibly apocryphal) story of inter-clan nastiness, when a war party of Macdonalds swooped out of the west and set fire to a church full of praying Mackenzies. According to Gaelic tradition, the Macdonald pipers strutted round the flaming building, playing their war-tunes, until the last of their shrieking victims was carbonised. "She herself was a Mackenzie," Miller says, "and her eyes flashed a wild fire when she spoke of the barbarous and brutal Macdonalds".

But to Mad Bell, there was a moral in the story. The Ancient Highlanders, she told Miller, were "bold and faithful dogs" and like dogs, ready to do "the most cruel and wicked actions" at the behest of their clan chiefs. And this was why, she told the bemused apprentice, the Gaelic Highlanders were in the sorry state they were. Whereas the pious martyrs of the south of Scotland had "contended in God's behalf", the Gaels of the north had "contended on behalf of their chiefs". And while the Good Lord had been kind to *his* servants, the Highland chiefs had been miserably unkind to *theirs*.

In the end Mad Bell's lunacy and haunted conversations became too much, even for the ever-curious Hugh Miller. After listening to her Miller says "I was always pained, and invariably quitted her, after each lengthened tête-a-tête in a state of low spirits, which I found difficult to shake off. There seems to be something peculiarly unwholesome in the society of a strong-minded maniac; and so contrived as much as possible—not a little, at times, to her mortification—to avoid her". Miller only saw the woman once after his sojourn on Cononside "when she told me that, though people could not understand *us*, there was meaning in both her thoughts and mine". Mad Bell was not destined to crouch in her hut, rattling her chains and reciting Flavel for much longer. "When fording the river Conon in one of her wilder moods", Miller relates, "she was swept away by the stream and drowned and her body cast upon the bank a day or two after".

It was on Cononside that spring of 1821 that Miller got his first taste of the raw, boisterous, crude, barrackroom life suffered by the itinerant masons of northern Scotland. In a letter to one of his friends he describes twenty-four workmen crowded into a dilapidated thirty-foot-long farm building with straw-filled beds ranged along the walls, a row of cooking fires along one gable, and bags of oatmeal suspended from the rafters to keep them out of reach of the rats. "The inmates, who exceeded twenty, had disposed themselves in every possible manner. Some were lounging in the beds, others were seated on the chests. Two of them were dancing on the floor to the whistling of a third. There was one employed in baking, another in making ready the bread. The chaos of sounds which reigned among them was more complete than that which appalled their prototypes, the builders of Babel. There was the gabbling of Saxon, the spluttering of Gaelic, the humming of church music, the whistling of the musician, and the stamping of the dancers". Miller also saw, for the first of many times, a "ramming", a curious mock-solemn punishment inflicted by the masons on one another, whereby the victim was grabbed by the arms and legs, and his backside battered against the wall.

Young Miller was plainly startled, and probably scared, by his introduction to barrack-life, but he realised there were lessons here "eminently worthy of being scanned". What he was seeing, he realised, was men cut loose from the softening effects of wives and families. "At home he is in all probability a quiet, rather dull-looking personage, not much given to a laugh or joke; whereas in the bothy, if the squad be a large one, he becomes wild and a humourist— laughs much, and grows ingenious in playing off pranks on his fellows". But there was, he knew, a feverishness about barrack-life that rang hollow. "And yet, amid all this wild merriment and license, there was not a workman who did not regret the comforts of his quiet home, and long for the happiness which was, he felt, to be enjoyed only there. It has long been known that gaiety is not a solid enjoyment".

One of Miller's closest friends of this period was William Ross, a consumptive youth, five years older than Miller, who described him as "a thin, pale lad, fairhaired, with a clear waxen complexion, flat chest and stooping figure". Ross was unfortunate in his parents; his mother was the wayward daughter of a God-fearing family, and his father was a semi-imbecile farm labourer. Despite these disadvantages, Ross seemed to brim with talent. He was a voracious reader with a taste for Dryden and Addison, and a gifted musician. He possessed a love of the rocks and woods that almost matched Miller's. Ross was also a talented draughtsman and painter, and like most youngsters with that bent in nineteenth-century Scotland, he became a house painter.

Miller returned to Cromarty after his first spell on Cononside to find that William Ross had been working at water-colour sketches of the "Runic obelisks of Ross" (Pictish slabs and monoliths with which Easter Ross was studded). What impressed Miller was that these were faithful representations, almost scale drawings of the Pictish stones "and looking with the eye of the stone-cutter at his preliminary sketches, I saw that, with such a series of drawings before me, I myself could learn to cut Runic obelisks, in all the integrity of the complex ancient style, in less than a fortnight".

Miller found his talented friend in dire straits, trying to scrape

Hugh Miller; one of the set of Hill/Adamson calotypes in the collection of the Scottish National Portrait Gallery. While Miller was an amiable, gentle, church-going family man, he also had a reputation as a fearsome opponent. According to David Masson who knew him, there was a "tremendous element of ferocity" in Miller which amounted to a disposition to kill. In Masson's view, "A duel of opinions was apt to become with him a duel of reputations and of persons". (Courtesy of the National Galleries of Scotland)

together enough money to take himself off to the south of Scotland where work was more plentiful. He had, he told Miller, been subsisting on a diet of potatoes, salt and water for a number of weeks. "A very poor friendless lad of genius," as Miller described him later, "diluting his thin consumptive blood on bad potatoes and water, and, at the same time, anticipating the labours of our antiquarian societies by his elaborate and truthful drawings of an interesting class of national antiquities, must be regarded as a melancholy object of contemplation . . . "

And there were other "melancholy objects of contemplation" in Miller's circle of friends. Perhaps the strangest was a doomed youth of twenty, known around Cromarty as "poor Danie", who lived with his widowed mother in a damp cottage. Miller describes Danie as "simply a human skeleton, bent double, and covered with yellow skin" and so crippled that he could hardly move from his chair or his bed. For all that, Danie seems to have had a decent intelligence and acted as a kind of "amanuensis and adviser general" to the love-lorn, or sexually-frustrated, young women of Cromarty. With unconscious cruelty, the girls of the town would troop into Danie's wretched home, and unburden themselves on the sexless youth, treating him, Miller noted, "simply as an intelligence coupled with sympathies that could write letters".

Surprisingly perhaps, Danie appeared to relish his role, although he did share the burden of confidence with his friend Miller who noted wryly that he could have filled "more than a couple of paragraphs" with the amorous history of the ladies of Cromarty, "some of whose daughters were courted and married ten years ago". Danie did not live for long, swept away suddenly by pneumonia, but the poignancy and helplessness of his life struck Miller strongly. "I have seen," he wrote, "in even our better works of fiction, less interesting characters portrayed than poor gentle-spirited Danie, the love-depository for the young dames of the village; and I learned a thing or two at his school."

The following spring, 1822, Miller was back in the barracks at Cononside where he found the rats more troublesome than ever. He ended the season in the most loathed of all masonry work "biggin dykes wi' dirty stanes", standing in ditches up to his knees in water, all his fingers oozing blood, shivering in the September rain, and, to his alarm, spitting out "a blood-stained mucoidal substance". As his depression deepened, the pain in his chest grew worse, and he began to fear for his life. The superstitious side of his personality took over. "One day when on the top of a tall building, part of which we were throwing down to supply us with materials for our work, I raised up a broad slab of red micaceous sandstone, thin as a roofing slate and exceedingly fragile, and, holding it out at arms length, dropped it over the wall". If the slab breaks, Miller told himself, then "I shall break up like that sandstone slab and perish as little known". But the thin slice of the sandstone did not break. A breeze took it, blew it over a heap of stones and it impaled itself upright in the soft grass. "I at once inferred that recovery awaited me," Miller wrote later. "I was to live and not die".

THE JOURNEYMAN

BY the spring of 1823 Miller had served his time to old David Williamson, and after running up a single-room cottage in Cromarty for his Aunt Jenny, the newly-fledged journeyman took himself off to the other side of the Cromarty Firth, ending up in Gairloch on the northwest coast. His main companions were a villainous carter known as "Click-Clack" (a skilled night-raider and scrounger) and a shrewd sarcastic old stone-mason called John Fraser, a legend in his trade, who could cut a stone with one strike, where other masons took a dozen, and who had the perfect eye "in fitting the interspaces between stones already laid". Miller's admiration for old John Fraser was immense. Even in the fearsome rain-soaked gales of northwest Scotland, John Fraser never failed to build a watertight wall.

Gairloch was a very different Scotland from the one Miller grew up in, and he soaked in as much of the geology, botany, and fast dying culture as his time and energy allowed. He found huge pleasure in the beautiful landscape, wandered the beaches looking for shells, enjoyed the amazing abundance of the wild flowers, and studied the alien gneiss-dominated geology. Although his Gaelic was scanty, he visited the drystone, peat-thatched cabins of the local people, noted the strange "mediocrity in their size" (also noted by Dr Johnson) and concluded that Gaelic women aged prematurely out of sheer hard work. "How these poor Highland women did toil! I have paused amid my labours under the hot sun to watch them as they passed, bending under their load of peat or manure, and at the same time twirling the spindle as they crept along, and drawing out the never-

ending thread from the distaff stuck in their girdles." Miller observed
that the boat-yard at Gairloch turned out craft remarkably like the
ones produced by the ancient Norse boat builders, that the people
still turned the soil with the primitive *cass-chron,* that they were
dangerously dependent on potatoes for their food and that the local
lairds extracted more rent in the way of fish and cereals than the
people could afford.

And while Miller found Highland men living up to their ancient
reputation for indolence, he saw nothing genetic in the cause. "Even
a previously industrious people", he wrote, "were they to be located
within the great north-western curve of thirty-five inch rain, to raise
corn and potatoes for the autumnal storms to blast, and to fish, on
the laird's behalf, herrings that year after year refused to be caught,
would, I suspect, in a short time, get nearly as indolent themselves."
And he pointed to the Macdonalds, McLeods and Mackays among
the masons, diligent, hard-working men who happen to have been
"bred in the eastern border of the Highlands in a sandstone district,
where they had the opportunity of acquiring a trade" and who had
been transformed into "industrious skilled mechanics of at least the
ordinary efficiency".

After his sojourn among the Gaels of Wester Ross, Miller found
himself in a very different environment. In the summer of 1824 he
shipped out of Cromarty to Edinburgh, partly to look for work, and
partly to get rid of a semi-derelict slum he had inherited (via his
father's estate) on Coal Hill in Leith. This eminently undesirable little
property—which was proving a drain on the family's funds—had
been in turn a dockside whisky-den, the roost for a series of
miserable lodgers who never paid the rent, a whorehouse (until the
authorities intervened) and home for "the ghost of a murdered
gentleman whose throat had been cut in an inner apartment by the
ladies, and his body flung by night into the deep mud of the
harbour".

The Edinburgh that Miller found in the June of 1824 was no
douce, settled, provincial place. It was still one of the intellectual
power houses of north Europe, where great names like Walter Scott
stalked the street. For more than thirty years the city had been in a
building fever, as the city fathers threw up the classic New Town, to
the designs of planners and architects like James Craig, Robert Reid,
William Playfair, and the great Robert Adam. It was a sustained
frenzy of building which was almost unmatched in Europe (and

which came near to bankrupting the city). It unleashed huge sums of money into the local economy.

Immigration from Ireland and from all over Scotland was running at a high level, and while the gentry and middle classes were trooping out of the Old Town and into the New, their places were being snapped up by poverty-stricken immigrants. Dispossesed Highland tribesmen clashed with Irish clansmen in the stews and whorehouses of the Canongate, Cowgate and High Street, while the always ineffective City Guard struggled to keep the lid on the violence. When Miller landed in Leith, he found his head "dizzied with the confused cries of watermen and carters, and my thoughts scattered by a multiplicity of objects, any of which I might have thought curious, but all of which only tended to confuse".

Miller was met on the quayside at Leith by his friend William Ross ("in pale moleskin, a good deal bespattered with paint") and after a quick survey of his derelict property on the Coal Hill, he plunged himself and the weak-lunged Ross into an enthusiastic pedestrian tour of the city. The next day, he was back seeing the Town Clerk of Leith, who said that the Coal Hill house could probably be dumped on the market so long as no great price was expected and mentioned that one of his master-builder friends was on the lookout for skilled masons. Miller leapt at the chance and found himself one of a party of sixteen stonemasons building a house at Niddry, south-east of Edinburgh.

It was an experience that Miller never forgot, and which rankled in his memory for the rest of his life. The Edinburgh masons were a breed entirely outwith Miller's experience. The serious young journeyman from Cromarty was used to quiet, hard-working men who could be boisterous and noisy in the barracks, but who were basically placid and responsible. The city workmen were different. They were hard-drinking, free-spending, irreligious and feckless, given to blowing a fortnight's wages in a weekend of whoring, badger-baiting, boozing and fighting in the dens of Edinburgh, returning late, penniless and legless, and incapable of real work. The Edinburgh masons shocked Miller to the core, and he found his first (and practically only) friend in one John Wilson, an elderly, pious and rather dim workman.

And the Edinburgh men twitted Miller (and his pious associate) mercilessly. He was, they told him "a Highlander newly come to Scotland" and unless they chased him back over the Highland line, half the money of Edinburgh would vanish into his pocket. John Wilson was told by one that if he tried to convert him to God, "I'll brak your face". Miller was particularly shocked by the irreligious wisecracks. One mason "aye liked to be in a kirk for the sake of decency once a twelvemonth", while another proclaimed he "hadna been kirked for the last ten months, he was only waiting for a rainy Sabbath to lay in his stock of divinity for the year".

All of which sounds suspiciously like the normal, sardonic humour of urban Scotland, and it is interesting that when the men were giving Miller too much of a hard time, one of the leading reprobates—a man known as Cha—stepped forward and brought it to an end. Cha was a six foot high, handsome, 23-year-old, who led the pack in any dicey adventure. "No man of the party squandered his gains more recklessly than Charles, or had looser notions regarding the legitimacy of the uses to which he often applied them," Miller recalled. "And yet, notwithstanding, he was a generous-hearted fellow; and, under the influence of religious principle, would, like Burns himself, have made a very noble man."

But the prospects of "religious principle" steering Cha and his mates onto the straight-and-narrow were not good. On Friday, with their wages in their pockets, the masons headed for Edinburgh "and until the evening of the following Monday or Tuesday, I saw no more of them. They would then come dropping in, pale, dirty, disconsolate looking—almost always in the reactionary state of unhappiness which succeeds intoxication—(they themselves used to term it 'the horrors')—and with their nervous system so shaken, that rarely until a day or two after did they recover their ordinary working ability."

And it was in Edinburgh that Miller had his first taste of industrial aggravation. That winter, the employers dropped the masons' wages from 24 shillings a week to 15 shillings a week. The masons judged this drop too steep and decided to organise a strike in Edinburgh. Miller accepted the justice of their cause but argued with them that they were totally unprepared, without a penny laid by to finance a strike. They were bound, he told them, to lose. Cha agreed, saying "if the masters don't give in by Saturday, it's all up with me; but never mind, let us have one day's fun".

And fun they had. The men marched into the city and joined an 800 strong meeting dominated by "crack orators" whose fluency cowed Cha into silence. After a few rousing speeches, the striking

Miller's great mentor Thomas Chalmers, astronomer, mathematician, theologian, and the first moderator of the Free Church of Scotland. When a faction within the Free Church tried to oust Miller from the editorship of The Witness *(or at least run Miller on a tighter rein), Chalmers thwarted the* coup *with the question, "Which of you could direct Hugh Miller?" (Courtesy of The National Galleries of Scotland)*

masons adjourned, having agreed to meet again that evening "in one of the humbler halls of the city". To pass the time, Miller and his mates found themselves in a "low tavern" somewhere in the Canongate, and once again, Miller was racked with horror at the *mores* of the Edinburgh working class. The pub, Miller says, was "a low roofed room into which the light of day never penetrated, and in which the gas was burning dimly in a slow, close, sluggish atmosphere, rendered still more stifling by tobacco smoke and a strong smell of ardent spirits". From a trap door in the middle of the floor came a bedlam of shouts and curses, screams and yelps. Miller discovered that the pub had a cellar in which customers used to pit their dogs against the pub-owner's badgers.

The cheap whisky, Miller noticed, told not so much on the younger men but on the middle-aged members of the squad "whose constitutions seemed undermined by a previous course of dissipation and debauchery. Their conversation became very loud, very involved, and although highly seasoned with emphatic oaths, very insipid." It was all too much for Miller who left some cash with Cha to cover his share of the drink, and wandered off to the King's Park to forage among the trap rocks. When he pumped Cha the next day as to how the evening's strike meeting had gone, he was told "we got upon the skuff after you left us, and grew deaf to time, and so none of us has seen the meeting yet".

This was very much as Miller expected. It was the prospect of political and economic power falling into the hands of men like the Edinburgh masons which instilled in Miller a dread of radicals, chartists and the universal franchise—a dread that never left him. He believed that the anarchy and barbarism which had haunted Scotland for so long, had been transferred from the Highlands into the cities (especially Edinburgh and Glasgow). "And it is in the great towns that Paganism now chiefly prevails. In at least their lapsed classes—a rapidly increasing proportion of their population—it is those cities of our country which first caught the light of religion and learning, that have become pre-eminently its dark parts." This injection of barbarity into the cities, he believed, was "preparing terrible convulsions for the future".

But there was a lot about Edinburgh which Miller clearly loved. The intricate urban landscape of the Old Town fascinated him as much, if not more, than the classical elegance of the New Town. He was transfixed and history-struck in front of Holyrood House (which he viewed "with the same emotion which a pilgrim feels when prostrating himself before the shrine of a favourite saint"). He was filled with admiration for Robert Adam's university building ("the finest building in Edinburgh, either taken in its parts or as a whole") and was contemptuous of the equestrian statue of Charles II in Parliament Square ("this lascivious and dissipated monarch"). The small bust of John Knox in the High Street, however, impressed him enormously and "I uncovered my head and bowed very low to his effigy".

He made several trips to the theatre ("I did not derive from theatrical representation half the pleasure I anticipated") but was taken with the circular wooden building on The Mound "where the good people of Edinburgh see shows and sights of all descriptions, from the smoking baboon to the giant of seven feet and a half". He was particularly enthusiastic about the *son et lumiere* representation of the Battle of Trafalgar in all its gory detail. In his more intellectual/pious moments, he travelled across the city to hear the sermons of Dr Thomas McCrie, "the elegant historian of Knox and Melville", and did not find the Presbyterian divine wanting.

But he did not overlook the squalor and virtual serfdom that existed in the little coal-towns that lined the Midlothian coal fields near Edinburgh. One such (now totally obliterated) existed near Niddry Mill and was "a wretched assemblage of dingy, low-roofed, tile-covered hovels, each of which perfectly resembled the others, and was inhabited by a rude and ignorant race of men that still bore about them the stain of recent slavery". And, once again, it was the plight of the women that appalled him. "How these poor women did labour, and how thoroughly, even at this time, were they characterised by the slave nature". It had been estimated by a man who knew them well that "one of their ordinary day's work was equal to the carrying of a hundredweight from the level of the sea to the top of Ben Lomond". The wretched women were marked, he said, "by traits of almost infantile weakness. I have seen these collier women crying like children, when toiling under their load along the upper rounds of the wooden stair that transversed the shaft; and then returning, scarce a minute after, with the empty creel, singing with glee".

In the autumn of 1825 Miller returned (fled?) to Cromarty, having finally managed to unload the rotting tenement on Coal Hill for £50. But the dust from the stones which built Niddry House had inflamed his silicosis and, as usual when the affliction flared up, he was overtaken by depression. He took to wandering the woods of Cromarty with his five-year-old half-sister Jean Williamson (the daughter of his mother's second marriage), convinced that his life was over and that he was about to topple into his grave. In fact he penned a poem to little Jean with the glum lines, "A few short weeks of pain shall fly/and asleep in that bed shall thy puir brither lie".

But he was overdoing it. Once again the big, powerfully-built young mason recovered his health and his optimism and started re-forging his links with Cromarty. He resumed his close friendship with John Swanson, a practical and energetic young man who had served his time as a grocer in London and was now building a flourishing business in Cromarty. Swanson—who was soon to embark on a career as a Church of Scotland Minister—was a Christian zealot, and impatient with Miller's lacklustre Christianity. It was Swanson who introduced Miller to metaphysics, and the pleasures of Locke, Hume, Berkeley and Reid (and Miller who taught Swanson some of the joys of lyric poetry).

In fact, John Swanson was an important influence on Miller. When he finally threw up his business, and took himself off to Aberdeen to learn to be a Minister, he kept up an intense, slightly odd, correspondence with his friend in Cromarty. Swanson's ambition was to convert Miller into the kind of zealous Christian he was himself. "Oh I pant after that time when I may be fully assured that you are travelling towards Zion," Swanson wrote to Miller from Aberdeen in July 1825. Two months later he was demanding to know "Dost thou believe? Do you believe that He lived? that He was sent of God? that He died to save sinners?" In January 1826 Swanson was still at it; "Go on, my dear Hugh, go on and the Lord Himself will bless you".

Miller was patient enough with his friend's religious ecstasy and pious badgering, but showed little sign of becoming the evangelical Christian that Swanson wanted. Swanson was not without subtlety, and his letters struck chords with Miller. Gradually he became more and more interested in religion, theology, religious affairs, and more importantly, in the interface between faith and politics which became so disruptive an issue in nineteenth-century Scotland. In this, he was encouraged by the Cromarty parish minister, Stewart, a friendly, humourous and intelligent man for whom Miller retained a high regard.

At the same time, Miller kept up a regular correspondence with his friend William Ross, the consumptive house-painter who was still living in Edinburgh, but fretting for the sights and sounds of Easter Ross. As his disease advanced, Ross grew increasingly melancholy and Miller tried—at long range—to spark some hope into the young man. But Ross was dying and he knew it. His wit and energy faltered as his future shortened. Ross was happy to do small chores for Miller, and he did try to sell one of Miller's ham-fisted Byronic poems *(Ode to Greece)* to *The Scotsman* newspaper who turned it down with little grace.

But Miller was determined to make his mark as a literary man. He had, in fact, been scribbling banal poetry for years, but it was not until 1829 that any of it saw the light of day (and then only because Miller paid for the publication himself). *Poems Written In The Leisure Hours of a Journeyman Mason,* the volume was called, and when it slipped off the presses of the *Inverness Courier* in the summer of 1829, it was roundly trounced.

"The time has gone by," wrote one critic, "when a literary mechanic used to be regarded as a phenomenon; were a second Burns to spring up now, he would not be entitled to so much praise as the first." Another critic was more blunt: "We are glad to understand," he wrote, "that our author has the good sense to rely more on his chisel than the Muses." Yet another took much the same line: "It is our duty to tell this writer, that he will make more in a week with his trowel than in half a century by his pen." Another thought Miller had "no chance whatever of being known beyond the limits of his native place", while someone else thought the book showed nothing "which sanctioned the expectation of better things to come".

Actually, Miller had anticipated the criticism. He had been told often enough—not least by William Ross—that he was no poet, and in a sly tailpiece to the volume of poems, he raised the suspicion himself. "It is more than possible," he wrote, "that I have completely failed in poetry. It may appear that, while grasping at originality of description and sentiment, and striving to attain propriety of expression, I have only been depicting common images, and embodying obvious thoughts, and this too, in inelegant language." But he added defiantly: "The pleasure which I enjoy in composing verses is quite independent of another man's opinion of them . . ."

Although Miller took a critical drubbing on the appearance of his poems, the volume did his reputation no harm at all. There were one or two kind reviews (one of which was downright fulsome) and the literary stir brought him to the attention of the *culturati* of the North of Scotland and beyond. One Isaac Forsyth of Elgin, descendent of William Forsyth, who had built so much of Cromarty, became interested in Miller, as did Sir Thomas Dick Lauder. And Miller found a genuine patron in Miss Dunbar of Boath, an elderly spinster of the gentry, who had a positively eighteenth century relish for encouraging poets and poetry. "Her mind was embued with literature," Miller wrote of his elderly friend later, "and stored with literary anecdotes; she conversed with elegance, she wrote pleasingly and with great facility in both prose and verse."

More to the point, Robert Carruthers, editor of the *Inverness Courier*, invited Miller to contribute to his newspaper, and Miller opted to do a series of five "letters" (articles) about the Cromarty herring fishery, on the sensible grounds that it was a subject he knew something about. When the letters appeared in the summer of 1829 they were hugely successful—so popular, in fact, that Robert Carruthers had them reprinted as pamphlets, which promptly sold out (and had Sir Walter Scott scrambling for a copy after the run was exhausted).

The five letters are stunning pieces of work. The conjunction of luminous descriptive passages, well-caught dialogue, and real insight into how the herring fishermen worked their trade, makes them minor masterpieces. "The breeze had died into a calm," Miller writes in one passage, "the heavens, no longer dark and grey, were glowing with stars; and the sea, from the smoothness of the surface, appeared a second sky, as bright and starry as the other; with this difference, however, that all its stars seemed to be comets; the slightly tremulous motion of the surface elongated the reflected images, and gave to each its tail." The rising of the herring shoals are described even more vividly. "A peculiar poppling noise, as if a thunder shower was beating on the surface with its multitudinous drops, rose around the boat; the water seemed sprinkled with an infinity of points of silver, that for an instant glittered in the sun and then resigned their places to other quick glancing points, that in turn were succeeded by yet others . . . . Shoal rose beyond shoal, till the whole bank of the Gulliam seemed beaten into foam, and the low poppling sounds were beaten into a roar, like that of the wind through some tall wood, that might be heard in the calm for miles."

It was good stuff, and Miller knew it. He had, he realised, found

Robert Chambers the Edinburgh author, journalist, bookseller and publisher. Chambers' books The Vestiges of Creation *and* Sequel to Vestiges of Creation *were huge publishing successes, and put forward theories of evolution fifteen years ahead of Darwin's* Origin of Species. *Hugh Miller felt that Chambers' success was "doing harm on both sides of the Atlantic" and as a counterblast wrote his own anti-evolution bestseller* Footprints of the Creator. *(Courtesy of The National Galleries of Scotland)*

his *metière*. "Let it be my business, I said, to know what is not generally known—let me qualify myself to stand as interpreter between nature and the public, while I strive to narrate as pleasingly and describe as vividly as I can, let truth, not fiction, be my walk; and if I succeed in uniting the novel to the true, in provinces of more general interest than the very humble one in which I have now partly succeeded, I shall succeed also in establishing myself in a position, which if not lofty, will yield me at least more solid footing than that which I might attain as a mere *litterateur.*"

It was a wise decision (although it upset his new-found aristocratic patron Miss Dunbar of Boath) and it rekindled his enthusiasm for geology and natural history. He resumed his habit of wandering about the rocks of Easter Ross and the Moray Firth with his geologist's hammer, cracking open stones, delighting at the fossil contents, and trying to make sense of the puzzles he found in the strata. At the Eathie Burn near Cromarty, he found a treasure-trove of fossil-studded rock about which he said, "I found I had work enough before me for the patient study of years." While he continued to ply his trade in and around Cromarty, his articles in the *Inverness Courier,* gave him a local reputation which attracted a small band of admirers from around Scotland.

In 1831 the north of Scotland was harried by cholera, and the people of Cromarty watched it creep closer down Scotland and stop on the other side of the Cromarty Firth. "Such was the general panic in the infected places," Miller wrote, "that the bodies of the dead were no longer carried to the churchyard, but huddled up in solitary holes and corners; and the pictures suggested to the fancy, of familiar faces lying uncoffined in the ground beside some lonely wood, or in some dark morass or heathy moor, were fraught to many with a terror stronger that that of death. We knew that the corpse of a young robust fisherman, who used occasionally to act as one of the Cromarty ferrymen, lay festering in a sandbank; that the iron frame of a brawny blacksmith was decomposing in a mossy hole beside a thorn-bush; that half the inhabitants of the little fishing village of Inver were strewn in shallow furrows along the arid waste which surrounded their dwellings."

In a vain attempt to keep the disease out of Cromarty, a public meeting decided to throw a *cordon sanitaire* round the town. A Defence Association was formed and pickets were organised to guard all the roads into the town and "all vagabonds and trampers were turned back without remorse" while more respectable travellers were wheeled into a wooden building and thoroughly fumigated with sulphur and chloride of lime ("though for my own part, I could not see how the demon of disease was to be expelled by the steam of a little sulphur and chloride").

But the disease crept in by sea. A local fisherman had died of cholera in Wick and while most of his clothes had been burnt by the authorities, his brother had purloined some and smuggled them back to Cromarty. The cholera leapt from the seaman's wardrobe, killed the wretched fisherman, and ran through the streets of the town for weeks. "The visitation," Miller recalled grimly, "had its wildly picturesque accompaniments. Pitch and tar were kept burning during the night in the openings of the infected lanes; and the unsteady light flickered with ghastly effect on house and wall, and tall chimney-top, and on the flitting figures of the watchers. By day, the frequent coffins, borne to the grave by but a few bearers, and the frequent smoke that rose outside the place from fires kindled to consume the clothes of the infected, had their sad and startling effect."

Shortly before the cholera epidemic, Miller met the young woman who was to become his wife. She was Lydia Fraser, daughter of an Inverness merchant who died after his business collapsed. She had come to live in Cromarty with her widowed mother. Lydia Fraser was only nineteen and, according to Miller, a fetching, fair-haired young woman who looked three years younger than she was. But she had been educated in England and Edinburgh, had a good mind (she later became a writer of children's books), and was an enthusiastic reader. For all his status as a Cromarty notable, Miller seems to have been bashful, and sexually inept, with little experience of women.*

For all her fragile looks and apparently winsome ways, Lydia Fraser knew what she wanted. She began to hang around whatever dyke, churchyard, cottage or manse Miller was working on, engaging

*Once again, the irate Hugh Miller Williamson, puts a very different complexion on the events surrounding Hugh Miller's courtship from the genteel idyll sketched by Bayne and Lydia in *The Life and Letters*. The meeting with Lydia Fraser, Williamson declares, was Hugh Miller's "evil fate". And Lydia's father, far from being the faintly aristocratic, "notably hansome", accomplished Highland gent, was a shady Inverness businessman known as "Snuffy Wull", who had an "odour of sanctity" that parted hapless old maids and widows from their savings, which "Snuffy Wull" sank into various dodgy enterprises and then went bankrupt. It was not Cupid that conjoined Hugh Miller with Lydia Fraser, Williamson wrote angrily, but "some evil-minded counterfeit of him".

him in conversation "on all manners of subjects connected with *belles-lettres* and the philosophy of the mind", or contriving to bump into him on evening walks in the Cromarty woods. The stately and somewhat metaphysical love-making went on for a number of years, to the horror of Lydia's mother who tried to knock it on the head. The respectable, and decidedly sniffish, widow Fraser was appalled at the thought of a girl of her daughter's taste and refinement taking up with a dust-covered mason. Ironically, Miller agreed with her; he vowed to himself that he would never marry Lydia until he could offer her a more respectable station in life. And *that,* he hoped, would come via his writings. He was busily putting together a series of semi-fictional essays, later known as *Scenes and Legends of the North of Scotland.* The tenacious Lydia, however, refused to be put off by either her mother or Hugh Miller, and eventually the couple agreed that if nothing came of his literary ambitions, they would collect the £300 which Miller's mother held for him, head for the United States "and share together in a strange land, whatever fate might be in store for us".

THE BANKER

WHEN help came, it came from a decidedly unexpected quarter. One morning at the end of 1834—when Miller was thirty-two years old—he was invited to have breakfast with one Robert Ross, who had just been appointed "agent" for the newly-opened branch of the Commercial Bank in Cromarty. During the meal Ross put a proposition to Miller. The bank needed an accountant, he said, would Miller take the job? Miller was startled. He knew nothing of business, he told Ross, and even less about banking or accounting. What use could he be? Ross assured him there was nothing in banking that a man of his intelligence could not learn. And the Commercial Bank would be happy to train him in its mysteries. After a moment's reflection, Miller accepted. The job was a purchase on respectability, a way into the middle classes, a way of marrying Lydia.

In November 1834, Miller was once again on a ship to Edinburgh to begin his training as a bank officer. This time, he was landing in the capital with a modest reputation as a writer and a list of potential contacts. "I see many changes in Edinburgh," he wrote to Lydia on landing, "there are large open spaces which were occupied ten years ago by lofty masses of buildings; and masses of buildings where there were then only open spaces. Some of the new statues I don't at all admire." Miller lost no time in making contact with his new found admirers among the *literati* of Edinburgh. He looked up Sir Thomas Dick Lauder at Grange House, was received with "great kindness" and invited to live there. The day after, he introduced himself to Adam Black the publisher, then Lord Provost of Edinburgh and MP for the city, and once again got a cordial welcome.

But the corner which the Commercial Bank had set aside for Hugh Miller was not in Edinburgh itself, it was in their branch at Linlithgow in West Lothian, seventeen miles west of the city. "I have never yet been in any part of the country where the surface is so broken into little hillocks," Miller soon wrote to Lydia. "Its geological character is highly interesting. Almost all the eminences are basaltic. In the hollows we meet with sandstone, lime and indurated clay. The lime is rich in animal remains, all of the earliest tribes." As Miller's enthusiastic letter suggests, he lost no opportunity of foraging about among the limestone quarries and coal seams of West Lothian. He dug up and carted back to his lodgings palaeozoic shells, carbonised lignite with traces of "woody structure", the fossil remains of palms, and the joints of flattened reeds ("possibly the vegetable to which the south of Scotland owes its coal").

And while he found the bank hard going at first (in fact he was denounced by his boss to the head office as an incompetent), he quickly mastered the system. At the same time his book on the *Scenes and Legends of Northern Scotland* was coming off the press and, with mounting excitement, he corrected the proofs and waited for the publication. He also found time to tour the antiquity-rich central belt of Scotland ("never before did I pass over so large a tract of the classic ground of Scotland") and to indulge his taste for Scottish history at Sheriffmuir, Falkirk, Stirling Bridge, Linlithgow Castle Palace, and the armoury of Stirling Castle.

At the beginning of 1835 after two months in Linlithgow and Edinburgh, Miller returned to Cromarty to take up the job as bank accountant. On the face of it, his four year stint behind the bank counter was an odd one, but by dealing with the nuts and bolts of economic life, he learned lessons that he later put to excellent use. "For the cultivation of a shrewd common sense," he wrote in *My Schools and Schoolmasters,* "a bank office is one of perhaps the best schools in the world . . . ingenuities, plausibilities, special pleadings, all that make the stump-orator great, must be brushed aside by the banker. The question with him comes always to be a sternly naked one:—Is, or is not, a person fit to be trusted with the bank's money?"

In the bank office, Miller learned at first hand how the economy of rural Scotland was changing, with a drift towards bigger farms, and bigger businesses: "the small farm system, so excellent in a past age, was getting altogether unsuited for the energetic competition of the present one; and that the *small* farmers—a comparatively comfortable class some sixty or eighty years before, who used to give dowries to their daughters, and leave well-stocked farms to their sons—were falling into straitened circumstances, and becoming, however respectable elsewhere, not very good men in the bank". Much the same was happening elsewhere in the district and he observed "how the business of its shopkeepers fell always into a very few hands" leaving to the remainder "only a mere show of custom". The fishing industry—and particularly the herring fishery—was in a precarious state "not more from the uncertainty of the fishings themselves than from the fluctuation of the markets".

One melancholy talent he developed, he said, was spotting bankruptcies coming. He claimed he always underestimated the time they took to happen because of the "desperate efforts which men of energetic temperament make in such circumstances, and which, to the single injury of their friends and the loss of their creditors, succeed usually in staving off the catastrophe for a season. In short, the school of the branch bank was a very admirable school; and I profited so much by its teachings, that when questions connected with banking are forced on the notice of the public, and my brother editors have to apply for articles on the subject to literary bankers, I find I can write my banking articles for myself."

It was not until January 1837 that Miller finally married Lydia Fraser—a contract that had to be steered through the dogged objections of Lydia's mother. After a brief, modest honeymoon in Elgin the Millers set up home in Cromarty in a modest house with one servant and an attic-room filled with books and fossils. His bank work left Miller enough mental energy to pursue his literary interests, and he began contributing regularly to *Chambers Journal,* and John Wilson's *Border Tales* for "as inadequate a remuneration as ever a poor writer got in the days of Grub Street".

As usual, Miller found his deepest pleasure in the fossil-rich deposits around Cromarty, "when fatigued by my calculations at the

Miller's friend and admirer Sir David Brewster, one-time editor of the Edinburgh Magazine, *and later principal of St Andrews and Edinburgh universities. A brilliant and original physicist, Brewster was fascinated by light, colour and optics (he invented both the kaleidoscope and the stereoscopic viewer). Brewster was one of the founder-members of the British Association which held its first meeting in York in 1831. (Courtesy of The National Galleries of Scotland).*

bank, I used to find it delightful relaxation to lay open its fish by the scores, and to study their peculiarities as exhibited in their various states of keeping, until I at length became able to determine their several genera and species from even the minutest fragments". He found an astonishing number of fish and fossils on the Old Red Sandstone and was struck by the "peculiarity of their organisation". Unlike any modern fish he could trace, his fossils all had their skeletons on the outside "where the crustaceans wear their shells, and were furnished inside with but frameworks of perishable cartilege". What puzzled and amazed him even more was that the scientific luminaries who occasionally crossed his path "seemed to know even less about my Old Red fishes and their peculiarities of structure, than I did myself".

But once again Miller's idyll was shattered by tragedy. In the spring of 1839 his first child, a little girl called Liza, was taken ill and died within days.

"She was," Lydia Miller wrote about Liza,"a delight and wonder to Hugh above all wonders. Her little smiles and caresses sent him away to his daily toil with a lighter heart." Lydia described how, "one lovely evening in April," the child pushed her mother away with the words "awa, awa," "while a startled, inquiring, almost terrible look came into her lovely eyes. All the time she lay dying, which was three days and three nights, her father was prostrate in the dust before God in an agony of tears. Whether he performed his daily bank duties, or any part of them, I do not remember. But such a personification of David the King at a like mournful time, it is impossible to imagine. All the strong man was bowed down. He wept, he mourned, he fasted, he prayed. He entreated God for her life."

But Liza Miller died and was buried beside the old chapel of St Regulus. The last piece of work Hugh Miller ever did as a stonemason was to carve her headstone. "Never again in the course of his life was he thus effected," Lydia Miller wrote. "He was an affectionate father and some of his children were at times near death, but he never again lost thus the calmness and dignity of the natural equipoise, as it were, of his manhood."

By the late 1830s, as Miller's interest in national affairs deepened, he found himself—like most other Presbyterians in Scotland—racked by resentment at the Patronage Act of 1712, which gave the Scottish gentry the right to appoint or "intrude" Parish ministers of their own choosing (a right which the English squirearchy had happily exercised for centuries). In the hierarchical and classbound structures of the Church of England, such a practice was accepted with hardly a murmur. But in the democratic and populist traditions of the Church of Scotland, the Patronage Act was anathema, and, as Scottish churchmen had been pointing out for generations, ran totally counter to the letter and spirit of the Treaty of Union of 1707.

The resentment raised by the Patronage Act was very powerful indeed, and was as much to do with a deep dislike of the gentry, suspicion of the English, and Scottish nationalism as it was to do with theology or Church affairs. The Lairds of Scotland, as Professor Christopher Smout points out in his *History of the Scottish People* were "a class increasingly looking to England for their cultural models, and therefore wanting to see someone in the Manse as polite and friendly to the laird as the average Anglican parson was to the squire". The result was a distinct tendency for the Anglicised Lairds to appoint parish ministers who were inclined "to share the landowner's outlook and social aims".

In many ways the "ten years conflict" (which culminated in the Disruption of the Church of Scotland in 1843) became quite nakedly political, as the "moderate" party of the Church were hounded year after year by the fast-growing and highly-vocal "evangelical" party led by the Presbyterian philosopher and theologian Thomas Chalmers. As James Young points out in his book *The Rousing of the Scottish Working Class,* the ten years conflict over the "intrusion" of ministers became a political catalyst. Far from diverting the passions and attention of the Scottish working people from politics, the disruption controversies radicalised them. Young cites the case of an East Lothian patroness who was horrified that the local presbytery had given her candidate the thumbs down. "Yes Ma'am," she was told by a local farmer, "but your appointing him was the very reason we wad' na' tak' him".

The Patronage Act was a grave injustice, but no matter how often, bitterly or loudly the Church of Scotland complained, or cried *foul!,* the English-dominated parliament and government paid no attention. In 1834 the Church took the matter into their own hands, and the General Assembly of the Church of Scotland passed a Veto Act decreeing that no Laird had the right to "intrude" a minister unless that minister had the support of a majority of the male communicants in the parish. Predictably, the Anglicised lairds were outraged at this assault on their diginity and power, and began resisting.

What brought Hugh Miller into the lists on the side of the "non-intrusionist" evangelicals was the historic "Auchterarder case", when Perthshire aristocrat Lord Kinnoull tried to foist the Rev. Robert Young on the parish of Auchterarder. The presbytery promptly organised a ballot in which the Rev Young got three votes, while forty people abstained, and nearly 300 of the faithful voted to tell the Laird's man to get lost. Lord Kinnoull and his legal advisers were outraged at this affront, and took the case to the Court of Session in Edinburgh. In March 1838 the judges voted by eight votes to five that Lord Kinnoull had right on his side, and that the presbytery and the parishioners had no right to dump his appointee. But the presbytery fought on, the case was taken to the House of Lords, and finally lost in 1839 when Lord Brougham and Vaux dismissed as preposterous the notion that the members of the Church of Scotland had the right to elect their own ministers.

Hugh Miller was incensed by Brougham's decision, and the tone with which it was delivered, and wrote in his autobiography that "it was only when the Church's hour of peril came that I realised how much I really valued her, and how strong and numerous the associations were that bound her to my affections". He had, he said, been interested in the arguments for the Reform Bill, the Catholic Emancipation Act, and the struggle to free Negro slaves "but they never cost me an hour's sleep. Now, however, I felt more deeply; and for at least one night after reading the speech of Lord Brougham, and the decision of the House of Lords in the Auchterarder case, I slept none . . . Could I not do something to bring up the people to their assistance? I tossed wakefully throughout a long night, in which I formed my plan of taking up the purely popular side of the question; and in the morning I sat down to state my views to the people, in the form of a letter addressed to Lord Brougham."

After a week's unremitting work in his spare time, Miller produced the manuscript which he called *A Letter to Lord Brougham from one of the Scotch People,* and which, though not the best, was probably the most important single piece that Hugh Miller ever wrote. He sent the manuscript of his "letter" to his bank colleague Robert Paul of Edinburgh (an ardent evangelical) who passed it on, almost by accident, to the Rev Dr Candlish, one of the evangelical party's leading lights. Candlish was so impressed by the ferocity and the eloquence of Hugh Miller's attack on Brougham and the House of

Lords, that he passed Miller's manuscript on to the Church's publishers, who brought it out as a pamphlet. The top brass of the evangelical party were also impressed by Miller's polemic and thought he might be the man to edit the new evangelical newspaper, to be called *The Witness,* which they were about to launch. Miller was invited to Edinburgh to discuss the job, and after some hesitation he agreed to give it a try.

Miller had other ambitions; he wanted to make his mark on the world as a serious author, and as a geologist. He knew that the demands of producing a twice-weekly newspaper on a shoe-string budget would be fearsome, and he quaked at the prospect of the wrath of the establishment that would come down on his head. "But believing the cause to be a good one," he wrote, "I prepared for a life of strife, toil, and comparative obscurity." Miller quit his job at the bank, and after a rousing testimonial dinner from his friends and associates in Cromarty (at which he was presented with an "elegant breakfast service of plate" and sent on his way to the tune of *A Man's a man for a' that)* Miller left Cromarty for Edinburgh at the end of 1839.

STURM UND DRANG

THE first issue of Hugh Miller's *Witness* made its appearance on the streets of Edinburgh on 15 January 1840 (under a slogan coined by John Knox: "I am in the place where I am demanded of conscience to speak the truth, and therefore the truth I speak, impugn it whoso list"). From the outset Miller made it plain he meant business. "We enter upon our labours at a period emphatically momentous," he wrote in his first, very wordy, editorial, "at the commencement, it is probable, of one of the most important eras, never forgotten by a country, which influences for ages the conditions and character of the people, and from which the events of their future history take colour and form." Miller went on to contrast the luke-warm, limp-wristed policies of the "moderates" inside the Church of Scotland, with the energy of the "evangelicals". "Here, then, on a distinction as obvious as it is important we take our stand. The cause of the unchanged party in the Church is that of the Church itself;— it is that of the people of Scotland, and the people know it . . . "

While the first issue of *The Witness* (like many issues thereafter) was dominated by Church affairs, Miller found space for much else. He carried reports,—on the opening of the provincial parliament in Upper Canada, fresh riots in Valencia, the draft constitution for the state of Hanover, more honours for the Prince Albert of Saxe-Coburg, the "cruel diseases" that were ravaging the Turkish fleet, the health of the Princess of Denmark, the build-up of "certain armaments" in Russia, and the fact that the authorities in Constantinople had introduced the guillotine to the intense curiosity of Turkish execution enthusiasts (and the apparent indifference of the condemned men).

The first issue was also liberally peppered with advertisements for, among other things, church meetings, religious tracts, useful books, temperance medals, and Mr Thalberg's "Third and Farewell Concert" to take place at the Assembly Halls and which was due to be strummed on "Erard's New Patent Grand Piano Forte brought from London expressly for the occasion". In addition, there were less edifying items for sale such as old whiskey, sherry from the butt, the newest style in "dress vests", straw-hat pressing machines, penny-postage letter-weighers, plus "an automatic singing bird, Chinese juggler, and a transparent clock with the invisible movement" (the last three items available from the Royal Bazaar at 19 Princes Street).

Interestingly, the first issue of *The Witness* also carried an advertisement for the *Scottish Standard,* a pro-Patronage newspaper which was launched on the same day as Hugh Miller's *Witness.* The publishers confidently expected that the *Scottish Standard* would satisfy "long cherished expectations felt and acknowledged by all classes and parties in the country; for it is a fact, lamented over on the one side, and boasted on the other, that the Conservative Newspapers, both in number and circulation fall greatly behind those which advocate the Destructive principle . . . " The *Scottish Standard,* their owners promised, would be devoted to "the support of the British Constitution in Church and State". This proved to be a very creaky platform in the Edinburgh of 1840; within a year the *Scottish Standard* had flopped, and Miller was able to report with some relish that it had been "converted into a cravat for the *Edinburgh Evening Post".*

In fact, Miller took to the knockabout world of periodical journalism like a duck to water. For months he produced *The Witness* almost single-handed (sometimes with the help of his wife Lydia, who joined him in April 1840) working deep into the night, churning out reams of copy to fill the papers gaping maw. That first year he

The two-storey thatched cottage in Cromarty where Hugh Miller was born and raised. The house was built in 1711 by Miller's great-grandfather John Feddes, a small-time privateer who made his money plundering Spanish cargo ships. Miller claims to have seen the apparition of John Feddes in the house, "a tall large, tall, very old man attired in a light-blue greatcoat. He seemed to be steadfastly regarding me with apparent complacency; but I was sadly frightened. . . ." (Courtesy of the National Trust for Scotland).

wrote a dazzling range and variety of articles from fiercely polemic pieces on Church politics (some of them enormously long) to crisp political commentary on the Navy estimates, capital punishment, the Edinburgh savings banks, the copyright bill, and the Queen's marriage. He also cooked up long, discursive pieces on, for example, China and the Chinese, and reviewed books such as Darwin's masterpiece *The Voyage of the Beagle*. (Miller waxed lyrical over

Darwin's ability to combine "high literary abilities and fine taste to many extensive acquirements as a man of science".)

Miller seldom hesitated to weigh in on foreign affairs. He was appalled at the oppression and torture of Jews in Rhodes and Damascus, claimed that it was the Roman Catholic hierarchy in Damascus that was whipping up the anti-semitism, and looked forward to the day when the Jews would give up their benighted religion and become good Christians (i.e. Presbyterians). He was equally appalled at the behaviour of the British mercenaries in Spain who had "burnt villages, and cut throats, and shot and stabbed a great many human creatures who never did them any harm, and who, but for their exertion as man-slayers, would have still been alive . . ." There was nothing, Miller pronounced, "very fine in the idea of a man-butcher hired to destroy life at the rate of 1s per day".

But for a man who was so patently and sincerely agitated by injustice and the miserable conditions of working people, Miller kept some of his deepest bile for political radicals like the Socialists and the Chartists. Socialist pamphlets he found "detestably obscene" and "horribly blasphemous" while the participants of a Chartist rally on Glasgow Green were "dirty, squalid and depressed . . . entirely broken men". So far as Miller was concerned the Chartist movement was a dangerous fraud, and he was convinced that "the worst friends of the people are those who drive their claims too far. Popular license is but despotism in its first stage—a great truth confirmed by the history of almost every European country." As for one man one vote: "Universal suffrage in the present state of public morals would ruin the country," he cried, "the masses are not fit for it."*

*In the course of his editorship, Miller regularly showed flashes of a latent Scottish nationalism, which ran counterpoint to his British patriotism. Reporting on the instigation of an early proto-nationalist movement called The Scottish Association, he wrote that "it is one thing to acquiesce in the Union (of 1707) and quite another to acquiesce in the treatment which Scotland almost ever since that event, has been receiving at the hands of the English. And the present is a most favourable time for the country to take its stand against further aggression." But Miller warned that it would not be easy as "it is one of the inevitable effects of treatment such as that to which Scotland has been subjected by the English, to produce disunion and diversity of opinion in the injured country". And on another instance he made the point that "It has been the tendency of English misgovernment and aggression to render us a divided people."

The Witness was an odd, but vigorous mix of radicalism, church infighting, philosophical comment, foreign news, decent reporting, book reviews, and small ads. And it worked! Miller's editorial recipe proved highly successful (to the delight of the evangelical party in the Chuch of Scotland). In 1841—having seen off the conservative *Scottish Standard*—Miller was boasting that the circulation of *The Witness* was climbing fast and had now reached "third place in point of circulation among the long-established newspapers in Edinburgh". By the beginning of 1842, *The Witness* circulation (which had started at 700) was heading towards 2,000, making it second only to *The Scotsman* (which then had a circulation of 2,577). Nine other Edinburgh papers (*Courant, Advertiser, Journal, Chronicle, Mercury, Post, Observer, Pilot* and *Messenger*) were all selling well below *The Witness*. "With such a circulation," he announced to the traders and merchants of Edinburgh, "Advertisers must see that by employing our columns they are promoting their own interests."

But the main thrust of *The Witness* was to champion the evangelical party in the long confrontation between the British state and the Church of Scotland over who should appoint parish ministers. By 1843 the argument was coming to a head, and Chalmers and the evangelicals had decided that they could no longer put up with the high-handed arrogance of the British establishment (or for that matter, with the hand-wringing feebleness of the "moderates" in the Church of Scotland). In the weeks before the General Assembly of the Church, due to be held on 18 May 1843, they let it be known that they planned to "disrupt" the Church by walking out, and setting up their own "Free" Church of Scotland. It was a momentous occasion for Scottish religious and political life, and the question buzzing round Edinburgh was how many ministers would throw up their livelihoods to follow Chalmers and the evangelicals? The establishment and the moderates were completely convinced it would be a mere handful. Others were not so sure.

When the day came Hugh Miller was there with his notebook, waiting in the gallery of the Church of St Andrew & St George in George Street, Edinburgh. The atmosphere was electric, and there was a huge crowd of people outside, pressing against the church doors in a struggle to get in. After the procession of dignitaries had descended from the High Church of St Giles the moderator, the Rev Dr Welsh started off with a "deeply impressive prayer" which the back of the Church could not hear because of the noise from outside.

Welsh then read out a formal statement which had been signed by 120 ministers and 74 church elders stating that a great, and intolerable infringement of the Church's constitution had been perpetrated, and that men of principle could stand for it no longer. He threw the document down on the table, and with Chalmers beside him, led the procession of four hundred or so ministers and elders out of the building and out of the establishment.

With the great men gone, Miller observed, "There suddenly glided into the front rows a small party of men who no-one knew, obscure, mediocre, blighted-looking men" who reminded Miller of the "thin and blasted corn of Pharoah's vision, and, like them too, seemed typical of a time of famine and destitution". In disgust, Miller left the Assembly to the "moderates" and followed the procession of determined evangelicals down the hill to the ramshackle Tanfield Hall in Canonmills, where they held the first General Assembly of the Free Church of Scotland. It was no empty gesture. About one-third of the Church's ministers walked out at the Disruption, cutting themselves off from state funds, their wages, their homes, their security, and risking their families in hard times in a poor country.

The years between 1840 and 1844 were hard going for Miller. The fledgling paper had to be nursed then coaxed to success, there were battles to be fought and campaigns to be won. It was, from all accounts, an exhausting business, and Miller never shook off the silicosis which he contracted working as a stone-mason in the quarries and building sites of Easter Ross and the Black Isle. But his idea of a holiday seems to have been to take off with his notepad to gather material for a book (with which he would then fill his free time). In the summer of 1844 Miller abandoned *The Witness* for a few weeks to cruise around the "small isles" (i.e. the Inner Hebrides) with his old friend John Swanson, then Free Church minister for the small isles. Swanson was one of the hundreds of Church of Scotland ministers who threw up their livings and homes at the Disruption. In his case he found himself with a widely scattered, but extremely pious flock, but with no permanent church building, and a Laird who refused to give him a site to build on. The Free Church had resorted to spending some of their scarce cash on a small yacht (called *Betsey*) in which Swanson and a crew of one sailed from island to island, tending his charges. Pleasant enough for much of the summer, perhaps, but a nasty, and sometimes near-lethal business in the Hebridean autumn and winter, when the westerly gales made the reef-strewn coast a nightmare. (*The Betsey* came close to being lost twice; once when Hugh Miller was on board).

In the middle of July 1844 Miller met up with Swanson at Tobermory on Mull, and for the next few weeks sailed the bound of Swanson's parish, flitting between Mull, Eigg, Skye, Rum and Pabba. And not in luxury; the cabin he and Swanson shared he describes as "the size of a common bed and just lofty enough under the beams to permit a man of 5ft 11ins to stand erect in his night cap". Miller was particularly fascinated by the beautiful and distinctly weird island of Eigg, situated between the southeast of Skye and the mainland at Ardnamurchan. Eigg was the island where Swanson had been the parish minister, and where, till the Disruption, he had expected to end his days. Miller was impressed by his friend's fluency in Gaelic (a language he had to learn the hard way), his oratory, and the loyalty he inspired among the population of the island. Although all that Swanson could offer the people was a dingy, peat-roofed cabin for a church, his services were invariably packed to the doors and beyond. Swanson seems to have had the characteristic zeal of the best of the evangelicals, and confirmed Miller's view that "Presbyterianism without the animating life is a poor shrunken thing. Without the vitality of evangelism it is nothing."

Miller was so intrigued by the geology, history, and people of Eigg (whom he describes as "an active, middle-sized race, with well-developed heads, acute intellects and singularly warm feelings") that he returned to the little island with Swanson the following year (1845). In his short book *The Cruise of the Betsey* Miller gives some insight into the poverty of much of the Inner Hebrides. The two men had dropped in to visit one of Swanson's parishioners, an old woman who had been bed-ridden for ten years, and Miller was outraged by what he found. "Scarce ever before had I seen so miserable a hovel," he wrote. "It was hardly larger than the cabin of the *Betsey*, and a thousand times less comfortable . . . The low chinky door opened direct into the one wretched apartment of the hovel, which we found lighted chiefly by holes in the roof . . . Within a foot of the bed-ridden woman's head there was a hole in the turf-wall, which was, we saw, usually stuffed with a bundle of rags . . . The little hole in the wall had formed the poor creature's only communication with the face of the external world for ten weary years."

Miller noticed that, on leaving, Swanson had slipped the woman a few coins. "I learned that not during the ten years in which she had

been bed-ridden had she received a single farthing from the
proprietor, nor, indeed, had any of the poor of the island, and that
the parish had no session funds. I saw her husband a few days
after,—an old, worn-out man, with famine written legibly in his
hollow cheek and eye, and on the shrivelled frame, that seemed lost
in his tattered dress; and he reiterated the same sad story. They had
no means of living, he said, save through the charity of their poor
neighbours, who had so little to spare; for the parish or the
proprietor had never given them anything. He had once, he added,
two fine boys, both sailors, who had helped them; but the one had
perished in a storm off the Mull of Cantyre[Kintyre], and the other
had died of fever when on a West India voyage; and though their
poor girl was very dutiful, and staid in their crazy hut to take care of
them in their helpless old age, what other could she do in a place like
Eigg than just share with them their sufferings?"

The wretchedness of the rural poor, the living and working
conditions of farm labourers, fisherman, Highland crofters, was
something which haunted Miller. Some of his finest, most powerful
essays are on the subject; *Peasant Properties, The Cottages of Our Hinds,
The Bothy System, The Highlands, the Scotch Poor Law, Pauper Labour, The
Felons of the Country,* and the superb *Sutherland As It Was And Is; Or How
A Country May Be Ruined.* There was something about their mute
suffering, their patience and silence that moved Miller more deeply
than the squalor of the Edinburgh and Glasgow working class, who
were turbulent, vocal, and often downright dangerous.

In the autumn of that same year (1845) Miller took eight weeks off
from *The Witness* to wander in England, the "sister kingdom" which
he had never visited. His account of his journey, called *First
Impressions of England and Its People,* is one of the most interesting and
least known of nineteenth century travel books. Despite choosing an
autumn which was "ungenial and lowering" and a progress
bedevilled by "indifferent health and consequent languor" Miller's
account of England and the English is perceptive, lively, and studded
with passages of power and insight. Putting up at mainly second class
railway hotels, coaching inns and lodgings, Miller wandered down
over the border to Newcastle, Durham, York, Manchester, Wolverhampton, Dudley, Stourbridge, Droitwich, Birmingham, Stratford,
Olney, London, Harrow, Liverpool, and then back to Edinburgh via
Glasgow.

Inevitably perhaps, the constant theme in *First Impressions* is a comparison between the Scots and the English, from which the Scots come rather badly. One Sunday evening in Manchester, he watched the day-trippers spill off the train and noted, "There was not much actual drunkenness among the crowd . . . not a tithe of what I would have witnessed on a similar occasion in my own country." He put this down to the very different Sabbath habits of the two nations. "With the humble Englishman trained to no regular habit of church-going, Sabbath is a pudding-day, a clean-shirt day, a day for lolling on the green opposite the sun . . . or, if in the neighbourhood of a railway, for taking a short trip to some country inn, famous for its cakes and ale; but to the humble Scot become English in his Sabbath views, the day is, in the most cases, a time of sheer recklessness and dissipation."

He was also much taken by English women, finding that "The English type of face and person seems particularly well adapted to the female countenance and figure; and the proportion of pretty women to the population—women with clear, fair complexions, well-turned arms, soft features and fine busts—seems very great."

But as a shrewd observer of rural people, he thought that the country English were distinctly less intellectual and curious than their Scottish equivalents. He had no hesitation "in affirming that their minds lie much more profoundly asleep than those of the common people of Scotland. We have no class north of the Tweed that corresponds with the class of ruddy, round-faced, vacant English, so abundant in the rural districts." The ordinary Scot, he felt, was "a naturally more inquisitive, more curious being, than the common Englishman; he asks many more questions, and accumulates much larger hoards of fact".

But what the ordinary Englishman lacked in curiosity and intellectual drive, Miller found he more than made up with stubborn independence. They possessed, he thought, "much of that natural independence which the Scotchman wants; and village Hampdens— men quite ready to do battle on behalf of their civil rights with the lord of the manor as the Scot with a foreign enemy—are comparatively common characters". The paradox was that the English possessed a much greater intellectual "range" than the Scots. "There is an order of the English mind to which Scotland has not attained," he felt, "our first men stand in the second rank, not a foot's breadth behind the foremost of England's second rank men; but there is a front rank of British intellect in which there stands no

Scotchman . . . Scotland has produced no Shakespeare; Burns and Sir Walter Scott united would fall short of the stature of the giant of Avon. Of Milton we have not even a representative."

Like most Scots, Miller relished the range and diversity of England (and of the four days he spent in London, two were devoted to wandering about the British Museum in a state of ecstasy). But he was fearful for the English establishment, and particularly for the powerful Church of England, which he thought was being eaten away from within by the "white ants" of "Puseyism", the Anglo-Catholic, High-Church revival, being led by the Oxford Movement (whose best propogandist was Edward Bouvier Pusey). The High-Church medievalists were taking over the upper reaches of English society, Miller concluded, "with whose Conservative leanings the servile politics of Puseyism agreed well . . . Schools had been erected in which the rising generation might at once be shown the excellence, and taught the trick of implicit submission to authority . . . " This disabling reactionary ecclesiasticism, he thought, would lead the Church of England into "antagonism to the tendencies of the age" and render the institution irrelevant, and in danger of withering away.

Back in Scotland, some of the larger egos in the Free Church were becoming increasingly irritated by Hugh Miller, particularly at his racy turn of phrase, his capacity of aggravation and trouble, his scant respect for many Free Church dignitaries, and his determination to run *The Witness* his own way. One such enemy was the Rev Dr Robert Candlish (who had recommended Miller for the job in the first place) who now felt that there was a positive lack of "taste or tact" in the way Hugh Miller was handling important and delicate matters, and that it was time *The Witness* was merged with one or two other Free Church newspapers, and tightly run by a proper editorial board instead of the vague committee who took an overview of Miller's work.

Falling foul of an accomplished church politician like Robert Candlish was no joke. Miller knew that everything he had worked for was under threat, and he moved swiftly. In January 1847 he had printed, very quietly, a pamphlet marked "Strictly Private and Confidential" which he circulated to the entire editorial committee of *The Witness*. Miller's memorandum (for that's what it was) is a beautiful piece of pre-emptive bureaucracy. He quoted from letters which Candlish had thought were private, accused him of being out of touch with the Free Church members outside Edinburgh, rubbished the notion of running *The Witness* via a committee of professional churchmen, and pointed out that the main reason the paper seemed to be flagging was that he was obliged to print so many long and boring articles on Church affairs (such as "Dr Candlish's speech on education") and that many of *those* were inserted at the last minute by bumbling meddlers. He ended with a flourish: "My faults have no doubt been many; but they have not been faults of principle; nor have they lost me the confidence of that portion of the people of Scotland to which I belong and which I represent. And possessing their confidence, I do not now feel myself justified in retiring from my post."

The handiest memo-shuffler in IBM could have done no better. Candlish was crushed. And when he tried to back away, and suggested that all his communications to Miller and to other Free Church brass should be "superseded, set aside, buried and held as non-existent", Miller would have none of it. He refused to let Candlish off the hook. He was in a foul temper at the way Candlish had tried to undermine his position by "private" letters to the Committee, then had complained when Miller laid his hands on a few. "The man who has let his neighbour understand, in strict secrecy, that he intends bleeding him for his benefit by sending a ball through him in the evening, has no reason to complain that his neighbour betrays his confidence by blabbing to the police," Miller wrote.

The speed with which Miller had moved to outflank Candlish convinced Thomas Chalmers for one that the idea of the committee running the day-to-day affairs of *The Witness* was a nonsense. He promptly convened a special meeting, delivered a fierce pro-Miller harangue, and then settled the matter by asking the sheepish churchmen, "which of you could direct Hugh Miller?" Having seen the way Miller disposed of Candlish none of them offered to try, the whole idea was dropped, and Miller's position was never challenged again. But Candlish's attempted *coup* did leave a sour taste in Miller's mouth, and thereafter he never quite trusted the divines of the Free Church in the same way. But it is entirely likely that the whole business did *The Witness* nothing but good; Miller lost some of his pre-occupation with Free Church affairs, cut back on the coverage, and replaced it with general features, literature, and more popular science.

The obverse of Hugh Miller's enthusiasm for the Free Church of

Scotland was a naked anti-Catholicism which flared up from time to time and did him no credit. While Miller never came near the mindless ranting of many of his compatriots (some of whom despaired of the soft line on Catholics Miller took in *The Witness,* and started their own anti-Catholic sheet called *The Rock*), a few of Miller's leaders and articles on Catholics and Catholicism were downright vicious. In September 1850, for example, he ran a long piece on *The Cowgate Flock,* the immigrant Irish who were flooding into Edinburgh's Cowgate in the 1840s. "They eschew cleanliness for that is a Protestant virtue," Miller wrote caustically. "They hate to be seen in unpatched garments because these are often the accompaniments of a mind defiled with deadly heresy. Rather than toil themselves, they not infrequently prefer living on the labour of others, especially Protestants."

He did identify the root differences between Protestantism and the Roman church. "Her name is mystery," he wrote of the Catholic Church, "and the power which she wields is not moral but mystical. The change she effects on those on whom she acts is not a moral or a spiritual reformation, but a mystic transformation . . . " But transformation or no, he thought, Catholicism was bad news. "The experience of the ages has demonstrated that wherever Popery comes, there too come beggary and wretchedness;— there the intellect is paralysed, genius droops, industry is smitten, learning takes flight, commerce decays, every source of wealth and natural greatness dries up, and nothing is left but a universal wreck."

But Miller was even more contemptuous of Catholicism in the Anglo-Catholic form reviving under the Oxford Movement of the aggressive Edward Pusey. To Miller "Puseyism" represented everything that he loathed and despised in religious life. He saw it as an abomination, neither Protestant nor properly Catholic, but a shadowy, obscure, elusive thing, dangerous because it was fast becoming the religion of the politically-powerful English upper classes, and probably a stalking horse for the Roman church. Miller filled many columns of *The Witness* with attacks on Puseyism, but was at his most scathing after encountering it at first hand on his trip through England. He was repelled by a High-Church Cathedral service in York Minster. "The coldly-read or fantastically-chanted prayers, common-placed by the twice-a-day repetition of the centuries—the mechanical responses—the correct inanity of the choristers who had not even the life of music in them— the total want of lay attendance . . . all conspired to show that the Cathedral service of the English Church does not represent a living devotion, but a devotion that perished centuries ago."

In lying down with the dead, Miller thought, the Church of England were putting themselves in some peril and "in dressing out their clerical brethren in the cerements of Popery and setting them a-walking, could hardly have foreseen that many of them were to become the actual ghosts which they had decked them to simulate". What particularly incensed Miller about the High-Church revival in England was its incessant, and sometimes effective, hostility to science. He shared the alarm expressed by Charles Lyell that the classes in chemistry and botany, astronomy, geology and mineralogy at Oxford University could hardly raise half a dozen students, when fifteen years previously they had been heavily over-subscribed. "The medieval miasma, originated in the bogs and fens of Oxford, has been blown aslant over the face of the country," he wrote bitterly, "and not only religious but scientific truth is to experience, it would seem, the influence of its poisonous blights and rotting mildew".

By the late 1840s Hugh Miller was one of Edinburgh's literary lions, and like most of the species, was greatly stalked by polite society. The Duke of Argyll, for example, was a keen science buff, and continually invited Miller to Inverary Castle to discuss Higher Things (an invitation that Miller politely declined). Socially, Miller seems to have been both genuinely shy and something of a showman. Why else would a respectable Edinburgh intellectual and churchman dress himself up in a tweed plaid (as Miller invariably did) and pound the streets of the Capital like an upland shepherd? Why else would he spend happy hours posing as a stonemason for the calotype photographs of his friends David Octavius Hill and Robert Adamson? He enjoyed giving little drawing-room lectures on fossils and geology to the ladies of Edinburgh, or creating a *frisson* of dread in them with his tales of North Highland ghosts, or hard times in the Black Isle. He took huge delight in challenging his (mainly bookish) friends to wrestling, jumping over burns, or putting heavy stones, knowing full well that he would win. According to David Masson, another of Miller's simple-minded conceits was to entice his friends to try on his broad-brimmed hat, then falling about laughing as it slipped down over their noses. A large head, it was generally thought, was a mark of superiority.

There was, however, a darker side to Miller's success as a literary man and celebrity as a newspaper editor. He quickly became convinced that the enemies he made through his pugnacious articles and leaders in *The Witness* were a physical threat, and were likely to set some of Edinburgh's foot-pads or cut-purses on him. This seems very unlikely, but Miller took the notion seriously. By the early 1840s he had taken to carrying a loaded handgun around with him. One evening Miller walked past two of his friends in the Meadows of Edinburgh without recognising them. As a joke one of them shouted after him, "There goes that rascally editor of *The Witness*", and was horrified to find himself looking down the barrel of a cocked revolver. An embarrassed Hugh Miller later explained to his friends that he expected to be attacked any day, and the revolver was his defence.

THE GEOLOGIST

ON 9 September 1840, when *The Witness* was only eight months old and still finding its feet, a remarkable article appeared in the paper. Written by Hugh Miller himself and entitled *The Old Red Sandstone,* it described the foragings of a young man in the sandstone quarries of the North of Scotland. "In the course of the first day's employment I picked up a nodular mass of blue limestone," Miller wrote, "and laid it open by a stroke of the hammer. Wonderful to relate, it contained inside a beautifully finished piece of sculpture,—one of the volutes, apparently, of an Ionic capital; and not the far-famed walnut of the fairy tale, had I broken the shell and found the little dog lying within, could have surprised me more. Was there another such curiosity in the whole world? I broke open a few other nodules of similar appearance,—for they lay pretty thickly on the shore,—and found that there might. In one of these there were what seemed to be the scales of fishes, and the impressions of a few minute bivalves, prettily striated; in the centre of another there was actually a piece of decayed wood. Of all Nature's riddles, these seemed to me to be at once the most interesting and the most difficult to expound."

The essay was the first of seven (the last was published on 17 October 1840) fresh, beguiling accounts of what Miller had found and collected in the years he spent wandering the rocks, beaches, caves, quarries and river beds of Easter Ross and the Black Isle. They were an instant success. In fact so popular were the Old Red

Sandstone essays, that Miller fleshed them out into a full-length book, which he published under the same title in 1841, and dedicated to the geologist Sir Roderick Murchison. In the preface Miller apologised to both the professional geologists for covering ground with which they were already too familiar, and to the general reader for descriptions that could "have been thrown off with perhaps less regard to minute detail than to pictorial effect. May I crave, while addressing myself, now to the one class and now to the other, the alternate forbearance of each."

He need not have worried. *The Old Red Sandstone* ran into twenty-six editions, became a classic of mid-Victorian popular science, and established Miller's reputation as a serious, but eloquent and entertaining, geologist. The importance of Miller's book was that it reminded the geological world that the Old Red Sandstone formations of northern Scotland, far from being "remarkably barren of fossils" (as had been claimed in a professional journal) was liberally sprinkled with some of the most interesting of fossilised life. In fact, ever since the early 1830s Hugh Miller had been gathering fragments of fossilised fishes, crustaceans, plants and trees, and trying to make some sense of what he had in front of him. "I was for some time greatly puzzled in my attempt to restore these ancient fishes, by the peculiarity of their organisation," he wrote in *My Schools and Schoolmasters*. And after years spent quizzing passing geologists and scientists, most of whom seemed to know less about his Old Red fishes than he did, Miller came to the startling conclusion "that I had got into a *terra incognita* in the geological field, the greater portion of whose organisms were still unconnected with human language".

Working on his own, with little or no help from scientific literature, Miller painstakingly put together his "Old Red fishes", shuffling the fossil fragments and pieces about like parts of a jigsaw, struggling to build up some kind of picture of the long-dead creatures that lurked in the sandstone rocks around Cromarty, "until at length, after my abortive effort, the creatures rose up before me in their strange unwonted proportions, as they had lived, untold ages before, in the primeval seas". Miller describes coming across one particularly important fossil fragment, which he lay open with a single blow of his hammer: "And there, on a ground of light-coloured limestone lay the effigy of a creature fashioned apparently out of jet, with a body covered with plates, two powerful-looking arms articulated at the shoulder, a head entirely lost in the trunk as that of the ray or the sun fish with a long angular tail. My first formed idea regarding it was I had discovered a connecting link between the tortoise and the fish . . . "

It was not. What Miller had discovered was an important variety of Pterichthys, the winged fish, which was confirmed when it was passed on to the the great Swiss palaeontologist Louis Agassiz (via Roderick Murchison). Agassiz was almost as excited by what Miller had dug up as Miller was himself. "It is impossible," the Swiss wrote, "to see aught more bizarre in all creation than the Pterichthyan genus; the same astonishment that Cuvier felt in examining that Plesiosauras, I myself experienced when Mr H. Miller, the first discoverer of these fossils showed me the specimens which he had detected in the Old Red Sandstone of Cromarty."

In fact, Hugh Miller's work on the Old Red Sandstone produced a serious contribution to nineteenth-century geology, as well as a stunningly beautiful book. At the annual meeting of the British Association for the Advancement of Science, held in Glasgow on 23 September 1840, Miller's work was held up for scrutiny and applause by the best scientists of the day. With Charles Lyell in the chair, Roderick Murchison had nothing but praise for Miller's skill, perseverance and insight, and invited Louis Agassiz to classify the fossils which Miller had dug out of the rocks. Agassiz was even more effusive in his praise than Murchison, and paid Miller the tribute of naming one of the best fossils after him—*Pterichthys Milleri*, Miller's winged fish. The English geologist Buckland (author of the *Bridgewater Treatise*) said that he "had never been so much astonished in his life by the powers of any man as he had been by the geological descriptions of Mr Miller", and added that he would "give his left hand to possess such powers of description as this man".

The literary and scientific journals of the day shared Buckland's enthusiasm for *The Old Red Sandstone*. "The geological formation known as the Old Red Sandstone was long supposed to be peculiarly barren of fossils," the *Westminster Review* reminded its readers. "The researches of geologists, especially those of Mr Miller, have, however, shown that formation to be as rich in organic remains as any that has been explored." *The Edinburgh Review* thought that Miller's book was "as admirable for the clearness of its descriptions and the sweetness of its composition, as for the purity and gracefulness that pervade it", while Mantell's *Medals of Creation* could not think of "a more fascinating volume on any branch of British Geology".

Nor was the praise confined to this side of the Atlantic. Professor

Silliman's *American Journal of Science* found that *The Old Red Sandstone* evinced "talent of the highest order, a deep and healthful moral feeling, a perfect command of the finest language, and a beautiful union of philosopy and poetry. No geologist can peruse this volume without instruction and delight." And when Sir Roderick Muchison came to address the Geological Society in 1842 he announced that in Miller "we have to hail the accession to geological writers of a man highly qualified to advance the science. His work, to a beginner, is worth a thousand didactic treatises . . . "

Although *The Old Red Sandstone* is, in many respects, the best of Miller's writings on geology, it was only the beginning. In the sixteen years between the publication of the first essay in *The Witness,* and his death in 1856, Miller produced hundreds of articles, lectures, papers, and thumb-nail sketches on geology and palaeontology, on the *minutiae* of field work, and its philosophical and religious implications. In his cruises around the inner Hebrides with his friend John Swanson in 1844 and 1845, Miller wrote about the geological oddities of Eigg, Rum, Skye and Pabba. He ranged all over Scotland from the Bass Rock and coalfields of the Lothians, to Cromarty, Sutherland, Caithness and Orkney, in an unflagging effort to chart the rocks of Scotland. In his wanderings in England in 1845 he was endlessly fascinated by the alien geology of the Dudley coal measures, the Aymestry limestone, the New Red Sandstone around Wolverhampton, the salt deposits at Droitwitch. The output was endless, and how Miller found the time, energy and mental reserves to do the scientific work *and* be the full-time editor of the crusading *Witness,* is one of the literary miracles of the nineteenth century.

Of course, Miller's passion for geology and palaeontology drove him deep into one of the central issues of nineteenth-century philosophy—how life, and in particular human life, came about. This in the end boiled down to a confrontation between the "creation" theory of life, and the "development" (i.e. evolutionary) theory. It was an issue that struck at the very roots of the system of beliefs that prevailed in nineteenth-century Europe. And while the argument raged at its most fierce after Charles Darwin published *The Origin of Species* in 1859 (three years after Hugh Miller's death), the debate had been going on since the end of the eighteenth century. As far back as 1750 the Frenchman de Maillet published a fanciful, but deeply intelligent work called *Telliamed* (one of the first science books that Miller ever read) which suggests that the sea is "the great and fruitful womb of nature". In 1802 his compatriot, the great chemist and zoologist Jean Baptiste De Lamarck published a paper called *Recherches Sur L'Origins De Corps Vivant* which suggested that changes in the environment could work changes in living creatures, and that those modifications could be passed on to offspring. Lamarck developed and refined this thesis in his work *Philosophe Zoologique,* which became one of the great works of nineteenth-century science (and is currently being rediscovered, reappraised, and revalued).

Twenty years later the Scots geologist Charles Lyell, one of Darwin's teachers, and mentors, set the geological framework for biological evolution in his *Principles of Geology.* Lyell argued that, from all the scientific evidence, the earth was very, very old, infinitely older than the received wisdom of the eighteenth century had decreed, and that evolution over a long period of time was entirely feasible. And in 1835, 1836 and 1837, the brilliant but wayward English biologist and natural historian Edward Blyth published in the *Magazine of Natural History* a series of close-argued papers that suggested the existence of a mechanism for natural selection, and posed the question, "May not then a large portion of what are described as species have descended from a common parentage?"

All of which was highly contentious and controversial, to say the least. In the three decades before Charles Darwin dropped his bombshell on the empire of ideas, a vigorous and sometimes acrimonious "development" versus "creation" debate had been going on, with scientists and interested laymen lining up in the respective camps. For many, of course, the argument reduced to faith versus infidelity, God versus the Random Factor, order versus chaos. And while the protagonists of the "development" theory were a lively and forceful lobby (and one that was growing fast) there is no doubt that the adherents of the "creation" theory were in the majority. And Hugh Miller was one of that majority.

In *The Old Red Sandstone* he made it very plain where he stood, and poured eloquent scorn on the great Lamarck and his idea that "in the vast course of ages, inferior have risen into superior natures, and lower into higher races; that molluscs and zoophytes have passed into fish and reptiles, and fish and reptiles into birds and quadrupeds; that unformed gelatinous bodies, with an organization scarcely traceable, have been metamorphosed into oaks and cedars; and that monkeys and apes have been transformed into human creatures, capable of understanding and admiring the theories of Lamarck".

Miller could just not square evolutionary theory with the evidence of his own eyes. So far as he could see, the rocks of the Old Red Sandstone disproved the development theory. "Now it is a geological fact," he writes, "that it is the fish of the higher orders that appear first on the stage, and that they are found to occupy exactly the same level during the vast period represented by five succeeding formations. There is no progression. If fish rose into reptiles, it must have been a sudden transformation—it must have been as if a man who had stood still for half a lifetime should bestir himself all at once, and take seven leagues in one stride—there is no getting rid of miracle in the case. There is no alternative between creation and metamorphosis. The infidel substitutes progression for Deity— Geology robs him of his God."

This, 140 years on, sounds reactionary, muddle-headed, and just plain wrong. But there was nothing obscure, or hyper-conservative, about Miller's opinions. His position was very much that of the mainstream Victorian scientists, most of whom managed quite happily to reconcile their scientific work with their religious faith. Miller had nothing but contempt for the religious obscurantists, most of whom were found inside the Anglo-Catholic church, who viewed every scientific advance as an assault on the mysteries of Christianity and the work of the Devil. Miller belonged to the Presbyterian tradition, where hard-headed scientific enquiry thrived inside a religious structure. Miller's great mentor Thomas Chalmers shocked ecclesiastical circles in 1806 when he told a lecture in St Andrews the prejudice against geology and geologists was a nonsense, that they had valuable things to say and that "the writings of Moses do not fix the antiquity of the globe".

Miller was quite happy to accept that the earth was billions of years old, and that the seven-day creation of the Old Testament was a beautiful metaphor and nothing more. He even accepted that the rigorous, carefully-crafted arguments of the arch-infidel David Hume had done scientific inquiry nothing but good by making it look to its methods. But he could not accept that man was some kind of biological accident. Till the day he put a bullet in his chest, he believed that, somewhere in the history of the earth, the Creator had shaped man and breathed life into his body and consciousness into his brain.

It was an intellectual position that Miller never abandoned, and which he spent an enormous amount of time and effort defending.

In 1849 he published an intriguing book called *The Footprints of the Creator* which was written in an attempt to "contravert" the arguments of a runaway publishing success called *The Vestiges of Creation*, published anonymously in 1844 by Miller's old acquaintance, Edinburgh publisher and bookseller Robert Chambers. The success of *The Vestiges of Creation* and of *Sequel to Vestiges of Creation* (published in 1846) frankly alarmed Hugh Miller. He saw it as the kind of specious argument propagating the development thesis which was "doing much harm on both sides of the Atlantic, especially among intelligent mechanics, and a class of young men engaged in the subordinate departments of trade and the law". (Miller was not alone in turning his ire on *The Vestiges of Creation;* the book was given a terrible drubbing by Thomas Huxley, who later became known as "Darwin's Bulldog" for his fierce defence of *The Origin of Species*.)

The Vestiges of Creation is basically a spirited re-run of the Lamarckian theory of evolution, with the added theological twist that God created natural laws, and then let them get on with it. Although Chambers' book is now almost totally unknown, it was one of the *causes célèbres* of the Victorian scientific/literary world, was widely translated, sold thousands of copies, and anticipated the row over *The Origin of Species* by more than fifteen years. Because the canny Chambers had a fair idea of the anger that his book was likely to bring down on him, he published it anonymously (and Hugh Miller never learned that the author was his old friend).

And while Chambers' book drew flak from the direction of the religious and the strictly scientific—it was riddled with minor errors—the book had its admirers. Alfred Russell Wallace, for example, the man who almost beat Darwin to the punch on evolution, thought that *The Vestiges of Creation* "has always been undervalued, and which, when it first appeared, was almost as much abused and for much the same reasons, as was Darwin's *Origin of Species* fifteen years later". The book also impressed Ralph Waldo Emerson, the naturalist Richard Owen and the German philosopher Schopenhauer, and even Darwin was kindly disposed to the Edinburgh journalist's work.

But Hugh Miller was not. With *The Footprints of the Creator* Miller hoped to demolish the arguments contained in the book (and he was plainly irritated by the fact that the author had not the nerve to stick his name to his work). In fact, of all the many "replies" to the *Vestiges,* Hugh Miller's was the most widely read, and most widely bought.

Ironically, in the process of struggling to refute the Lamarck/ Chambers version of mankind's origins Miller comes up with a description of evolution that is superior to the one drawn by Chambers. In *The Footprints of the Creator* Miller found it absurd that "the creatures now human have been rising, by *almost* infinitesimals, from compound microscopic cells—minute, vital globules, begot by electricity on dead gelatinous matter—until they have at length become the men and women we see around us . . . " If this were so, then the implications were horrendous, because it meant that either "all the vitalities, whether those of monads or of mites, of fish or of reptiles, of birds or of beasts, are individually or inherently immortal and undying, or that human souls are *not* so". In other words if the "development" theory held, and man came down from remote biological ancestors, then either *every* living creature and plant had an immortal soul, or *none* had souls.

Miller was too much of a scientist to overlook the evidence there was for some kind of evolutionary process. But he went on to argue that "where the record does seem to speak of development and progression" it was in the "insensate" geology of the earth. "It is in the style and character of the *dwelling place* that gradual improvement seems to have taken place," he contended, "not in the functions or the rank of any of its inhabitants." This was a neat and ingenious solution to his problem. It squared the facts of science with his own religious beliefs. The Lord had shaped and changed the earth, experimenting with various species of animals until he had the conditions just right for man, and then—The Miracle! Miller seems to have been quite pleased with this theory, and thought that "there is no geological fact nor revealed doctrine with which this special scheme of development does not agree . . . It has no quarrel with the facts of even *The Vestiges* in their character as realities."

(Interestingly, in his attack on *Vestiges* Miller seems to have latched on to the very flaws in the evolution argument that have been bothering modern geologists and palaeontologists in the past few years. From the evidence of his own eyes Miller could see no justice in the claim that lower species evolved into higher species, *very slowly and very gradually.* So far as Miller could judge from the fossil evidence, when these changes happened, they happened with remarkable suddenness. To Hugh Miller this was evidence of the hand of God, and he described these points of change as "elevatory fiats". But it was a well-taken point and one which is still troubling scientists. Most now think that when evolutionary mutations occur, they happen with remarkable speed and suddenness, and not with infinite slowness.)

Miller was, it seems, genuinely surprised by the success of his assault on *The Vestiges of Creation.* "Unpopular as I supposed my little book was to prove, the first thousand has gone off bravely, and I am passing the second through the press," he wrote to one of his female friends. He was, he said, particularly gratified by a note he had received from the anatomist Richard Owen who felt that Miller's book was "almost the first contemporary work in which I have found some of my own favourite ideas weighed out and pronounced upon". Lord Ellesmere, a well-known amateur scientist, was even more enthusiastic, and congratulated Miller on the way *The Footprints of the Creator* had worked to "neutralize the emanations of a poisonous book" and thanked the author for operating as "a sanitary commissioner of science".

But for all Miller's national and international success as a geologist, as a populariser of science, and as editor of *The Witness,* he had made many enemies, and some of them were well-placed in the Scottish establishment. When the Chair of Natural History at Edinburgh University fell empty in 1853, Hugh Miller was tipped as the next Professor. It was a job he would have dearly loved, and for which he had some powerful support. Lord Dalhousie, for instance, had been lobbying for Miller, and had written to Lord Aberdeen that "I shall consider that the best man amongst us for this chair is passed over if he (Hugh Miller) is not chosen". The best man was passed over, however, and the Chair was given to the hard-working biologist, Edward Forbes, thirteen years Miller's junior. Miller was deeply hurt at being overlooked (although he had nothing but regard for Edward Forbes).

The University's snub was all the more remarkable given Miller's large and growing popularity. In the spring of 1854, for instance, he gave a lecture to a huge audience (estimated by the press at 5,000) at Exeter Hall, in London. His subject was "The Two Creations, Mosaic and Geological" and Miller was amazed to find that his audience was with him from the outset, "which I hardly expected as my preliminary matter was somewhat scientific and dry". At the end, he says, the audience were "rapturous in their applause" and he concluded that "on the whole a more successful address was never delivered in the great hall". A year later, in 1855, Miller was offered a sinecure and £800 a year as the Distributor of Stamps and Collector of Property Tax for Perthshire by Lord Breadalbane. Breadalbane's main reason for offering Miller the job was to "know him and to cultivate his acquaintance." Miller turned the job down.*

Miller returned to his theme of reconciling geology, palaeontology and religion in his last book *Testimony of the Rocks* which was published in 1857 (shortly after his death). In the dedication (to his old friend James Miller, Professor of Surgery at Edinburgh University), Miller describes the book as an attempt at "answering to the best of the author's knowledge and ability the various questions which the old theology of Scotland has been asking for the last few years of the newest of the sciences". In many ways the *Testimony of the Rocks* is Miller's most interesting book; it is beautifully illustrated in some editions, eclectic and quirky, and Miller slips from finely-honed argument on, for instance, the palaeontology of plants to a rambling discourse on the mythological bases of Noah's flood, the cosmogonies of the Buddhists and Hindus, and the problems faced by astronomers such as Galileo, Tyco Brahe, and Kepler.

One of the most entertaining essays in the book is *The Geology of the Anti-Geologists,* which is a brisk and amusing sideswipe at the quack philosophers, religious buffoons and plain cranks who have always plagued serious scientists. As examples, he holds up the French philosophers who rejected the idea that the earth was revolving, because if it were, the birds in the air would be left behind; the Edinburgh lecturer who argued that if God made the beasts of the field, then it was Satan who must have made the nasty sharp-toothed carnivores; the Anglican clergyman who firmly believed that all fossils were made of stone to start with, and inserted into rocks by the Creator as some kind of elaborate joke to fool the "development" theorists. Miller's clear favourite was the Scots eccentric who bombarded the press with his theory that the earth was a hollow metal ball "supported inside by a framework of metal wrought into hexagonal reticulations, somewhat like the framework of the great iron bridge over the River Wear at Sunderland". While enjoying the joke, Miller makes the point that the real story of creation is infinitely more subtle and beautiful than anything cooked up in a crank's

---

*Hugh Miller Williamson claims that, sometime in the 1850s, his uncle was offered a Knighthood, but turned it down to the intense fury of Lydia who wanted nothing better than to be known as "Lady" Miller.

study, or in the monasteries or Cathedral closes of England which
would "huddle the whole into a few literal days, and convert the
incalculably ancient universe into a hastily run-up erection of
yesterday".

Miller ends the *Testimony of the Rocks* with a marvellous essay on the
fossil flora of Scotland, in which he returns at the end to the eternal
question. "Who shall declare what, throughout these long ages, the
history of creation has been?" he asks. "We see only detached bits of
that green web which has covered our earth ever since the dry land
first appeared; but the web itself seems to have been continuous
throughout all time; though ever, as breadth after breadth issued
from the creative loom, the pattern has altered, and the
sculpturesque and graceful forms that illustrated its first beginnings
and its middle spaces have yielded to flowers of richer colour and
blow, and fruits of fairer shade and outline; and for gigantic club-
mosses stretching forth their hirsute arms, goodly trees of the Lord
have expanded their great boughs; and for the barren fern and the
calamite, clustering in thickets beside the waters, or spreading on the
flowerless hill-slopes, luxuriant orchards have yielded their ruddy
flush, and rich harvests their golden gleam."

Underpinning all Hugh Miller's writing on geology and palaeontology was his fierce belief in the First Great Cause, his unswerving
loyalty to the idea that the creation was the work of a Creator.
Nothing that any of the Lamarckians—or their propagandists like
Robert Chambers—could say, would ever shake his belief in the First
Great Cause. That cause had no harder-fighting champion than
Hugh Miller. He believed passionately that God had to be defended
out in the open, that the faithful had to pit their logic and intelligence
against the logic and intelligence of the Infidels of science. He
believed that the Puseyites and the Catholics were doing the
Creator's cause no service by retreating into blind faith, medievalism,
and a disingenuous anti-scientism. As well as being intellectually
dishonest, Miller thought it bad strategy, because it allowed the
Deists to be backed into a corner where they could be (and were
being) easily picked off by the advancing Infidels. Faith, doctrine,
and atheology were not enough.

Nor were the philosophies, metaphysics or any of the "purely
mental sciences" being taught at the Schools and Universities. To
Hugh Miller these were valuable as "gymnastics of the mind" (as he
said in accepting the Presidency of the Royal Physical Society in 1852)

but were not be confused with real work. And they carried with them the danger of "turning the mind in upon itself, instead of exercising it on things external to it, as if we had been engaged in turning the *eye* upon itself instead of directing it on all the objects which it has been specially framed to see". That is why Miller thought the cosmogonies of the theologians (or at least most theologians) were paltry: "The mere theologian," he writes in *First Impressions of England and Its People* takes a view based on only *one* creation, whereas "to the eye purged and strengthened by the euphrasy of science, the many vast regions of other creations,— promontory beyond promontory—island beyond island—stretch out in sublime succession into that boundless ocean of eternity . . . "

Compared to the devastating insights into creation and the Creator offered by practical science, to Miller the sophistry and metaphysics of the universities, and the piety and scripture-quoting of the Cathedral closes were mere "laughing gas". And laughing gas would not prevail against the armoured assaults of the Infidels. Only bolts of hard and heavy facts, energetically delivered, could turn the tide. To the end of his life, Miller went on firing the bolts. "We cannot link a single recent shell to a single extinct one," he wrote in his last book *The Testimony of The Rocks*. "*Up* to a certain point we find recent shells exhibiting all their present scientific peculiarities, and beyond that point they cease to appear. *Down* to a certain point the extinct shells also exhibit all *their* specific peculiarities, and then they disappear for ever. There are no intermediate species,— no connecting links,— no such connected series of specimens to be found as enables us to trace the trilobite through all its metamorphoses from youth to age. All geologic history is full of the beginnings and the ends of species,— of their first and last days; but it exhibits no genealogies of development. The Lamarckian sets himself to grapple, in his dream with the history of all creation: we awaken him, and ask him to grapple, instead, with the history of but a few individual species,— with that of the mussell or the whelk, the clam or the oyster; and we find from his helpless ignorance and incapacity what a mere pretender he is."

THE RETURN OF THE WITCH

THE *Testimony of the Rocks*   was the last book that Miller ever
wrote. By the time the proof copies were in his hands at the end of
1856, his health and his mind were beginning to falter. He worked
on the proofs with a feverishness that Lydia had never seen before,
and she began to dread that he would be felled by apoplexy.
Normally, Miller was a quiet and steady worker who liked to start
early and enjoyed relaxing in the afternoon with long walks. But now,
in late 1856, he was restless, unsettled, easily distracted and almost
unable to work during the day. At night he seemed to pull himself
together and spent long hours tidying the proofs, doing the bits of re-
writing and the literary chores.

The morbid and melancholy dimension to his personality began to
assert itself. Miller grew increasingly paranoid. He fell prey to fears
about his family's safety, his house, his beloved museum, which had
been built in the garden of Shrub Mount to house his collection, and
his own safety. He began to scour the newspapers for stories about
footpads, cut-purses, "ticket of leave" men, and nineteenth-century
muggers with which Edinburgh abounded. After being told by his
son that he thought he had heard voices and seen a light in the
garden, Miller acquired a man-trap and set it on the porch of his
museum. Everywhere he went, his six-shot revolver, fully loaded,
went too; and he took to supplementing his armoury at night with a
razor-sharp, broad-bladed *sgian,* and a Highland broadsword. One
night he crashed into Lydia's bedroom waving pistol and
broadsword, swearing that he had heard voices and footsteps in the
house.

Lydia's alarm deepened when, on Monday 22 December, Miller
came down to breakfast pale and shaken, and told her of terrible,
vague dreams and a fear that he had been sleepwalking. "It was a
strange night," Miller said. "There was something I didn't like. I shall
just throw on my plaid and step out to see Dr Balfour." This did
nothing to reassure his wife. Miller had never before volunteered to
see a doctor. His distaste for the profession was matched only by his
distaste for drugs.

And Dr Balfour—who was the Miller family's friend as well as their
doctor—was astonished by what his patient had to tell him. "My
brain is giving way," Miller told Balfour. "I cannot put two things
together today. But when I awoke this morning I was trembling all

over and quite confused in my brain. On rising, I felt as if a stiletto was suddenly . . . passed through my brain from front to back." Miller went on to explain that while passing through the Edinburgh Exchange a few days previously, he had been overcome by a spasm of nausea and dizziness, and had passed out while leaning against a wall.

Lydia, meanwhile, had taken the coach into Edinburgh to see her husband's friend Professor James Miller of Edinburgh University. Professor Miller agreed to come down to Portobello and made an appointment to see Miller—and Dr Balfour—at Shrub Mount the next day.

When Miller was examined by Dr Balfour and Professor Miller that Tuesday afternoon, they found him in reasonable physical shape, although clearly exhausted and strained from overwork. Professor Miller recalled vividly Hugh Miller's account of the mental disturbance plaguing his nights. " 'It was no dream,' he said. He saw no distinct vision and could remember nothing of what had passed accurately. It was a sense of vague and yet intense terror, with a conviction of being abroad in the night wind, and dragged through places as if by some invisible power. 'Last night,' he said, I felt as if I had been ridden by a witch for fifty miles, and rose more wearied in mind and body than when I lay down.' "

The doctors were unanimous in their diagnosis. Miller was suffering "from an overworked mind, disordering his digestive organs, enervating his whole frame." They ordered him to stop work, read lightly, thin down his great thatch of hair, lay off heavy suppers and drinking at night, take warm baths before he went to bed, and prescribed a sleeping draught. If Miller followed their advice, they said, the fevered imaginings would fade away. Miller agreed to do so. But when a servant went into the dining room to set the table a few hours later, she found Miller on a couch, his face contorted in agony, burying his head in a pillow.

After dinner, Miller spent a few hours with Lydia and his eldest daughter Elizabeth, who was then sixteen and attending verse-making classes in Edinburgh. The conversation moved towards Cowper—Miller's favourite poet—and then Lydia's little "Christmas book" on Cats and Dogs which had just been published. Did they know Cowper's poem *To a Retired Cat?* From there, the conversation drifted to Cowper's poem *The Castaway* and Lydia heard him read ("in tones of anguish", as she later recalled):

At length, his transient respite past,
His comrades, who before
Had heard his voice in every blast,
Could catch the sound no more.
For then, by toil subdued he drank
The Stifling wave, and then he sank.

The mood passed, and Miller turned to Cowper's touching poem
Lines to Mary which, Lydia says, he read with delicacy and with glances
at her. The poem ends:

And still to love, though pressed with ill,
In wintry age to feel no chill,
With me is to be lovely still,
      My Mary!*

Some time in the night, Miller's dream returned, and driven to
despair and anguish, he rose and killed himself with his revolver.
Nearly two hundred miles away in Cromarty, his mother, the granddaughter of the Gaelic seer Donald "Roy" Ross, sat up in bed to
watch a ball of bright light float around her room. According to the
old woman's account it floated from one item of furniture to another,
as if looking for somewhere to alight. In dread, she began to wonder
what it meant. Then the ball of light hovered, stopped, began to fade
and was suddenly extinguished, "leaving utter blackness behind, and
in her frame, the thrilling effect of a sudden and awful calamity".

The Scottish press and establishment were shaken by the news of
Miller's suicide. A black-trimmed late edition of *The Witness* carried a
brief report talking vaguely about Miller's "aggravated attacks of
nightmare" and ended plaintively: "We cannot, at present, dwell
further on this sad calamity." By the following day the newspapers
had had time to crank out their obituaries. "It is not often," wrote
the *Edinburgh Evening Courant* "that the reasoning and imaginative

---

*If Hugh Miller Williamson is to be believed, that mawkish cameo is more likely to
be bad Victorian art re-shaping events. According to Williamson, Lydia was a "selfish
hypochondriac, bound up almost entirely in herself", and far from organising Miller's
bath, and coaxing him to take his sleeping draft, she took herself off to bed and left
him alone. He had no bath, just boiled a kettle of water and sponged himself down.
Williamson also claims that his father—Miller's half-brother Andrew Williamson—
tried to hush up the circumstances of Miller's suicide, but Lydia would have none of
it. Playing the tragic heroine, she insisted on releasing the suicide note to the press,
probably because it contained a reference to herself as the "dear, dear wife" of the
freshly-killed Miller.

powers are found combined in so large a measure in the same mind; and in this rare union lay the secret of his strength as an author."

On Saturday 27 December *The Witness*, still trimmed in black, carried a detailed report of Miller's suicide, and the events leading up to it. The writer found himself groping for an explanation, and came up with the bleak irony, that Miller's powerful imagination was at the root. "The terrible idea that his brain was deeply and hopelessly diseased—that his mind was on the verge of ruin—took hold of him, and stood out before his eye in all that appalling magnitude in which such imagination as his alone could picture it."

Even the weather was depressing for Hugh Miller's funeral on the afternoon of Monday 29 December 1856. "The wintry aspect of the day," lamented *The Witness* reporter, "and the heavy laden sky like a pall, was spreading across the face of nature." Sixty individuals— including the Lord Provost of Edinburgh, two MPs, a large number of Free Church luminaries, and Miller's family and friends— gathered at Miller's Portobello house at 12.45 that afternoon. After a brief Presbyterian service officiated by the Rev Dr Thomas Guthrie, the mourners climbed into thirteen mourning coaches and followed the ornately-decked four-horse hearse in the direction of Edinburgh.

At the east end of Princes Street the little procession of coaches was met by a huge crowd of mourners. Half of Edinburgh, it seemed, had turned out to see Hugh Miller's last journey. Among them were the entire Kirk Session and most of the congregation of Free St John's (Miller's own church), a large delegation of scientists and science- buffs from the Royal Physical Society, parties of Free Church mourners from all over Scotland (and some from England) and clerks, salesmen, typographers from *The Witness*. All the shops on the route up the North Bridge to the Grange Cemetery were closed. The Edinburgh press calculated that upwards of 4,000 people had turned out to watch Miller's cortege pass. It was a bigger crowd than the one which had watched the departure of Thomas Chalmers.

A few minutes before the Hugh Miller cortege arrived at the Grange Cemetery, they buried the body of Thomas Leslie, 52, an Edinburgh gunsmith. Leslie's death was a grim footnote to the Miller tragedy. When Miller shot himself, the gun fell into the bath where it lay for a number of hours growing rusty. Professor James Miller needed to learn exactly how many shots had been fired, and knowing nothing of firearms, and fearful of the rusty revolver, he gingerly transported the weapon to the gunsmith who had sold it to Hugh

Miller, the firm of Alexander Thomson & Son of 16 Union Place, Edinburgh.

When Professor Miller arrived at the shop at lunchtime on Friday the 26th, the man in charge was Thomas Leslie, a foreman who had worked for Thomson & Son for more than twenty-five years (and a married man with eight children). Professor Miller explained what he wanted and handed the gun over to Leslie with the words, "Mind it is loaded." Leslie fingered the rusted safety catch, lifted the hammer of the revolver, turned the gun towards himself to count the bullets in the chamber, and the revolver went off, shooting the luckless Leslie through the right eye, and blowing his brains out. Leslie was buried in the same cemetery, on the same day, and almost at the same time, as Hugh Miller.

They dug Hugh Miller a grave at the northwest corner of the Grange Cemetery and cemented a large, ill-shaped, and faintly vulgar headstone of polished pink granite into the cemetery wall. The stone carries the inscription "Hugh Miller Born 1802 Died 1856", and is positioned near the end of a row which contains many Free Church notables, including Thomas Chalmers himself. The reporter from *The Witness* adduced that Miller's presence "added a new feature of attraction" to the spot. Miller's coffin was lowered into his grave by his eldest son William (then aged 16), two local MPs, his half-brother Andrew Williamson, Henry Fairly, the co-owner of *The Witness*, Miller's friend Robert Paul, and the Reverends Guthrie and Hanna, and Principal Cunningham of Edinburgh University.

When the *Testimony of the Rocks* was published a few months later, Lydia sent copies of the book to a long list of the British intelligensia. The replies were prompt. "Believe me," wrote Charles Dickens, "it will find no neglected place in my book shelves, but will always be precious to me, in remembrance of a delightful writer, an accomplished follower of science, and an upright and good man." Thomas Carlyle—with whom Miller had corresponded—was effusive. "The book itself," Carlyle writes, "is full of grave and manly talent, cleverness, eloquence, faithful conviction, knowledge; and will teach me and others much in reading it." Miller's death, Carlyle told Lydia, was "the world's great loss" but "the ways of God are high and dark and yet there is a mercy hidden in them".

John Ruskin took the opportunity to wax philosophical in his long letter to Lydia. "To all of us who knew your husband's genius," Ruskin wrote, "it seems to me that the bitterest cruelty of the trial must lie in . . . the littleness of the thing that brought about his illness and death. It seems so hard that a little overwork, a few more commas to be put into a page of type, a paragraph to be shortened or added, in the last moment should make the difference between life and death." "God," said Ruskin, "gave the mind to do certain work and withdrew it when that work was done. We are all too apt to think everything has been right if a man lives to be old, and everything lost if he dies young."

After his death, Hugh Miller's literary career and reputation began to flourish as never before. Under Lydia's shrewd and watchful eye, a steady stream of Miller's work began to run off the presses of London and Edinburgh, beginning with the *Testimony Of The Rocks* in 1857. "Its intrinsic value is superlative," opined the *Edinburgh Weekly Review.* "We cannot lay down the book without formally assuring readers of the rare entertainment its grandly descriptive, argumentative, reflective, and speculative pages afford, or without repeating our intense regret that we have no more of such works to expect." The London *Athenaeum* paid tribute to the late author's powers of imagination. "Fossil species, however long extinct, live again in Mr Miller's pages," their reviewer enthused. "His fossil fishes swim and gambol as if they were creatures of today . . . We commend the book as a fitting memorial of the mind of a man remarkable for his self-culture, literary ability, accurate science, and manly assertions of his convictions of the truth."

The influential *Saturday Review* joined in the accolade: "The style is easy, the knowledge brought to bear upon the subject is varied and extensive, and the purpose of the whole is throughly honourable and good . . . " *The Atlas* thought the book "eloquently written, and will afford its readers a great body of fact and philosophy". *The British and Foreign Evangelical Review* was even more impressed: "The most remarkable work of perhaps the most remarkable man of the age," their reviewer wrote, "a magnificient epic, and the Principia of Geology . . . "

By the time the firm of William P. Nimmo & Co., got round to publishing a fourteen-volume set of Miller's collected works (in 1875 and 1876) most of Miller's work had gone into many editions; *Old Red Sandstone,* 20; *Footprints of the Creator,* 18. And the various collections of essays and lectures did almost as well: *Sketchbook of Popular Geology,* 8; *Leading Articles,* 6; *The Headship of Christ,* 8; *Essays Historical and Biographical,* 7. And in the next thirty or so years

Miller's own books were joined by books of biography, criticism and commentary. By the early 1870s Miller's work was being widely translated, and the firm of Gould & Nelson of Boston, Mass., were pumping copies out into the USA where, according to the geologist Sir Archibald Geikie "they were to be found in the remotest log huts of the Far West . . . "

But by the turn of the century Miller's image and reputation had begun to fade and blur. When the town of Cromarty staged a celebration in 1902 to mark the centenary of Hugh Miller's birth, the main eulogist Sir Archibald Geikie regretted the fact. The debt which modern geology owed to Hugh Miller, he said, "has never been sufficiently acknowledged," and he felt that Miller's works "ought to be far more widely read than they are now . . . " Since about 1910 virtually nothing has been written about Hugh Miller. Apart from a modest, and faintly grudging, pamphlet published by the National Trust for Scotland in 1966, and a modest opera by Reginald Barret-Ayres and Colin Maclean (performed in 1974 at the Edinburgh Festival), a kind of eery silence has hung over Hugh Miller's reputation.

But why? Just what happened to Hugh Miller? Why did the Cromarty stonemason drop out of sight? He was, after all, the man whose "patient sagacity" and "natural insight" had impressed Thomas Huxley, and for whose powers of description Buckland would have given his left hand. Sir Roderick Murchison thought that Miller's popular science was worth "a thousand learned tracts", while Thomas Carlyle thought Miller's "peaceful radical heat" was "beautiful to see". Miller impressed Dickens and Richard Owen, Charles Lyell and Charles Darwin, Leigh Hunt and Thomas Chalmers, Louis Agassiz, Charles Kingsley, Robert Chambers, and almost the entire literary and scientific establishment of Victorian Britain. Yet in the twentieth century Miller's powerful journalism, dazzling scientific writing, and fierce Presbyterian polemic has gone largely unread.

Possibly Miller has suffered from having come down on the "wrong" side of the evolution vs creation arguments of the 1860s. Perhaps, terrible irony, Miller was tarred in the public mind with the same brush as Bishop "Soapy" Wilberforce, and the forces of Anglo-Catholic obscurantism? Maybe Miller's brand of fiery journalism was out of tune with his times? Certainly Miller's nineteenth-century biographer (or hagiographer) Peter Bayne is apologetic about the stone-mason's regrettable lapses of taste and delicacy. Possibly his reputation suffered from the sheer complexity and paradox of his temperament; to the Victorian radicals and socialists Miller must have seemed like a conservative; to the High Tories of the shires Miller must have seemed like a flaming radical.

But the range and quality of the work that poured from Miller's pen in the sixteen years between 1840 and 1856 was astonishing. When Miller's biographer Peter Bayne was ploughing his way through the files of *The Witness* to ferret out essays for the collection, he was frankly awed by what he found. "Having surveyed this vast field," Bayne wrote later, "I retain the impression of a magificient expenditure of intellectual energy—an expenditure of which the world will never estimate the sum."

Part Two
Selected Writings of Hugh Miller

A SENSE OF OUTRAGE

IF Hugh Miller is remembered, it is as a writer of dazzling essays on natural history, fossil life, and geology. But many of Miller's most telling and powerful pieces of writing were those inspired by sheer outrage at the poverty, misery, and injustice he found around him. He never forgot the lessons he learned as an itinerant journeyman mason in the 1820s. The long hours, the grinding back-breaking work, and the wretched weeks spent in rat-infested bothies, damp outhouses, and cramped "barracks" burned themselves on his memory. And the acute young workman noted (and wrote down) almost everything he saw on his wanderings across Scotland. What he learned about life and conditions of people in Gairloch, Lairg, Cononside, the Black Isle, and in the coal-rich countryside around Edinburgh, he later put to good use in a series of essays which can only be described as "radical" (although Miller would have loathed the adjective).

In The Highlands, *for example, Miller writes bitterly of the way in which the Gaelic people were ousted from the reasonably fertile straths and glens by the "improving" gentry, and forced on to the emigrant ships, or down onto the coasts to eke out a living in a "sort of amphibious life as crofters and fishermen". It was, Miller thought a monstrous injustice, made worse by the accusation that the people were flopping economically because they were incurably idle. The plague of the Highlands, Miller believed, were the Highland landowners who were in the process of selling a once loyal people down the river.*

The attempts by some of the Highland grandees such as the Duke of Atholl and the Duke of Leeds, to stop the public using the old drove roads across their hunting and shooting grounds, made Miller furious. In Glen Tilt Tabooed *he warns that if the Duke of Atholl got away with his plan to close off Glen Tilt, it might end up "shutting the Scotch out of Scotland" and that if the Scots allowed it to happen "they will richly deserve to be shut out of their country altogether". (In the event, the amenity and rights-of-way lobby won the ensuing court case, and Glen Tilt was kept open).* The Legislative Court *is a sardonic commentary on a Highland gent's attempt to prove that the Cromarty Firth is a river (and the salmon in it his property).*

The Cottages of Our Hinds *and* The Bothy System *are both grim accounts of the living conditions of farm labourers and workers in the South of Scotland. In some respects, Miller argues, the living conditions of southern "hinds" (i.e. farm labourers) were worse than the conditions of the crofters in the Highlands where at least people knew how to thatch a roof with peat, or repair a wall with dry stone. Miller contrasts the damp, ramshackle, miserably-furnished hovels of the farm labourers with the plump countryside, and the "jealous neatness of the homes of the gentlemen farmers of Lothian.* The Bothy System *is how the agriculture of lowland Scotland housed its single farmworkers—eight or ten men to a grim little outhouse, spending their evenings trying to cook a small meal with damp firewood. The result, Miller said, was a breed of men who loathed their employers, and gloried in their ruin.*

It is interesting that some of Miller's warmest admirers found the level of aggravation in these articles distasteful. In the pieces of biography which were written on Miller in the latter half of the nineteenth century, these essays tend to be glossed over as regrettable lapses of taste and decorum. But Miller was plainly a very angry man, and in one of the best pen sketches of him (by Prof David Masson, published in Memories of Two Cities) *Masson writes about Miller's "tremendous ferocity" which "amounted to a disposition to kill" (although even Masson thought it led him into "a few immense exaggerations of the polemical spirit"). But in the booklet published by the National Trust for Scotland in 1966, the author Charles Waterston complains that Miller's journalism is "like shot hardly cool from the battle", and that most of it demonstrates "a bitterness and lack of moderation which makes much of his writing distasteful to today's reader".*

Maybe! But it seems more likely that "today's reader" would be impressed by the angry, but well-researched and well-argued essays with which Hugh Miller hammered the aristocratic "clearers" of the Highlands, the tight-fisted farmers of the Lothians, the grafting manufacturers, and the miserable master chimney-sweeps who preferred using seven-year-old "climbing boys" to the sweeping machines which were on the market (as Miller points out in Climbing Boys— Chimney Sweeping). *And some of the arguments described by Miller—such as the face-off between amenity and scientific interests and the gentry's shooting rights—are still raging.*

The Highlands

"IT is very sad that the people of this fine wild country have not got enough to eat; but depend on't, we will collect no more money for them in England. We have already done our best to help them, and they must now help themselves." Such was the remark of a comfortable-looking Englishman whom we encountered a few weeks ago among the wilds of the northern Highlands; and, judging from the indifferent success which has attended the recent efforts to form a second fund on behalf of the suffering Highlander, it seems to represent pretty fairly the average feeling and general determination of his country on the subject. Charity on a large scale, and directed on distant objects, soon exhausts itself.

The difficulty is certainly very great, and it has been vastly enhanced by the late years of famine. We are old enough to remember the northern Highlands, rather more than thirty years ago, when there were whole districts of the interior, untouched by the clearing system, in possession of the aboriginal inhabitants. And if asked to sum up in one word the main difference between the circumstances of the Highlander in these and in later times, our one word would be, that most important of all vocables to the political economist,—*capital*. The Highlander was never wealthy: the inhabitants of a wild mountainous district, formed of the primary rocks, never are. But he possessed on the average his six, or eight, or ten head of cattle, and his small flock of sheep, and, when—as sometimes happened in the high-lying districts—the corn-crop turned out a failure, the sale of a few cattle or sheep more than served to clear scores with the landlord, and enabled him to purchase his winter and spring supply of meal in the Lowlands. He was thus a capitalist, and possessed the capitalist's peculiar advantage of not living "from hand to mouth," but on an accumulated fund, which always stood between him and absolute want, though not between him and positive hardship, and enabled him to rest during a year of scarcity on his own resources, instead of throwing himself on the charity of his Lowland neighbours. And in these times he never *did* throw himself on the charity of his Lowland neighbours. And as his mode of life was favourable to the development of the military spirit,—a spirit which the traditions of the country served mightily to foster,—great numbers of the young men of the country, of a very different class from those that usually enlist in England and the Lowlands, entered the army, and our Highland regiments were composed of at once the best men and the best soldiers in the service.

With the wars of the French Revolution their was a great change introduced into the country. The wheels of its industry were quickened by the pressure of taxation, and by the introduction of a system of competition with machinery, on the one hand, that lengthened the term of labour by reducing its remuneration, and with the "estimate system" on the other. Nor was it in the nature of things that the Highlands should long remain unaffected by this change. The price of provisions rose in England and the low country; and, with the price of provisions, the rent of land. The Highland proprietor naturally enough bethought him how his rental was also to be increased; and, as a consequence of the conclusion at which he arrived, the sheep-farm and clearing system began.

Many thousand Highlanders, ejected from their snug holdings, employed their little capital in emigrating to Canada or the States; and there, in most cases, save in very inhospitable localities, as in the Cape Breton district, the little capital increased, and a rude plenty continues to be enjoyed by their descendants. Many thousands more, however, fell down upon the coasts of the country, and, on moss-covered moors or bare exposed promontories, little suited for the labours of the agriculturist, commenced a sort of amphibious life as crofters and fishermen; and there, located on an ungenial soil, and prosecuting with but indifferent skill a precarious trade, their little capital dribbled out of their hands, and they became the poorest of men.

It required, however, another drop to make the full cup run over. The potato is of comparatively modern introduction into the Highlands. We were intimate in early life with several individuals who had seen potatoes first transferred from the gardens of Sutherland and Ross to the fields. But during the present century potatoes had become the staple food of the Highlander. In little more than forty years their culture had increased fivefold; for every twenty bolls reared in 1801, there were a hundred reared in 1846; and when in the latter year the potato blight came on, the poor people, previously stripped of their little capitals, and divested of their employment, were deprived of their food, and ruined at a blow. The same stroke which did little more than slightly infringe on the comforts of the people of the Lowlands, utterly prostrated those of the Highlands; and ever since, the sufferings of famine have become chronic along the bleak shores and rugged islands of at least the north-western portion of our country. It is a more disastrous though less obtrusive fact, that so heavily has the famine borne on a class that were not absolutely the poor when it came on, that they are the absolutely poor now. It has dissipated the last remains of capital possessed by the *people* of the Highlands, and placed them in circumstances of prostration too extreme to leave them any very great chance of recovering themselves, or rather in circumstances from which, in the present state of the country, recovery for them as a *people* is an impossibility.

In travelling over an extensive Highland tract last autumn, we had a good deal of conversation with the people themselves. Passing through wild districts of the western coast, where the rounded hills and scratched and polished rocks gave evidence that the country had once been wrapped up in a winding-sheet of ice, we saw the soil for many miles together,—where the bare rock had any covering at all,—composed of two almost equally hopeless ingredients. The subsoil was formed of glacial debris,—the mere scrapings of the barren primary rocks; and over it there lay a stratum, varying generally from six inches to six feet, of cold, wet, inert moss, over which there grew scârce even a useful grass, except perhaps the "deer's hair" of the sheep-farmer. And yet, on this ungenial soil, representative of but vegetable and mineral death,—the dead ice-rubbish and the dead peat,—we saw numerous cultivated patches, in which the thin green corn or sickly-looking potatoes struggled with aquatic plants,—the common reed and the dwarf water-flag. No agriculturist, with all the appliances of modern science at command, would once think of investing capital in such a soil; and yet here were the poor Highlanders investing at least labour in it, and their modicum of seed-corn.

"How," we have frequently enquired of the poor people, "are you spending your strength on patches so miserably unproductive as these? You are said to be lazy. For our own part, what we chiefly wonder at is your great industry. Were we at least in your circumstances, we would improve upon your indolence, by striking work, and not labouring at all." The usual reply used to be,—"Ah, there is good land in the country, but *they* will not give it to us." And certainly we did see in the Highlands many tracts of kindly-looking soil. Green margins, along the sides of long-withdrawing valleys, which still bore the marks of the plough, but now under natural grass, seemed much better fitted to be, as of old, scenes of human industry, than the cold ungenial mosses or the barren moors. But in at least nineteen cases out of every twenty we found the green patches bound by lease to some extensive sheep-farmer, and as unavailable for the purposes of the present emergency, even to the proprietor, as if they lay in the United States or the Canadas.

We were much struck by the casual statement in a newspaper paragraph, that of several hundred emigrants from Lewis who arrived in Canada this season, there was scarce one who was not under thirty. It was the *elite* of the island that went, while its pauperism staid behind. We regretted to find, during our late visit, that the military spirit is at present so dead in the Highlands, that the recruiting party of one of the most respectable Highland regiments under the Crown succeeded in enlisting, during a stay of several months, only some ten or twelve young men, in a country charged with an unemployed and suffering population. The condition of the British army is at the present time one of comfort and plenty, compared with that of the general population of the north-western parts of Scotland; the prospect of retirement with a snug pension some one-and-twenty years hence, is a better prospect than any poor Highland crofter or cottar can rationally entertain; and we would much prefer seeing some twenty thousand of our brave countrymen enrolled in the army, as at once its best soldiers and best Protestants, than lost for ever to the country in a colony that in a few years hence may exist as one of the States of the great North American republic. *September 20, 1851*

Glen Tilt Tabooed

A rencounter of a somewhat singular character has taken place in Glen Tilt between the Duke of Atholl, backed by a body of his gillies, and a party of naturalists headed by a learned Professor from Edinburgh. The general question regarding right of way in Scotland seems fast drawing to issue between the people and the exclusives among the aristocracy, and this in a form, we should fain hope, rather unfavourable to the latter, seeing that the popular cause represents very generally, that of the sentiment and intellect of the country, while the cause of the exclusives represents merely the country's brute force,—luckily a considerably smaller portion of even that than falls to the share of even our physical-force Chartists. Should thews and muscle come to bear sway among us, the *regime* must prove a very miserable one for Dukes of Leeds and of Atholl.

From time immemorial the public road between Blair-Athole and Braemar has lain through Glen Tilt. In most questions regarding right of roadway witnesses have to be examined; the line of communication at issue is of too local and obscure a character to be generally known; and so the claim respecting it has to be decided on

A West Highland woman of the nineteenth century, burdened with a wickerwork creel of peat. "How these poor Highland women did toil!" Miller wrote. "I have paused among my labour under the hot sun to watch them as they passed, bending under their load of peat or manure, and at the same time twirling the spindle as they crept along." (Courtesy of the National Museum of Antiquities of Scotland).

the evidence of people who live in the immediate neighbourhood. Not such, however, the case with Glen Tilt. There is scarce in the kingdom a better-known piece of roadway than that which runs through the glen; and all our ampler Guide-Books and Travellers' Companions assume the character of witnesses in its behalf. The reader will find it marked in every better map of Scotland. In the "National Atlas,"—a work worthy of its name,—it may be seen striking off, on the authority of the geographer to the Queen, at an acute angle from the highway at Blair-Athole; then running on for some twelve or thirteen miles parallel to the Tilt; and then, after scaling the heights of the upper part of the glen, deflecting into the valley of the Dee, and terminating at Castleton of Braemar. The track which it lays open is peculiarly a favourite one with the botanist, for the many interesting plants which it furnishes; and so much so with the geologist, that what may be termed the classic literature of the science might, with the guide-books of the country, be brought as evidence into court in the case. There is not a man of science in the world who has not heard of it.

We understand that when Agassiz was last in this country, he accompanied to the locality an Edinburgh professor, well known both in the worlds of letters and of science, with the intention of visiting a quarry on the grounds of his Grace; but, on addressing his Grace for permission, there was no answer returned to his letter, and the distinguished foreigner had to turn back disappointed, to say how much more liberally he had ever been dealt with elsewhere, and to contrast, not very favourably for our country, the portion of *liberty* doled out to even the learned and celebrated among the Scottish people, with that enjoyed under the comparably free and kindly despotisms of the Continent. The incident happily illustrates the taste and understanding of his Grace the Duke of Atholl, and intimates the kind of measures which the public should keep with such a man. If the Scottish people yield up to his Grace the right of way through Glen Tilt, they will richly deserve to be shut out of their country altogether: and be it remarked, that to this state of things matters are fast coming with regard to the Scottish Highlands.

It is said of one of the Queens of England, that in a moment of irritation, she threatened to make Scotland a hunting-park; and we know that the tyranny of the Norman Conqueror did actually produce such a result over extensive tracts of England. The pleasures of the chase are necessarily jealous and unsocial. The shepherd can

A West Highland crofter with a soil-breaking device known as a "cass chron" one of the many "arts and implements" which lingered in the Western Highlands and which elsewhere "would have been regarded by the antiquary as belonging to a very remote period." (Courtesy of Aberdeen University Library)

carry on his useful profession without quarrel with the chance
traveller; the agriculturist in an open country has merely to fence
against the encroachments of the vagrant foot the patches actually
under cultivation at the time; whereas it is the tendency of the
huntsman possessed of the necessary power, to "empty" the "wilds
and woods" of their human inhabitants. The traveller he regards as a
rival or an enemy: he looks upon him as come to lessen his sport,
either by sharing in it or by disturbing it. And into this state of savage
nature and jealous appropriation,—characteristic, in the sister kingdom, of the time of the Conquest,—many districts in the Highlands
of Scotland are fast passing. The great sheep-farms were permitted,
in the first instance, to swallow up the old agricultural holdings; and
now the let shootings and game-parks are fast swallowing up the
great sheep-farms. The ancient inhabitants were cleared off, in the
first process, to make way for the sheep; and now the people of
Scotland generally are to be shut out from these vast tracts, lest they
should disturb the game.

There is no exception to be made by cat-witted dukes and illiterate
lords in favour of the man of letters, however elegant his tastes and
pursuits; or the man of science, however profound his talents and
acquirements, or however important the objects to which he is
applying them. The Duke of Leeds has already shut up the
Grampians, and the Duke of Atholl has *tabooed* Glen Tilt. The
gentleman and scholar who, in quest of knowledge, and on the
strength of the prescriptive right enjoyed from time immemorial by
even the humblest of the people, enters these districts, finds himself
subjected to insult and injury; and should the evil be suffered to go
on unchecked, we shall by and by see the most interesting portions
of our country barred up against us by parishes and counties. If one
proprietor shut up Glen Tilt, why may not a combination of
proprietors shut up Perthshire? Or if one sporting tenant bar against
us the Grampians, why, when the system of shooting-farms and
game-parks has become completed, might not the sporting tenants
united shut up against us the entire Highlands?

September 1847

The Legislative Court

WE have a case before us in which the decision arrived at by the

Court traverses not quite so palpably the laws of the country, as the fixed laws of nature. We submitted to our readers, rather more than a week since, the report of a trial which had taken place a short time previous before the Court in Edinburgh, regarding a right to the fishing of salmon in the Frith of Dornoch, and which had gone against the defendant. We stated further, that a similar case, involving a similar right to the fishing of salmon in the Frith of Cromarty, had been tried with a similar result a few years before.

The principles of both cases may be stated in a few words. Salmon, according to the statutory laws of Scotland, may be fished for in the sea with wears, yairs, and other such fixed machinery; but it is illegal to fish for them after this fashion in rivers. The statutes, however, which refer to the case are ancient and brief, and contain no definition of what is river or what sea. They leave the matter altogether to the natural sense of men. But not such the mode pursued by the Court of Session. In its judicial capacity it can but decide that salmon are not to be fished for in rivers after a certain manner in which they may be fished for in the sea. In its legislative capacity it sets itself to say what is sea and what river, and proves so eminently happy in its definition, that we are now able to enumerate among the rivers of Scotland, the Frith of Dornoch and the Frith of Cromarty.

Yes, gentle reader, it has been legally declared by that "infallible civil court" to which there lies an appeal from all the decisions of our poor "fallible Church," that Scotland possesses two rivers of considerably greater volume and breadth than either the St Lawrence or the Mississippi. Genius of Buchanan! It is well that thou, who didst so philosophically describe the Court of Session, didst describe also, like a fine old poet as thou wert, the glorious bay of Cromarty!

Some of our readers must be acquainted with the powerful writing of Tacitus in his "Life of Agricola," in which he describes the Roman galleys as struggling for the first time with the tides and winds of our northern seas. The wave rose sluggish and heavy to the oars of the rowers, and they saw all around them, in the indented shores scooped into far withdrawing arms of the sea, evidences of its ponderous and irresistible force. Buchanan must have had the passage in his mind when he drew the bay of Cromarty. He tells us how "the waters of the German Ocean, opening to themselves a way through the stupendous cliffs of the most lofty precipices, expand within into a spacious basin, affording certain refuge against every tempest, and in which the greatest navies may rest secure from winds and waves."

The Court of Session, in the wise exercise of its legislative functions, reverses the very basis of this description. The rowers of Agricola must have been miserably in error: the old shrewd historian must have fallen into a gross mistake. The Frith of Cromarty is not the inlet of a mighty sea: it is merely the outlet of an inconsiderable river. It is not an arm of the German Ocean: it is simply a prolongation of the Conon. Why, we know a little of both. We have waded a hundred times mid-leg deep across the one, and picked up the large brown pearl mussels from the bottom without wetting our sleeve. We have guided our little shallop a thousand times along the green depths of the other, and have seen the long sea-line burying patch after patch, as it hurried downwards, and downwards, and downwards, till, far below, the lead rested in the darkness, amid shells, and weeds and zoophites, rare indeed so near the shore, and whose proper habitat is the profound depths of the ocean. We have seen the river coming down, red in flood, with its dark whirling eddies and its patches of yellow foam, and then seen it driven back by the tidal wave, within even its own banks, like a braggart overmastered and struck down in his own dwelling. We have seen, too, the frith agitated by storm, the giant waves dashing against its stately portals, to the height of an hundred feet; and where on earth was the power that could curb or stay them? The Frith of Cromarty a prolongation of the Conon! Were the Court of Session to put the Conon in its pocket, the Frith of Cromarty would be in every respect exactly what it is,—the noble *Portus Salutis* of Buchanan,—the wide ocean bay, in which the whole British navy could ride at anchor. Is it not a curious enough circumstance, that much about the same time in which the Court of Session, in the due exercise of its legislative functions, stirred up the Church to rebellion, it so laid down the law with respect to the Frith of Cromarty, in the exercise of exactly the same functions, that it stirred it up to rebellion also?

Yes, it is a melancholy fact, but it cannot be denied, that this splendid sheet of water has been in a state of open rebellion for the last four years. In obedience to its own ocean laws, it has been going on producing its own ocean products,—its prickly sea-urchins, its sea-anemones, its dulce, its tangle, its "roarin' buckies," and its "dead men's fingers," when, like a good subject, it should have been river-mouth to all intents and purposes, nor have ventured on growing anything less decidedly fluviatile than a lymnea or a cyclas, or a fresh-water polypus.

We can satisfactorily prove, that no farther back than last year, this frith gave admission, in utter contempt of Court, to so vast a body of herrings, that all its multitudinous waves seemed as if actually heaving with life; nay, that it permitted them, by millions and thousands of millions, to remain and spawn within its precincts. We can prove, further, that it suffered a plump of whales, —vast of back and huge of fin,—to pursue after the shoal, rolling, and blowing, and splashing the white spray against the sun; and that it furnished them with ample depth and ample verge for their gambols, though the very smallest of them was larger considerably—strange as the fact may seem—than the present Dean of Faculty. Is all this to be suffered? The Lords of Session must assuredly either bring the rebel to its senses, or be content to leave their own legislative wisdom sadly in question. For ourselves, we humbly propose that, until they make good their authority, they be provided daily with a pail of its clear *fresh* water, drawn from depths not more than thirty fathoms from the surface, and be left, one and all, to make their toddy out of the best of it, and to keep the rest for their tea. Nothing like river-water for such purposes, and the waters of the Conon are peculiarly light and excellent.

December 21, 1842.

The Cottages of our Hinds

WE presented to the reader on Saturday last, in our report of the late half-yearly meeting of the Highland and Agricultural Society, the remarks of two very estimable noblemen on the cottages of the country, especially the cottages of hinds, and on the best means of improving them. It was stated by the one noble speaker, and reiterated by the other, that in order to render cottages immensely better than they are at present, it is not at all necessary that they should be rebuilt. The rebuilding of them, in the greater number of instances, might be impossible, and in all cases it would be at least very inconvenient.

But if proprietors had thus little in their power regarding them, much might be done by the humble inmates in the way of dividing their single rooms when their accommodation chanced to be greater, and imparting to them an air of general comfort. It was held that on this point, therefore, the premiums of the Society ought specially to be directed. The proprietary of the country could not be expected to help their poor labourers on a large scale, by providing them with suitable dwellings (a single cottage might cost fifty pounds); but then they were ready to encourage them in any feasible way of helping themselves.

A room twelve feet by sixteen might be regarded as a very pretty sort of problem; and if a man and his wife, with some eight or ten children, could contrive to solve the difficulty by residing in it with comfort and decency, they should be by all means rewarded for their ingenuity by a premium from the Society.

We passed the summer and autumn of 1823 in one of the wildest and least accessible districts of the north-western Highlands. The nearest public road at that period was a long day's journey away. Among the humbler people we met with only a single man turned of forty who understood English. It was, in truth, a wild, uncultivated region, brown and sterile, studded with rock, blackened with morasses, and cursed with an ever-weeping climate. Every little village had its few boats and its few green patches of cultivation. Some of the latter, scarcely larger than onion beds, seemed to stand out from amid the brown heath like islands in the ocean; and both the boats and the patches served as indices to show how the poor inhabitants of so barren a region contrived to live. Could we travel back into the past, amid the rich fields of the Lothians, for full ten centuries, we would fail to arrive at so primitive a state of things with regard to the common arts of life as existed only nineteen years ago in this wild district. A man of some little imagination might have supposed that one of the many Scotch witches of the seventeenth century had passed the way in the time of harvest, and transformed all the newly-reaped shocks into accumulations of stone. Such was the agriculture of the district: it was the agriculture of the first ages,— the fruit of the very first lesson which man had derived from experience, on setting himself to force a living from the soil.

On the first evening of our arrival in the district, we accompanied an acquaintance, to secure the services of a Highlander whom we were desirous to engage as a labourer, and who lived in the nearer village. Twilight was falling, but there remained light enough to enable us to examine the surrounding forms of things. The cottage we sought was a low, long, dark building, whose roof and walls

Crofter's Cottage, Lewis

A West Highland croft or "black house", a species of domestic building that remained unchanged for many centuries. Primitive, but in Miller's eyes, warm, waterproof, and comfortable, and easily repaired (or extended) by local materials. Miller compared the black houses favourably with the leaking, ramshackle "bothies" of the Lowland agricultural workers whose homes had "sunk below the level of semi-civilisation".
(Courtesy of National Museum of Antiquities of Scotland)

sloped in nearly the same angle, without any aperture for windows, except along the ridge of the roof, and with a door raised little more than four feet above the threshold. In these north-western regions, where there falls about twice as much rain as on any part of the eastern coast, and where, at some seasons, the almost incessant showers beat at an angle of inclination varying from thirty to sixty, it is imperatively necessary to render the side-walls of a building as impervious as the roof, and hence the slope of the walls,—a slope given them by filling up a bulwark of solid turf against the comparatively erect line of stone.

Our first step into the interior was into a pit fully two feet in depth. In this outer chamber, according to the custom of the district, the ashes produced by the turf and peat burnt during the year had been suffered to accumulate, for the purposes of manure; and as it was now early in summer, the place had been but lately cleared out. It was intensely dark, and filled with smoke; and we had some difficulty in finding the inner door, the threshold of which we found raised to the level of the door without. A step brought us into what proved to be the middle apartment of the cottage. A fire of turf, enlivened by a few pieces of moss fir, blazed on a flat stone in the middle of the floor, with no protecting back to screen any part of the building, so that the flames shone equally all around on the rude walls and the equally rude furniture. A cloud of smoke, thick and flat as a ceiling, rested overhead; and there hung, as if dropping out of it, a dark drapery of herring-nets.

The inner walls, as shown by the red glare of the fire, were formed of undressed stone, uncemented by mortar; but the interstices had been carefully caulked with dried moss. The furniture was somewhat of the scantiest. There were a few deal-seats, and a rude bed-frame in a corner, half-filled with heath,—the sleeping-place of the boys; a few wooden cogs occupied a recess behind the woman; and there was a large pot suspended over the fire from the roof. But what we chiefly remarked was, that the place, rude as it was, had what by much the greater number of the dwellings of our south-country hinds have not,—the luxury of an inner apartment: the wicker door opened through a stone-wall; the thick turf roof was at least water-tight, except where, beside the gables (not over the fire), there were two openings to admit air and light, and to give egress to smoke.

Our reader would smile were we to associate ideas of comfort with such a dwelling. Certain it was, however, that its inmates could do so; and all can at least associate ideas of decency with it. The construction of Red Murouch's house was quite as primitive as the tillage of his little croft, or the tackle of his boat, or the distaff and spindle employed by his wife. His grandfather removed by twenty generations had lived, in all probability, in just such another; but it served Murouch quite as well as its antitype had served his remote ancestor. Besides, if he wished it better or larger, could he not improve or add to it? There was space enough outside; vast abundance of stone everywhere, and wood in the neighbouring hollow; and Murouch, unsophisticated, like all his neighbours, by the scheme of dividing labour, which, while it adds to the skill of the community, lowers mightily that of the individual, was a master of the entire art of building such houses.

Just six months after quitting the Highlands, we were residing in one of the richest districts in the Lowlands of Scotland,—one of those centres of cultivation from which the art of the agriculturist has spread itself over all the more accessible portions of the kingdom. Considerably more than two hundred miles intervened between us and the scene of our last year's labour. We have often thought whether it would not be equally correct to say that we had travelled in advance of it at least a thousand years. The whole seemed, viewed in recollection from amid the fertile fields of the south, as if belonging rather to the remote past than to the present. Even the most unpractised eye could not fail being struck by the superior style of the husbandry in the *modern* district. How very close the plough had contrived to skirt the well-dressed fences! How straight the furrows!—how equal the braird! How thoroughly had the land been cleared of weeds! And then, what an air of snugness seemed to pervade the farm-houses of the district, and how palpably had the experience of ages been concentrated on the means and appliances of their several steadings.

The jealous neatness, too, with which the various gentlemen's seats in the neighbourhood were kept, their general style, the appearance of the surrounding grounds, their woods, and gardens, and belts of shrubbery,—all testified to the elegant tastes and habits of the possessors. Whatever belonged immediately to the upper classes had but one character,—comfort gilded by the beautiful. And there was much, doubtless, in the very sight of all this for the poor man to enjoy. We still entertain a vivid recollection, distinct as a picture, of the beautiful vista in a gentleman's woods,—tall, green, finely arched, close over head as the roof of a cathedral,—through which we could see, almost every evening, as the twilight faded into darkness, the Inchkeith light twinkling afar off, like a star rising out of the sea. The noble grove through which it shone was scarce a hundred yards distant from the humble cottage in which we lodged.

But the cottage was an exceedingly humble one. It was one of a line on the way-side, inhabited chiefly by common labourers and farm-servants,—a cold uncomfortable hovel, consisting of only a single apartment,—by many degrees less a dwelling to our mind, and certainly less warm and snug, than the cottage of the west-coast Highlander. The tenant, our landlord, was an old farm-servant, who had been found guilty of declining health and vigour about a twelve month before, and had been discharged in consequence. He was permitted to retain his dwelling, on the express understanding that the proprietor was not to be burdened with repairs; and the thatch, which was giving way in several places, he had painfully laboured to patch against the weather by mud and turf gathered from the way-side. But he wanted both the art and the materials of Red Murouch.

With every heavy shower the rain found its way through, and the curtains of his two beds, otherwise so neatly kept, were stained by dark-coloured blotches. The earthen floor was damp and uneven; the walls, of undressed stone, had never been hard-cast; but, by dint of repeated whitewashings, the interstices had gradually filled up. They were now, however, all variegated by the stains from the roof. Nor had the pride of the apartment, its old-fashioned eight-day clock or its chest of drawers, escaped. From the top of the drawers the veneers were beginning to start, in consequence of the damp; and the clock gave warning, by its frequent stops and irregularities, that it would very soon cease to take further note of the time.

The old man's wife, still a neat tidy woman, though turned of sixty, was a martyr to rheumatism; and her one damp and gousty room, with its mere apron-breadth of partition interposed between it and the chinky outer door, was not at all the place for her declining years or her racking complaint. She did her best, however, to keep things in order, and to attend to the comforts of her husband and her two lodgers; but the bad roof and the single apartment were disqualifying circumstances, and they pressed on her very severely.

It was well remarked by his Grace the Duke of Buccleuch, that "the keeping of lodgers along with families in cottages where there is scarce room for the family itself, is a great evil." It is even so,—a very great evil. But, my Lord Duke, there are still greater evils which press upon the indignant. These poor old people had very slender means of living, and they found it necessary to eke them out in any honest way. Their lodgers, too,—humble, hard-working men,—could not afford a very sumptous lodging-place, nor were there any such in the neighbourhood, even if they could. There are stern necessities that press upon the poor in matters of this kind, which we sincerely trust your Grace may never experience, but of which all would be the better of knowing just a very little.

And this was all that civilization, in the midst of a well-nigh perfect agriculture, and amid the exercise of every useful and elegant art, had done for the dwelling of the poor hind. The rude husbandry of the western-coast Highlander had been left more than a thousand years behind; manufacturers had made marvellous advances since the relinquishment of the distaff and spindle; trade had imported many a luxury since woollen sails and wooden anchors had been abandoned; every umbrageous recess had it scene of elegance and comfort: the homes of the poor had alone remained stationary, and

The interior of a black house. The fire in the centre of the room "shone equally on the rude walls and the equally rude furniture", but for all its drawbacks possessed "the luxury of an inner apartment". (Courtesy of the National Museum of Antiquities of Scotland).

worse than stationary;—they had sunk below the level of semi-civilization.
January 22, 1842

The Bothy System

MOST of our readers must know what the bothy system is. A very considerable number of the farm-steadings of the country, built on the most approved plan, with roomy courts and sheds for the breeding of cattle, and stables constructed on the best possible principle for the horses,—with all, in short, that the modern system of agriculture demands,—have no adequate accommodation for the labourers by whom the farms attached to them are wrought. The horses and cattle are well provided for, but not the men. A wretched out-house,—the genuine bothy,—furnished with a few rude stools, a few deal bedsteads, a few bowls of tin or earthenware, a water-pail, and a pot,—serves miserably to accommodate some eight or ten labourers, all of them, of course, single men. Here they kindle their own fire, cook their own victuals, make their own beds.

The labours of the farm employ them from nine to ten hours daily; the grooming and feeding of their horses at least an hour more. The rest of their time falls to be passed in their miserable home. They return to it often wet and fatigued, especially in the briefer and stormier months of the year, just as the evening has fallen, and find all dark and chill: the fire has to be lighted,—in some districts even the very fuel to be procured; the water to be brought from the well; the hasty and unsavoury meal to be prepared. It is scarce possible to imagine circumstances of greater discomfort. The staple food of the labourer is generally oatmeal cooked in careless haste,—as might be anticipated in the circumsances,—by mixing a portion in a bowl with hot water and a little salt; and often for weeks and months together there is no change in either the materials of this his necessarily heating and unwholesome meal, or in the mode of preparing it. The farmer, his master, in too many instances takes no further care of him after his labours for the day are over. He represents merely a certain quantum of power purchased at a certain price, and applied to a certain purpose; and as it is, unluckily, power purchased by the half-year, and abundant in the market, there is no necessity that it should be husbanded from motives of economy, like that of the farmer's horses or of his steam-engine; and therefore little heed is taken though it should thus run to waste. The consequences are in most cases deplorable.

Nearly twenty years ago, we lived for a short time in an agricultural district in the north of Scotland, on the farm of one of the first introducers of the bothy system into that part of the country. He has been dead for years, nor do we know that any of his relatives survive. He had been a bold speculator in his time, and had risen, with the rise of the large-farm system, into the enjoyment of a very considerable income; but instead of regarding it as mere capital in the forming,—the merchant's true estimate of his gains,—he had dealt by it as the landed gentleman does in most cases with his yearly rental. His style of living had more than kept pace with his means; a change had taken place in his circumstances at that eventful period, so very trying to many of similar character, when England, at the close of her long war with France, ceased to be the workshop and general agency-office of Europe; and he was now an old man, and on the eve of bankruptcy.

The appearance of his steadings and fields consorted well at the time with his general circumstances. The stone-fences were ruinous; the hedges gapped by the half-tended cattle. Harvest was just over, and on his farm at least it had been a miserably scanty one; but it would have been somewhat better with a little more care. In walking over one of his fields, we counted well-nigh a dozen sheaves scattered about among the stubble, that seemed to have fallen from the carts at loading time, and were now fastened to the earth by the grains having struck their shoots downward and taken root. His steadings, though they wore a neglected look, were of modern substantial masonry, and well designed,—the stables roomy, the cattle-courts and sheds formed on the most approved plan. Very different, however, was the appearance of the building in which his farm-servants found their sort of half-shelter. Some twenty or thirty years before it had been a barn; for it had formed part of an older steading, of which all the other buildings had been pulled down, to make way for the more modern erection. It was a dingy, low, thatched building, bulged in the side-walls in a dozen different places, and green atop with chickweed and stone-crop. One long apartment without parti-tion or ceiling, occupied the interior from the gable to gable. A row of undressed deal-beds ran along the sides. There was a fire at each gable, or rather a place at which fires might be lighted, for there were no chimneys; the narrow slits in the walls were crammed with turf; the roof leaked in a dozen different places; and along the ridge the sky might be seen from end to end of the apartment. We learned to know what o'clock it was, when we awoke in the night-time, by the stars which we saw glimmering through the opening.

It was, in truth, a comfortless habitation for human creatures in a wet and gusty November, and the inmates were as rugged as their dwelling-place was rude. We need hardly say that none of them could regard it as a home. It was the gloomy season of the year, when the night falls fast, abridging the labours of the day; and ere they returned to their miserable hovel in the evening, all was deep twilight without, and all darkness within. The fuel had to be procured, the fire to be kindled, water to be brought from the well, and the unsavoury meal to be prepared; and all this by men stiff with fatigue, and not unfrequently soaked with wet. It was no easy matter at times to light the fire: the fuel often got damp, and, when at length lighted, burnt dead and cheerless. There was a singular want, too, of the ordinary providence among the inmates, and it could be shown in a matter slight as this. No provision was made in the morning for the fire of the night. If the rain fell, their fuel and their tempers were just so much the worse in consequence; and that was all. It seems natural for men in such circumstances to be careless of themselves, and equally natural for them to avenge on the cause of their general discomfort the irritating effects of their own indifferency and lack of care. There was a large amount of rude sarcasm in the bothy; and, strange as it may seem, a great deal of laughter. It has been remarked by, we think, a French writer, that the people of despotic Governments laugh more than those of free States.

We never heard the name of the farmer mentioned among his servants without some accompanying expression of dislike; we never saw one of them manifest the slightest regard for his interest. They ill-treated his horses, neglected his cattle, left his corn to rot in the fields. Some of them could speak of his approaching ruin with positive glee. What we would fain have said to him then may not be without its use to others now. "You, in your utter selfishness, have spoiled the men whom you employ; and they, in turn, are spoiling your horses, and cattle, and corn, and glorying in the ruin which is just on the eve of overtaking you. All right. There is no getting above the natural laws. Alkalies neutralize acids; dense bodies invariably descend when placed in fluids lighter than themselves; and men, when they are spoiled, spoil all other things."
September 22, 1841

Climbing Boys—Chimney Sweeping

HE must have been no humane man who first thought of forcing an infant up a chimney; the process is more than barbarous—it is unnatural; and the status of the people must have been very different from what it is at present ere chimney-sweeping on this plan could have become a trade. We do not see how it could have originated among Christians in the true sense of the term, though custom reconciles good men to it now. Observe the train of evils which arises out of its unnaturalness and inhumanity, and the consequent repugnance of children to engage in it. Climbing boys, in the great majority of cases, are either bought or stolen. No child, it is stated in one of the papers before us (from The Society For Superseding The Necessity of Climbing Boys) is ever made a chimney sweeper by fair means.

Families have been visited when in a state of the utmost destitution,—the children huddled together in rags in the corner of a loft, and on the very edge of starvation. The poor little things have risen "like hungry unfledged birds at the prospect of food," when the visitor has told them of an opening for one of their number; and no sooner have they learned the nature of the provided employment,— no sooner has the word chimney been mentioned to them, than they have all cowered back again into their corner. An honest man, a Methodist, states that he has looked about for an apprentice in this way for months together, but with always the same result;—no apprentice could he find.

The usual mode of obtaining children is by buying them from their parents, poor dissolute creatures whose natural affection has been drained off to the dregs in a long course of heart-hardening dissipation. The prices vary, it is stated, from two to four pounds; boys, small for their age, are preferred, and bring a higher price; the ages at which they are usually taken vary from five to seven years. One poor little creature, dressed in a cotton frock, was brought before the Recorder of Dublin in October last, one of its feet burned by climbing where fires had just been extinguished, its body torn, from an inability, through want of strength, to support itself in the flues, and covered all over with bruises from the kicks and chastisements of its brutal master. It had been purchased for ten shillings shortly before, and was under six years of age.

But this case is merely a specimen of a numerous class. Climbing boys, in the early part of their apprenticeship, are invariably forced up the flues, threatened, kicked, flogged, pinched in the feet, stripped naked, and then sent up. Their knees and elbows soon become sore, the skin breaks; but they are still forced to climb notwithstanding, and in course of time the parts become callous; they grow up, however, more stunted and deformed than any other class of children. The care taken of them when unemployed agrees in general with the rest of their treatment. Accidents are continually thinning their number, and accidents of the most frightful kind. We shall not harrow up the feelings of our readers with the more horrible details; page after page of two of the documents before us have more the look of being written with blood than any portion of almost any other production we ever saw.

Will it be credited that boys are sometimes forced up flues only seven inches square, and sometimes thrust down flues on fire to be literally roasted alive. It seems from the evidence, however, that too many of the poor creatures survive notwithstanding. One journeyman can superintend a number of boys; there is no employment in the trade, in consequence, for more than half those who serve their time in it, and these, to use the language given in evidence by a chimney sweeper, "get often into a roving way, and come to no good end at last." They associate, in many instances, with thieves, to whom, their habits of climbing render them valuable; and the convictions and confessions at the Old Bailey serve to sum up their stories of wretchedness and crime.

Great numbers, too, of the journeymen and master sweepers are characters of the worst description. A superintendent of police, examined before the House of Lords in 1834, stated in evidence, that there were eleven persons pursuing this miserable trade as masters within his district; of these, three were confirmed and known thieves; the greater part of the others stole, it was suspected, when they could, to eke out their living; they in general treated persons in their employment very ill; and all of them were drunkards.

Now, the object of the "Superseding Society" is to put down the trade of sweeping chimneys by means of boys or girls, for these last are sometimes also employed, and, by a positive prohibitory enactment, to substitute mechanical means. Why they should have opponents or opposers among the respectable classes, we do not very clearly see. Can it be alleged, in what has been so emphatically termed the mechanical age,—the age of Babbage's calculating machine—that chimneys cannot be swept by mechanical means? It is the direct interest of master sweeps to say so. Their boys cost them almost nothing but the first price; they live mostly on broken victuals, which they receive in charity at the houses at which they are employed, and one paid journeyman can superintend half a dozen of them.

But when, on the contrary, the machines recommended by the Society are employed, one paid journeyman is required for the working of each. The master sweeps, therefore, make use of every possible means to thwart the introduction of these. In the words of one of the sweepers examined—"they do not like the machine, and give it as bad a name as they can; and some of them use it unfairly on purpose to show that it cannot accomplish the object intended."

The right course of legislation in such a case seems sufficiently plain. If the use of climbing boys be rendered illegal, and the law guarded by severe penalties, and strictly enforced, means will soon be found to sweep chimneys without them, and thus a large amount of suffering, degradation, and crime, will be struck from off the general mass.

We find arguments of a truly singular cast adduced by the advocates of the system. The hapless children employed by the trade in this trade are "merry little fellows, it is said, and continually showing their white teeth in high glee." Well, we doubt it not. It has been told us by one who knew well, that when slavery was at the worst in the colonies, and the crack of the horse whip and the shrieks of the sufferer were to be heard in the fields by day, no sooner had the evening closed than the slave huts became scenes of gaiety, and the passer by might hear the frequent sound of the dance and the song. We have read, too, that when the bigot Dominican, or the wild Indian, have ceased but for a few minutes from inflicting their tortures, the worn-out victims of their cruelty have fallen asleep in their hands. Should man derive an apology for his wickedness from the great goodness of God, and defend slavery and tortures because He interposes in his mercy to lighten the miseries of the sufferer? Surely not!

MILLER'S Letter To Lord Brougham *was one of the most important pieces he ever wrote. Intended as a response to the announcement in the House of Lords by Lord Brougham and Vaux that the House had upheld the right of the gentry to "intrude" ministers into Church of Scotland parishes, it is a piece of long and angry polemic. When it found its way to the "evagelical" dignitaries of the Church, they quickly realised that the fiery author (who had a small reputation as a poet in the North of Scotland) was the man they were looking for to edit their planned newspaper* The Witness. *Miller began his tirade by telling Brougham, "I am a plain working man in rather humble circumstances," but then went on to remind his Lordship that "the opinions which I hold regarding the law of patronage are those entertained by the great bulk of my countrymen and entitled on that account to some respect. I shall state them as clearly and as simply as I can." This he did.*

Letter to Lord Brougham

My Lord,

I am a plain working man, in rather humble circumstances, a native of the north of Scotland, and a member of the Established Church. I am acquainted with no other language than the one in which I address your Lordship; and the very limited knowledge which I possess has been won slowly and painfully, from observation and reflection, with now and then the assistance of a stray volume, in the intervals of a laborious life. I am a plain untaught man; but the opinions which I hold regarding the law of patronage are those entertained by the great bulk of my countrymen, and entitled on that account to some little respect. I shall state them as clearly and as simply as I can.

Now, with many thousands of my countrymen, I have been accustomed to ask, Where is the place which patronage occupies in this Church of the people and of Christ? I read in the First Book of Discipline (as drawn up by Knox and his brethren), that "no man should enter the ministry without a lawful vocation; and that a lawful vocation standeth in the *election of the people,* examination of the ministry, and admission by them both." I find in the Second Book, as sanctioned by our earlier Assemblies, and sworn to in our National Covenant, that as this liberty of election was observed and respected so long as the primitive Church maintained its purity, it should be also observed and respected by the Reformed Church of Scotland; and that neither by the king himself, nor by any inferior person, should ministers be intruded on congregations, contrary to the will of the people.

I find *patronage* mentioned in this Second Book for the first time, and mentioned only to be denounced as "an abuse flowing from the Pope and the corruption of the canon law," and as contrary to the liberty of election, the light of reformation, the Word of God. Where is the flaw in our logic when we infer that the members of our Church constitute our Church, and that it is the part and right of these members in their collective capacity to elect their ministers? I, my Lord, am an integral part of the Church of Scotland, and of such integral parts, and of nothing else, is the body of this Church composed; nor do we look to the high places of the earth when we address ourselves to its adorable Head.

The Earl of Kinnoull is not the Church, nor any of the other patrons of Scotland. Why, then, are these men suffered to exercise, and that so exclusively, one of the Church's most sacred privileges? You tell us of "existing institutions, vested rights, positive interests." Do we not know that the slaveholders, who have so long and so stubbornly withstood your Lordship's truly noble appeals in behalf of the African bondsmen, have been employing an exactly similar language for the last fifty years; and that the onward progress of man to the high place which God has willed him to occupy has been impeded at every step by "existing institutions, vested rights, positive interests?"

My grandfather was a grown man at a period when the neighbouring proprietor could have dragged him from his cottage, and hung him up on the gallows-hill of the barony. It is not yet a century since the colliers of our southern districts were serfs bound to the soil. The mischievous and intolerant law of patronage still presses its dead weight on our consciences. But what of all that, My Lord? Is it not in accordance with the high destiny of the species that the fit and the right should triumph over the established?

It is impossible your Lordship can hold, with men of a lower order, that there is any necessary connection between the law of patronage and our existence as an Establishment. The public money can only be legitimately employed in furthering the public good; and we recognise the improvement and conservation of the morals of the people as the sole condition on which our ministers receive the support of the State. Where is the inevitable connection between rights of patronage (which, as the law now exists, may be exercised by fools, debauchees, infidels) and principles such as these? Nay, what is there subversive of such principles in a Christian liberty of election as complete as that enjoyed of old by the first fathers of the Reformation, or exercised in the present day by our Protestant Dissenters? I may surely add, that what is good for the Dissenters in this matter cannot be very bad for us; that I can find none of the much-dreaded evils of popular election,—the divisions, the heart-burnings, the endless law-suits, the dominancy of the fanatical spirit,—exemplified in them; and that there can surely be little to censure in a principle which could have secured to them the labours of such ministers as Baxter and Bunyan, Watts and Doddridge, Robert Hall and Thomas McCrie. Even you yourself, my Lord, will hardly venture to assert that our Scottish patrons could have provided them with better or more useful clergymen than they have been enabled to choose for themselves.

But on these points we are not at issue with your Lordship. You tell us, however, that we are protected against the abuses of patronage by the provision that patrons can present only qualified persons,—clergymen whose literature the Church has pronounced sufficient, and their morals not bad. And when, under the suspension of our higher privileges, we challenge for ourselves the *right of rejecting ministers thus selected without our assigning our reasons,* you ungenerously insinuate, that we are perhaps anxious to employ this liberty in the rejection of good men, too strict in morals, and too diligent in duty, to please our vitiated tastes. "Have a care, my Lord. "You are a philosopher of the inductive school. Look well to your facts. Put our lives to the question.

We challenge, as our right, *liberty of rejection without statement of reasons.* What is there so absurd in this as to provoke ridicule? or what so unfair as to justify the imputation of sinister design? It is *positive,* not *negative,* character we expect in a clergyman. We are suspicious of the *"not proven;"* we are dissatisfied with even the *"not guilty:"* we look in him for qualities which we can love, powers which we can respect, graces which we can revere. It matters not that we should have no grounds on which to condemn;—we are justified in our rejection if we cannot approve.

I have striven, my Lord, to acquaint myself with the history of my Church. I have met with a few old books, and have found time to read them; and, as the histories of Knox, Calderwood, and Wodrow have been among the number, I do not find myself much at the mercy of any man on questions connected with our ecclesiastical institutions, or the spirit which animated them. The Union had sunk the Presbyterian representation of Scotland into a feeble and singularly inefficient minority. Toryism in its worst form, acquired an overpowering ascendancy in the councils of the nation; Bolingbroke engaged in his deep-laid conspiracy against the Protestant succession and our popular liberties; and the law of patronage was again established.

Historical evidence is often of a vague and indeterminate character; there are disputed questions of fact which divide the probabilities in directions diametrically opposite; but on the question before us it is comparatively easy to decide. The law which re-established patronage in Scotland,—which has rendered Christianity inefficient in well-nigh half her parishes,—which has separated some of her better clergymen from her Church,—and many of her better people from her clergymen,—the law through which Robertson ruled in the General Assembly and which Brougham has eulogized in the House of Lords,—that identical law formed, in its first enactment, no unessential portion of a deep and dangerous conspiracy against the liberties of our country.

The Church has offended many of her noblest and wealthiest, it is said, and they are flying from her in crowds. Well, what matters it?— let the chaff fly! We care not though she shake off, in her wholesome exercise, some of the indolent humours which have hung about her so long. The vital principle will act with all the more vigour when they are gone. She may yet have to pour forth her life's blood through some incurable and deadly wound; for do we not know that though *the Church* be eternal, Churches are born and die? But the blow will be dealt in a different quarrel, and on other and lower ground,—not when her ministers, for the sake of the spiritual, lessen their hold of the secular, not when, convinced of the justice of the old quarrel, they take up their position on the well-trodden battle-field of her saints and her martyrs,—not when they stand side by side with her people, to contend for their common rights, in accordance with the dictates of their consciences, and agreeably to the law of their God. The reforming spirit is vigorous within her, and her hour is not yet come.

June 1839

SUTHERLAND As It Was and Is, *which Miller subtitled* How A Country May Be Ruined *is a minor masterpiece of sustained outrage. The essay is a long (23,000 words), seven-part attack on the folly, and callousness, of the hugely-wealthy Sutherland family on two counts; the 'clearing' of the people from the straths and glens to make way for the lowland sheep, and the refusal of the Duke (who was an Episcopalian, like most of the gentry) to allow the Free Church to build churches on any of his vast lands. In the course of his piece Miller traces the history of the Highland system of land tenure, describes (and documents) the superb performance of the Sutherland Highlanders as British soldiers, which he contrasts with the wretchedness of their families trying to scrape a living from the coastal strip. He rails against the ingratitude of the British state, and the iron hostility of the Anglicised Sutherland family. And as if the Duke and his family were not bad enough " . . . . there creep around them creatures whose business it is to anticipate their wishes; but who, at times, doubtless, instead of anticipating them, misinterpret them". To Miller this loathsome breed of factors and under-factors ". . . impart to whatever they do the impress of their own low and menial natures . . . "*

"It is a defect of the British Constitution" Miller fulminates in his concluding paragraphs "strongly exemplified by the case of Sutherland, that the rights of property may be so stretched as to overbear the rights of conscience . . . " In his final flourish, Miller makes an extraordinary appeal to the media of the United States to use the misery of Sutherland to embarrass the British government. He invites America to " . . . direct her aim where her darts, instead of provoking national hostility, or exciting bitter spirit among the entire people of a country would but subserve the general cause of liberty and human improvement". There was, he felt, little point in satirising the manners, mores, or modes of thinking of the British. "But there are matters of a different kind, regarding which the country bears a conscience, and is not quite at ease, and there we are vulnerable".

Sutherland As It Was and Is

SUCH of our readers as are acquainted with the memoir of Lady Glenorchy, must remember a deeply melancholy incident which occurred in the history of this excellent woman, in connection with the noble family of Sutherland. Her only sister had been married to William, seventeenth Earl of Sutherland,—'the last of the good Earls'; "a noble man", says the Rev. Dr. Jones, in his Memoir, "who to the finest person united all the dignity and amenity of manners and character which give lustre to greatness." But his sun was destined soon to go down. Five years after his marriage, which proved one of the happiest, and was blessed with two children, the elder of the two, the young Lady Catherine, a singularly engaging child, was taken from him by death, in his old hereditary castle of Dunrobin. The event deeply affected both parents, and preyed on their health and spirits. It had taken place amid the gloom of a severe northern winter, and in the solitude of the Highlands; and, acquiescing in the advice of friends, the Earl and his Lady quitted the family seat, where there was so much to remind them of their bereavement, and sought relief in the more cheerful atmosphere of Bath.

But they were not to find it there. Shortly after their arrival, the Earl was seized by a malignant fever, with which, upheld by a powerful constitution, he struggled for fifty-four days, and then expired. "For the first twenty-one days and nights of these," says Dr.

Jones, "Lady Sutherland never left his bedside; and then at last, overcome with fatigue, anxiety, and grief, she sank an unavailing victim to an amiable but excessive attachment, seventeen days before the death of her lord." The period, though not very remote, was one in which the intelligence of events travelled slowly; and in this instance the distraction of the family must have served to retard it beyond the ordinary time. Her Ladyship's mother, when hastening from Edinburgh to her assistance, alighted one day from her carriage at an inn, and, on seeing two hearses standing by the wayside, inquired of an attendant whose remains they contained? The remains, was the reply, of Lord and Lady Sutherland, on their way for interment to the Royal Chapel of Holyrood House. And such was the first intimation which the lady received of the death of her daughter and son-in-law.

The event was pregnant with disaster to Sutherland, though many years elapsed ere the ruin which it involved fell on that hapless county. The sole survivor and heir of the family was a female infant of but a year old. Her maternal grandmother, an ambitious, intriguing woman of the world, had the chief share in her general training and education; and she was brought up in the south of Scotland, of which her grandmother was a native, far removed from the influence of those genial sympathies with the people of her clan, for which the old Lords of Sutherland had been so remarkable, and, what was a sorer evil still, from the influence of the vitalities of that religion which, for five generation together, her fathers had illustrated and adorned.

The special mode in which the disaster told first, was through the patronages of the county, the larger part of which are vested in the family of Sutherland. Some of the old Earls had been content, as we have seen, to place themselves on the level of the Christian men of their parishes, and thus to unite with them in calling to their churches the Christian ministers of their choice. They knew,—what regenerate natures can alone know with the proper emphasis,—that in Christ Jesus the vassal ranks with his lord, and they conscientiously acted on the conviction. But matters were now regulated differently. The presentation supplanted the call, and ministers came to be placed in the parishes of Sutherland without the consent and contrary to the will of the people. Churches, well filled hitherto, were deserted by their congregations, just because a respectable woman of the world, making free use of what she

deemed her own, had planted them with men of the world who were
only tolerably respectable; and in houses and barns the devout men
of the district learned to hold numerously-attended Sabbath
meetings for reading the Scriptures, and mutual exhortation and
prayer, as a sort of substitute for the public services, in which they
found they could no longer join with profit. The spirit awakened by
the old Earls had survived themselves and ran directly counter to the
policy of their descendants.

Strongly attached to the Establishment, the people, though they
thus forsook their old places of worship, still remained members of
the national Church, and travelled far in the summer season to
attend the better ministers of their own and the neighbouring
counties. We have been assured, too, from the men whose judgment
we respect, that under all their disadvantages, religion continued
peculiarly to flourish among them,—a deep-toned evangelism
prevailed; so that perhaps the visible Church throughout the world at
the time could furnish no more striking contrasts than that which
obtained between the cold, bald, commonplace services of the pulpit
in some of these parishes, and the fervid prayers and exhortations
which give life and interest to these humble meetings of the people.
What a pity it is that differences such as these the Duke of Sutherland
cannot see!

The marriage of the young countess into a noble English family
was fraught with further disaster to the county. There are many
Englishmen quite intelligent enough to perceive the difference
between a smoky cottage of turf and a whitewashed cottage of stone,
whose judgment on their respective inhabitants would be of but little
value. Sutherland, as a country of *men,* stood higher at this period
than perhaps any other district in the British empire; but it by no
means stood high as a country of farms and cottages. The marriage
of the countess brought a new set of eyes upon it,—eyes accustomed
to quite a different face of things. It seemed a wild, rude country,
where all was wrong, and all had to be set right,—a sort of Russia on
a small scale, that had just got another Peter the Great to civilise it,—
or a sort of barbarous Egypt, with an energetic Ali Pasha at its head.

Even the vast wealth and great liberality of the Stafford family
militated against this hapless county: it enabled them to treat it as the
mere subject of an interesting experiment, in which gain to
themselves was really no object,—nearly as little so as if they had
resolved on dissecting a dog alive for the benefit of science. It was a

still further disadvantage, that they had to carry on their experiments by the hands, and to watch its first effects with the eyes, of others. The agonies of the dog might have had their softening influence on a dissector who held the knife himself; but there could be no such influence exerted over him, did he merely issue orders to his footman that the dissection should be completed, remaining himself, meanwhile, out of sight and out of hearing.

The plan of improvement sketched out by his English family was a plan exceedingly easy of conception. Here is a vast tract of land, furnished with two distinct sources of wealth. Its shores may be made the seats of extensive fisheries, and the whole of its interior parcelled out into productive sheep-farms. All is waste in its present state: it has no fisheries, and two-thirds of its internal produce is consumed by the inhabitants. It had contributed, for the use of the community and the landlord, its large herds of black cattle; but the English family saw, and, we believe, saw truly, that for every one pound of beef which it produced, it could be made to produce two pounds of mutton, and perhaps a pound of fish in addition. And it was resolved, therefore, that the inhabitants of the central districts, who, *as they were mere Celts,* could not be transformed, it was held, into store-farmers, should be marched down to the sea-side, there to convert themselves into fishermen, on the shortest possible notice, and that a few farmers of capital, of the industrious Lowland race, should be invited to occupy the new sub-divisions of the interior.

And, pray, what objections can be urged against so liberal and large-minded a scheme? The poor inhabitants of the interior had *very* serious objections to urge against it. Their humble dwellings were of their own rearing; it was they themselves who had broken in their little fields from the waste; from time immemorial, far beyond the reach of history, had they possessed their mountain holdings,—they had defended them so well of old that the soil was still virgin ground, in which the invader had found only a grave; and their young men were now in foreign lands, fighting, at the command of their chieftainess, the battles of their country, not in the character of hired soldiers, but men who regarded these very holdings as their stake in the quarrel.

To them, then, the scheme seemed fraught with the most flagrant, the most monstrous injustice. Were it to be suggested by some Chartist convention in a time of revolution, that Sutherland might be still further improved—that it was really a piece of great waste to suffer the revenues of so extensive a district to be squandered by one individual—that it would.be better to appropriate them to the use of the community in general—that the community in general might be still further benefitted by the removal of the one said individual from Dunrobin to a road-side, where he might be profitably employed in breaking stones—and that this new arrangement could not be entered on too soon—the noble Duke would not be a whit more astonished, or rendered a whit more indignant, by the scheme, than were the Highlanders of Sutherland by the scheme of his predecessor.

The reader must keep in view, therefore, that if atrocities unexampled in Britain for at least a century were perpetrated in the *clearing* of Sutherland, there was a species of at least passive resistance on the part of the people (for active resistance there was none), which in some degree provoked them. Had the Highlanders, on receiving orders, marched down to the sea-coast, and become fishermen, with the readiness with which a regiment deploys on review day, the atrocities would, we doubt not, have been much fewer. But though the orders were very distinct, the Highlanders were very unwilling to obey; and the severities formed merely a part of the means through which the necessary obedience was ultimately secured. We shall instance a single case, as illustrative of the process.

In the month of March 1814, a large proportion of the Highlanders of Farr and Kildonan, two parishes in Sutherland, were summoned to quit their farms in the following May. In a few days after, the surrounding heaths on which they pastured their cattle, and from which at that season the sole supply of herbage is derived (for in those northern districts the grass springs late, and the cattle-feeder in the spring months depends chiefly on the heather), were set on fire and burnt up. There was that sort of policy in the stroke which men deem allowable in a state of war. The starving cattle went roaming over the burnt pastures, and found nothing to eat. Many of them perished, and the greater part of what remained, though in miserable condition, the Highlanders had to sell perforce. Most of the able-bodied men were engaged in this latter business at a distance from home, when the dreaded term-day came on. The pasturage had been destroyed before the legal term, and while, in even the eye of the law, it was still the property of the poor Highlanders; but ere disturbing them in their dwellings, term-day was suffered to pass.

The work of demolition then began. A numerous party of men,

with a factor at their head, entered the district, and commenced pulling down the houses over the heads of the inhabitants. In an extensive tract of country not a human dwelling was left standing, and then, the more effectually to prevent their temporary re-erection, the destroyers set fire to the wreck. In one-day were the people deprived of home and shelter and left exposed to the elements. Many deaths were said to have ensued from alarm, fatigue, and cold. Pregnant women were taken with premature labour in the open air. There were old men who took to the woods and rocks in a state of partial insanity. An aged bedridden man, named Macbeath, had his house unroofed over his head, and was left exposed to the wind and rain till death put a period to his sufferings. Another man lying ill with fever met with no tenderer treatment, but in his case the die turned up life. A bedridden woman, nearly a hundred years of age, had her house fired over her head, and ere she could be extricated from the burning wreck, the sheets in which she was carried were on fire. She survived but for five days after.

In a critique on the work of Sismondi, which appeared a few months since in the *Westminster Review,* the writer tells us, "it has even been said that an old man, having refused to quit his cabin, perished in the flames." But such was not the case. The constituted authorities interfered; a precognition was taken by the Sheriff-substitute of the county, and the case tried before the Justiciary Court at Inverness; but the trial terminated in the acquittal of the pannels. There was no punishable crime proven to attach to the agents of the proprietor.

Their acquittal was followed by scenes of a similar character with the scene described, and even greater atrocity. But we must borrow the description of one of these from the historian of the *clearing* of Sutherland,—Donald McLeod, a native of the county, and himself a sufferer in the experimental process to which it was subjected:—

"The work of devastation was begun by setting fire to the houses of the small tenants in extensive districts—Farr, Rogart, Golspie, and the whole parish of Kildonan. I was an eye-witness of the scene. The calamity came on the people quite unexpectedly. Strong parties for each district, furnished with faggots and other combustibles, rushed on the dwellings of the devoted people, and immediately commenced setting fire to them, proceeding in their work with the greatest rapidity, till about three hundred houses were in flames. Little or no time was given for the removal of persons or property—

the consternation and confusion were extreme—the people striving
to remove the sick and helpless before the fire should reach them—
next struggling to save the most valuable of their effects—the cries of
the women and children—the roaring of the affrighted cattle, hunted
by the dogs of the shepherds amid the smoke and the fire—
altogether composed a scene that completely baffles description. A
dense cloud of smoke enveloped the whole country by day, and even
extended far on the sea. At night, an awfully grand but terrific scene
presented itself—all the houses in an extensive district in flames at
once.

I myself ascended a height about eleven o'clock in the evening,
and counted two hundred and fifty blazing houses, many of the
owners of which were my relations, and all of whom I personally
knew, but whose present condition I could not tell. The conflagration
lasted six days, till the whole of the dwellings were reduced to ashes
or smoking ruins. During one of these days, a boat lost her way in the
dense smoke as she approached the shore, but at night she was
enabled to reach a landing-place by the light of the flames."

But, to employ the language of Southey, "Things such as these, we
know, must be
At every famous victory".

And in this instance the victory of the lord of the soil over the
children of the soil was signal and complete. In little more than nine
years a population of fifteen thousand individuals were removed
from the interior of Sutherland to its sea-coasts, or had emigrated to
America. The inland districts were converted into deserts, through
which the traveller may take a long day's journey, amid ruins that still
bear the scathe of fire, and grassy patches betraying, when the
evening sun casts aslant its long deep shadows, the half-effaced lines
of the plough.

The writer of the singularly striking passage we have just quoted,
revisited his native place (Kildonan) in the year 1828, and attended
the divine service in the parish church. A numerous and devout
congregation had once worshipped there: the congregation now
consisted of eight shepherds and their *dogs*. In a neighbouring
district—the barony of Strathnaver, a portion of the parish of Farr—
the church, no longer found necessary, was razed to the ground. The
timber was carried away to be used in the erection of an inn, and the
minister's house converted into the dwelling of a fox-hunter. "A
woman well known in the parish," says McLeod, "happening to

traverse the Strath the year after the burning, was asked, on her return, What news? 'Oh', said she, 'sgeul bronach, sgeul bronach! sad news, sad news! I have seen the timber of our kirk covering the inn at Altnaharran; I have seen the kirkyard, where our friends are mouldering, filled with tarry sheep, and Mr. Sage's study-room a kennel for Robert Gun's dogs'."

A SENSE OF ORDER

BUT Hugh Miller was no radical. While no one was more quickly moved to outrage by poverty and injustice, squalor and oppression, and no one could fulminate to greater effect against the rich south-country farmers and Highland grandees, Miller was convinced that the radicals had no solutions. The Chartists and the Socialists he thought, were nudging the British working class down the road to perdition, and for them he saved his most stinging attacks. On Socialist pamphlets, for instance, he could not imagine that "anything more grossly disgusting, more detestably obscene—more horribly blashphemous—neither does, nor can exist in any language". (Although he was author enough to point out that they were not without literary merit: "But the smile does not render them a whit the less formidable"). In Miller's opinion the Chartist clamour for "one man, one vote" was the path to ruin which "would lead directly first to anarchy and then to despotism".

This, in retrospect, seems a baffling paradox. But Miller never seems to have forgotten, or forgiven, the time he spent with the ebullient, sardonic and spendthrift Edinburgh masons during 1824 and 1825. Although he was not blind to their talents he regarded them en masse *as buffoons, and totally unfitted to any kind of political responsibility. And too easily led astray by stump orators and "combination" leaders. The working class, he thought, had an unerring instinct for picking the wrong leader: "Benjamin Franklin himself," he wrote in his autobiography, "was deemed a much more ordinary man in the printing house or in Bartholomew Close, where he was teased and laughed at as the* Water American, *than in the House of Representatives, the Royal Society, or the Court of France." At the same time, Miller is on the record as having "great sympathy with the poor Chartists and Radicals who, having to work sixteen hours per day for a meagre livelihood, avenge their hard fate on all and sundry when they break loose".*

Miller's politics, such as they were, appear to have been a species of eighteenth century Whiggism, that mistrusted violent revolution as much as it disliked the High-Tory gentry who dominated so much of the country. Even the brand of law and order which they *represented was to Miller a better option than the bloodshed and chaos he saw in the political programmes of the radicals. (And with the Jacobin terror just over fifty years old, the threat seemed real enough). Things would improve when the moral quality of the individuals in the population improved. Miller espoused "a Whiggism of the future world", and was one of the large band who thought that "the liberty of preparing themselves for heaven was the only liberty they deemed worth fighting for".*

All of which amounted to a powerful sense of order *in Hugh Miller, and produced a theme in his work which ran counterpoint to the great "radical" essays like* Sutherland At It Was and Is, *the* Cottages of Our Hinds, *or* The Highlands. *In* The Franchise, *for example, he explains his "dread of universal suffrage" and goes on to argue that the vote should be restricted to men who owned property worth £5 (or paid rents of £10 a year). Such men were "well-hafted in society, and possessed a considerable stake in the stability of the country". In* Our Working Classes *he worries about the erosion of home and family life that was going on in the squalor of the cities, which he thought was probably subverting the efforts of the philanthropists and state charities. His analysis of* The Strikes *is fascinating, and makes points which the Monetarists of the 1980s are making; he saw them as inevitable in a free society, but regrettable and dangerous because "by the stoppage of a single wheel or pin, the whole engine is brought to a stand". In* An Unspoken Speech *Miller is very much the eminent Victorian, advocating the delights of hard work, self-reliance, temperance, and a cool head.*

OUR WORKING CLASSES

NEVER in the history of the world have so many efforts been made to improve the condition of the working classes as at the present time. The legislator, the philanthropist, the city missionary, the theorist, who would do his best to uproot the very foundations of our social system, and the man of practice, who would spare no exertion to ameliorate its actual condition, have been at work, each in his several direction, honestly, earnestly, and unremittingly toiling to a single purpose,—the elevation of our working people. We have passed laws; we have devised model dwellings; we have sent pious men to hunt out ignorance and vice; we have schemed out theories that would mow down the institutions of ages; we have speculated in the direction of secular socialism and in the direction of Christian socialism; we have tried co-operative societies, building societies, and model lodgings; we have written, lectured, and taught; we have appointed commissions, printed acres of reports; pried into every hole and corner of society (except the convents); we have exported hundreds of thousands of what we termed, only a year or two back, our "surplus population;" we have raised wages, diminished competition, and founded magnificent colonies with those who were too many at home; we have done these and many other things. And what has been the result? Have we moved the living mass of our workpeople a single step higher in the scale of moral existence? Have we taught them wisdom as well as knowledge? Have we taught them to be provident, and to manage their own affairs with prudence and discretion? Have we placed them in circumstances where they fulfil their duties as men? Have we, in fact, succeeded, after all our labours, in promoting the genuine welfare of the working population? To answer this question either with a summary affirmative or with an emphatic No, would be out of place. That all the expended labour has been wasted and thrown away, we cannot for a moment believe; but it is equally certain that the present condition of our working classes is pre-eminently unsatisfactory, and that no such general improvement has taken place as would entitle us to say that we had arrived at the true solution of this great social problem.

Two things there are which, in every condition of life, mark the well-being of society, namely, the integrity of the family and the sufficiency of the dwelling. The family is the foundation of everything,—the root out of which the social world grows. Break it up and you have as certainly introduced a corrupting poison into the framework of the community, as if you had inoculated the human frame with a deadly and malignant agent, that destroys the very issues of life. The whole of our factory system where women are employed is merely a systematic destruction of the family,— practical socialism, in fact, which prepares the way for theoretic socialism of the direst and most disastrous tendency, atheistic and material, without natural affection, without law, without order, without the thousand amenities of domestic life. It matters little whether the women are employed as married or only as unmarried. If married women are engaged in factory works, they, of course, neglect their children, who, between the period of childhood and that of labour, have the education of the public streets, with its unconcealed vice, its oaths and curses, its idleness and its vagabondism. We have only to go into our streets in the lower quarters of any of our towns, to be painfully assured that every one is a broad road to destruction for the young, and that no mere school-education can ever effectually compete with the force of evil habit, any more than wholesome food will effectually nourish those who dwell continually in a polluted atmosphere.

We are all aware that the decent portion of our country population look with absolute horror on the habitual circumstances of a town life. And why so? Is it not because in their country dwellings they have been accustomed to the sacred integrity of the family, and that their isolated cottage was a *home*, containing father, mother, and children; God's first institute,—a family? The cottage may be small, ill thatched, ill-ventilated, ill-floored, and smokey; it may have its dubs, its puddles, and its national *midden*; it may be high up on a hill, where winter blasts and winter snows are more familiar than blue skies or green fields; or it may be down in a glen, miles away from other mortal habitation, so solitary, that every stranger who appears is a spectacle and amazement to the children. No matter: wherever or whatever it may be, it is, a home, and contains a family every member of which would look with instinctive horror at the indiscriminate sort of existence common in many of our towns.

Thanks to the bothy system, however, this feeling of family sacredness is beginning to be eradicated out of even our rural population; and perhaps in time a certain portion of our peasantry may be duly brought to believe that the family is a superfluous invention, after which they will be fit for anything, and good for nothing. The same principle pervades every rank of society, high or low. Wherever the family is broken up,—whether from what are termed the necessities of trade, from polygamous customs, from fashionable usages, or from particular accidents,—evil follows as a regular and constant effect. Of all the social laws that have ever been discovered, this is the most indisputably certain, that the family is an institution of nature, an organized association established immutably by God's providence for the welfare of mankind.

The preservation of the family in its full integrity we regard as the first absolute requisite, without which there can be no permanent improvement, and without which all efforts to ameliorate the condition of our working classes must certainly fail.

Next to the family comes the dwelling. As dress is the clothing of the individual, so is the house the clothing of the family. It ought to be sufficient,—sufficient for all the purposes of family life,—for decency, for convenience, for warmth, for shelter, for washing and cooking, for retirement, and for the separation of the sexes. Here society has failed. It is idle to speak of sanitary reform, and almost idle to speak of moral reform, when we contemplate the dwellings of a large portion of the working population. We can no more expect propriety of conduct in the individual if we clothe him in rags, and keep him in rags, than we can expect propriety of conduct in the family that lives habitually in the wretched lodgements which disgrace our towns and cities. For our towns, however, there is some excuse. They have increased so rapidly in population, that the supply of house-room did not, and could not, under the ordinary course of private speculation, equal the demand.

When Ireland was pouring her thousands into Glasgow, and the Highlands were undergoing the process of clearing, it could not be expected that more than the very meanest accommodation should be obtained by such a class. The past must be palliated; but now that the pressure is in a great measure over, and a breathing-time is afforded by the stream of emigration setting no longer from the country to the town, but out of the kingdom into the colonies and the United States, we can conceive no object on which society may more profitably fix its attention than on the systematic improvement of the dwellings of the industrial classes. A universal crusade against every tenement that did not afford the proper requisites of domestic life would be at least one step towards the desirable result.

But this would be insufficient. It would be only a negative reform, and all negative reforms are insufficient. It would be only cutting off the evil, whereas the true object is to produce the good. If we were to pull down every tenement that did not fulfil even the moderate conditions that would in all probability be fixed by the Government, we should only have rendered our working people houseless. We must devise some plan by which proper buildings shall be erected, and insure the future well-being of the people by a systematic scheme, that could not legally be departed from within the limits of any town containing a given number of inhabitants.

What is already evil we must reform as best we may; but what is future we ought intelligently to design,—to leave nothing to accident, nothing to the hazards of a voracious speculation; but, duly considering what is needed, to provide for it beforehand with a wise precaution, which in course of time would re-act powerfully in the whole habits and manners of the labouring community. We believe, however, that we have reached a turning point in our downward course,—that we have passed the worst,—and that there is, both in the legislature and in society at large, a very general desire to favour the requisite improvements, provided it could be clearly shown what the improvements should consist of, and upon what principle they should be undertaken.

When we find men like the Duke of Buccleuch candidly confessing,—to his honour be it spoken,—that he had done wrong in so long neglecting the dwellings of the smaller tenantry, cottars, and bothymen,—when we find Mr Stuart of Oathlaw succeeding in banding together some of the most influential and extensive landed proprietors, for the purpose of improving the dwellings in the country districts,—and when we find the Rev. Mr Mackenzie of North Leith only stopped in his career of practical benevolence by the absurd and antiquated usages of feudal lawyerism,—we are not without ground for hope that a general movement may be made at no very distant period, and that we may see model towns not only projected, but actually erected, inhabited, and in vital operation. Without the integrity of the family and the sufficency of the dwelling there can be no satisfactory reform, either in a sanitary or a moral aspect.

Among all the experiments that have been made, at least in this country, it is plainly evident that a vast field, and *that* certainly not the most unpromising, has been left untouched and unexplored. To promote the habit of providence in our working classes, it is not only necessary to exhibit a moral restriction which cautions them from going wrong, but to present a positive stimulus which induces them to go right,—to exhibit something good before their eyes, after which they shall strive,—and to make them act of their own free will, as if they had an object to attain. This stimulus may possibly be found in the desire to possess real property; and although no mere change of laws or circumstances may ever do more than facilitate the progress of good, it is quite possible that a change of circumstances might eminently promote a change of habits, and lead gradually but surely to a more enlightened appreciation of the advantages that might accrue if the present recklessness and extravagance were exchanged for prudence and economy.

June 17, 1854

An Unspoken Speech

WE enjoyed the honour on Wednesday last of being present as a guest at the annual soiree of the Scottish Young Men's Society, and derived much pleasure from the general appearance of the meeting, and the addresses of the members and their friends. The body of the great Waterloo Room was crowded on the occasion with a respectable, intellectual-looking audience, including from about a hundred and fifty to two hundred members of the Society, all of them young men banded together for mutual improvement, and most of them in that important decade of life—by far the most important of the appointed seven—which intervenes between the fifteenth and the five-and-twentieth year.

We found ourself, after leaving the room, addressing them, *in imagination,* in a few plain words regarding some of the rocks, and shoals, and insidious currents, which we knew lay in their course. Men whose words come slowly and painfully when among their fellows, can be quite fluent enough when they speak inwards without breaking silence, and have merely an imaginary assemblage for their audience; and so our short address went off glibly, without break or interruption, in the style of ordinary conversational gossip. "Members of the Scottish Young Men's Society," we said, "it is rather late in life for the individual who now addresses you to attempt acquiring the art of the public speaker. You will at once see—to borrow from one of the best and most ancient of writers—that we are not 'eloquent', but 'a man of slow speech, and of a slow tongue.' And yet we think we may venture addressing ourselves, in a few plain words, to an association of young men united for the purpose of mutual improvement.

Let no young man ever beguile himself with the hope that he is to make a figure in society, or rise in the world, unless, as the apostle expresses it, he be 'temperate in all things.' Scotland has produced not a few distinguished men who were unfortunately *not* temperate; but it is well known that one of the greatest of them all—perhaps one of the most vigorous-minded men our country ever produced—Robert Burns, up till his twenty-sixth year, when he had mastered all his powers, and produced some of his finest poems, was an eminently sober man. Climbing requires not only a steady foot, but a strong head; and we question whether any one ever climbed the perilous steep, who did not keep his head cool during the process. So far as our own experience goes, we can truly state, that though we have known not a few working men, possessed some of them of strong intellects, and some of them of fine taste, and even of genius, not one have we ever known who rose either to eminence or a competency under early formed habits of intemperance.

Rather more than thirty years ago, the drinking usages of the country were more numerous than they are now. In the mechanical profession in which we laboured they were many: when a foundation was laid, the workmen were treated to a drink; they were treated to

drink when the walls were levelled; they were treated to drink when
the building was finished; they were treated to drink when an
apprentice joined the squad; treated to drink when his apron was
washed; treated to drink when his 'time was out;' and occasionally
they learned to treat one another to drink.

At the first house upon which we were engaged as a slim
apprentice boy, the workmen had a royal founding-pint, and two
whole glasses of whisky came to our share. A full-grown man might
not deem a gill of *usquebhae* (whisky) an over-dose, but it was too
much for a boy unaccustomed to strong drink; and when the party
broke· up, and we got home to our few books, we found, as we
opened the page of a favourite author, the letters dancing before our
eyes, and that we could no longer master his sense. The state was
perhaps a not very favourable one for forming a resolution in, but we
believe the effort served to sober us. We determined in that hour that
never more would we sacrifice our capacity of intellectual enjoyment
to a drinking usage; and during the fifteen years which we spent as an
operative mason, we held, through God's help, by the determination.

But there are other kinds of intoxication than that which it is the
nature of strong drink or of drugs to produce. Bacon speaks of a
"natural drunkenness.' And the hallucinations of this natural
drunkenness must be avoided if you would prosper. Let us specify
one of these. Never let yourself be beguiled by the idea that fate has
misplaced you in life, and that were you in some other sphere you
would rise. There are few such prisons in which a young man of
energy and a brave heart can be placed, in which he will not gain
more by taking kindly to his work, and looking well about him, than
by wasting himself in convulsive endeavours to escape. If he but
learn to think of his prison as a school, there is a good hope of his
ultimately getting out of it. Were a butcher's boy to ask us how we
thought he could best escape from his miserable employment, we
would at once say, 'You have rare opportunities of observation; you
may be a butcher's boy in body, but in mind you may become an
adept in one of the profoundest of the sciences, that of comparative
anatomy;—think of yourself as not in a prison, but in a school, and
there is no fear but you will rise.'

There is another delusion of that 'natural drunkenness' referred
to, against which you must also be warned. Never sacrifice your
independence to a phantom. We have seen young men utterly ruin
themselves through the vain belief that they were too good for their

work. They were mostly lads of a literary turn, who had got a knack of versifying, and who, in the fond belief they were poets and men of genius, and that poets and men of genius should be above the soil and drudgery of mechanical labour, gave up the profession by which they had lived, poorly mayhap, but independently, and got none other to set in its place. A mistake of this character is always a fatal one; and we trust all of you will ever remember, that though a man may think himself above his work, no man *is,* or no man ought to think himself, above the high dignity of being independent. In truth, he is but a sorry, weak fellow who measures himself by the conventional status of the labour by which he lives.

There is another advice which we would fain give you, though it may be regarded as of a somewhat equivocal kind: Rely upon yourselves. The man who sets his hopes upon patronage, or the exertions of others in his behalf, is never so respectable a man, and, save in very occasional instances, rarely so *lucky* a man, as he who bends his exertions to compel fortune in his behalf, by making himself worthy of her favours. Some of the greatest wrecks we have seen in life have been those of waiters on patronage; and the greatest discontents which we have seen in corporations, churches, and states, have arisen from the exercise of patronage. Patronage is twice cursed,—cursed in the incompetency which it places where merit ought to be, and in the incompetency which it creates among the class who make it their trust. But the curse which you have mainly to avoid is that which so often falls on those who waste their time and suffer their energies to evaporate in weakly and obsequiously waiting upon it. We therefore say, Rely upon yourselves.

With regard to the conduct of your studies, we simply say, Strive to be catholic in your tastes. Some of you will have a leaning to science; some to literature. To the one class we would say, Your literature will be all the more solid if you can get a vein of true science to run through it; and to the other, Your science will be all the more fascinating if you temper and garnish it with literature. In truth, almost all the greater subjects of man's contemplation belong to both fields. Of subjects such as astronomy and geology, for instance, the poetry is as sublime as the science is profound. As a pretty general rule, you will perhaps find literature most engaging in youth, and science as you grow in years. But faculties for both have been given you by the great Taskmaster, and it is your bounden duty that these be exercised aright."

The Strikes

THE last twelve month has been peculiarly marked in the manufacturing world as a year of strikes and combinations; nor, though there are adjustments taking place, and bands of operatives returning to their employment after months of voluntary idleness, are they by any means yet at an end. Great fires and disastrous shipwrecks are both very terrible things; but, so far as the mere waste of property is involved, a protracted strike is at least as formidable as either, and its permanent effects are often incalculably more mischievous. Wreck or conflagration never yet ruined any branch of industry. Were all the manufactured goods in London to be destroyed in one fell blaze, a few months of accelerated industry would repair the loss. The greatest calamity of the kind which could possibly take place would resemble merely the emptying of a reservoir fed by a perennial steam, that would continue flowing till it had filled it again. But the loss occasioned by a long-protracted strike is often of a deeper kind. It not only empties the reservoir, but in some instances cuts off the spring, and in this way robs of its means of supply the town or district whose only source the spring had constituted. Nations have in this way, when there were competing nations in the field, been permanently stripped of lucrative branches of industry, and become the mere importers of articles with which they had been accustomed to supply their neighbours.

In other instances the effects are disastrous, not to the nation generally, but to merely a class of its workers. A partial strike of one section of workmen, on the product of whose labours certain other sections are dependent for employment, disturbs the social machine, and arrests its progress. By a stoppage in the movements of a single wheel or pinion, the whole engine is brought to a stand. The inventive power is quickened, through the necessity thus created, to originate some mode of supplying the place of the refractory bit or segment; the ingenuity exerted at length proves successful; wood, iron, and leather, are made to perform the work of human nerve and muscle; and a province of industry is divested of its living workmen, and occupied by dead machines.

During the season of strikes and combinations that followed the passing of the Reform Bill, a combination of the ship-carpenters of Dublin, accompanied by more than the ordinary Irish violence and coercion, was completely successful. The terrified masters broke

down, and, yielding to the terms imposed, gave their workmen the
wages they demanded. But though they escaped, in consequence, the
bludgeon and the brick-bat, they could not escape the ordinary laws
of trade and manufacture. They of course looked for the proper
return from the capital invested in their business; they expected the
proper remuneration for the time, anxiety, and trouble which it cost
them. Profit was as indispensable to them as wages to their
operatives.

They found, further, that on the new terms, and with the
competition of the western coast of Britain, especially that of the
ship-builders of Liverpool and the Clyde, to contend with, profit
could no longer be realised, and so they had to shut up their work-
yards, one after another; and Dublin has now scarce any trade in
ship-building. Its ship-carpenters have become very few, and, of
consequence, very weak; and, no longer able to dictate terms as
before, they have to work for wages quite as low as in any other part
of the United Kingdom. But though carpenter-work can now be had
as cheaply in the Irish capital as in Liverpool or Glasgow, the trade,
fairly scared away, failed to return; the dock-masters of the Clyde and
the Mersey kept a firm hold of what they had got; and all that was
accomplished by the successful strike of the Dublin ship-carpenters
was simply the ruin of the ship-carpentry of Dublin.

Nor would the result have been different had the combination
been more extensive. Had it included all the carpenters of Britain
and Ireland, the competition on ship-building would have lain
between, not the opposite sides of the Irish Channel, but the
opposite sides of the German Ocean: our merchants would have
purchased their vessels, not from the Clyde and the Mersey, but from
the dockyards of the Baltic and Zuyder Zee; and our British
carpenters, instead of being, as of old, the fabricators of navies, might
set out, shovel in hand, for the railways, and become navvies
themselves.

And yet, disastrous as strikes almost always are, it cannot be
questioned that the general principle which they involve is a just
one,—quite as just as that of the masters who continue to resist them.
In the labour-market, as in every other, it is as fair to sell dear as to
buy cheap; and it is in no degree more unjust for five hundred, five
thousand, of fifty thousand men to agree together that they shall
demand a high price for their labour, than it is for five or for one.
The laws framed to compel working men to labour at whatever rate

or remuneration legislators may choose to fix,—and in this country
the terms the *legislators* and *employers* have in the main been ever
synonymous,—are properly regarded as evidence of a barbarous and
unscrupulous time.

The unquestioned right of the working man is, however, of all
others one of the most liable to abuse. It is greatly more so than the
corresponding right of his employers. Both possess the same
common nature; and it is quite as much the desire of the one to buy
labour cheaply as of the other to sell it dear. But there is an amount
of responsibility attached to the position of the masters, which has
always the effect, in at least a free age and country, of keeping their
combinations within comparatively safe bounds. Masters of a
morally inferior cast cannot control their fellows. Should they even
be a majority, and should they agree to fix a rate of wages
disproportionately low compared with their own profits, a few honest
employers, instead of incurring loss by entering into competition
with them, and raising the hire of their workmen, would soon
appropriate to themselves their gains, by robbing them at once of
their workers and their trade. Competition on the side of the masters
forms always the wholesome corrective of combination.

Nor dare the combiners take undue means to overawe and control
the competitors. Their amount of property, and their general
standing in consequence, give them a stake in their country which
they dare not forfeit by any scheme of intimidation; a regard too, to
the general interests of their trade imposes upon them its limits; and
this, supposing them to be quite as unscrupulous and selfish as the
worst workmen that ever lived,—as no doubt some of them are,—
there is in the nature of things restrictions set upon them, which the
workman, often to his disadvantage, escapes. On him the lowliness of
circumstances virtually confers a power, if he has but the hardihood
to assert it, of overawing competition. And we find, from the history
of all strikes, that he always does attempt to overawe it. During the
last thirty years he has shot at it, thrown vitriol upon it, rolled it in
the kennel, sent it to Coventry, persecuted it with clumsy but very
relentless ridicule, and subjected it, where he could, to illegal fines.

Masters have no doubt the same nature in them as their men; but
from their position they cannot, or dare not, attempt putting down
competition in this way. Their position is that of the responsible few,
while that occupied by the operative classes is the position of the
comparatively irresponsible many; and, from the little stake which

the latter possess in the property of the country individually, and
from their conscious power in the mass, they are ever under the
temptation of overstretching their proper liberties of combining to
carry out their own intentions, into a wild licence, which demands
that their neighbours and fellows shall not, either singly or in parties,
exercise the liberty of carrying out theirs. There have been several
glaring instances of this species of tyranny during even the present
strikes; but one instance may serve as a specimen of the class. We
quote from the Stockport correspondent of a London paper:—

"At a large mill not three miles from this, where upwards of a
thousand hands are engaged, one of the weavers did not choose to
subscribe to the weekly delegate's tax towards the unfortunate
Preston strike. In consequence, one evening this week, when the mill
was stopped, he was watched in passing through the large gates into
the road, was immediately knocked down and blindfolded, his arms
pinioned, and his legs tied fast together, and, thus disabled, was
carried through the population of the place, mobbed by hundreds
upon hundreds, shouting, yelling and execrating, not a soul daring
to interfere, as any resistance to these proceedings would probably
have cost the poor fellow his life. I know the man well, as an honest,
sober, hard-working operative, and feel grieved that he should be
thus persecuted. You may say, Why do not the masters protect such
men, and put down such tyranny? Simply because *they dare not;* such
interference being sure to be followed by a general turn-out, and,
very likely, by destruction of property by fire or otherwise. These are
sad realities; and I cannot but conclude that the above outrage has
been a natural sequence to the visit of one of the Preston delegates to
the heads of that very mill during last week. My own life would not
be safe, were it known that I had told this circumstance to one
connected with what the delegates call the 'vile hireling press'."

It is one of the grand disadvantages of these strikes, that their
management and direction are almost always thrown into the hands
of a class of men widely different in character from the country's
more solid and respectable mechanics. Inferior often as workmen,
low in the moral sense, fluent as talkers, but very unwise as
counsellors, they rarely fail to land in ruin the men who, smit by
their stump oratory, make choice of them as their directors and
guides. Too little wise to see that the most formidable opponent
which any party can arouse is the moral sense of a community,
violence and coercion form invariably the clumsy expedients of their

policy. And so, for the success which a well-timed strike, founded on just principles, would be almost always certain to secure, they succeed in but achieving from their unfortunate constituencies discomfiture either immediate or ultimate.

We find in strikes, as they ordinarily occur, the disastrous working of exactly the same principle which has rendered the revolutions of the Continent such unhappy abortions. Who can doubt that the revolutions, like some of the strikes, had their basis of real grievances? But their leaders lacked sense and virtue; their wild licence became more intolerable than the torpid despotism which it had supplanted; and in the re-action that ensued, the sober citizen, the quiet mechanic, the industrious tiller of the soil, all the representatives of very influential classes, found it better, on the whole, again to submit themselves to the old tyranny, than to prostrate themselves before the new.

January 21, 1854

The Franchise

ONE of the most remarkable sayings of which the discussion in Parliament on the Reform Bill proved the occasion was that of Lord Jeffrey, then Lord Advocate for Scotland. "It was a measure," he said, "that would separate the waters above the firmament from the waters below." The remark embodied both a striking figure and a solid truth,—a figure which, by appealing to the imagination, has sunk deeper into the memory of the country than any other produced at the time; and a truth which recent events have served peculiarly to substantiate and elucidate.

It was in consequence of this separation of the waters that, while the revolutionary hurricane raged wide upon the Continent, dashing into one wild weltering ocean of anarchy and confusion the dense and ponderous masses, whose inherent strength no such measure had divided into antagonistic, self-balancing forces, Britain escaped at least all the more terrible consequences of the storm. It is doubtful, however, whether we are permanently to escape. We are told by men of science that, save for that continuous belt of ocean which girdles the globe in the southern hemisphere, we of the northern regions would have scarce any tides. In the equatorial and arctic oceans, the rise of the sea, in obedience to the attractive impulsion of the sun and moon, is checked by the great continents that stretch from north to south, before the tidal wave becomes in the least considerable; but in the southern belt that wave rolls round the world without break or interruption, and then, travelling northwards laterally, in obedience to the law through which water always seeks its level, it rises and falls every twenty-four hours on the most northern shores of Europe, Asia and America.

It has been thus with the tidal wave of revolution. The Reform Bill in this country stretched abreast of the privileged classes like a vast continent, and would have effectually checked every rising tide of revolution that originated in the country itself. But there lay in the neighbouring States great unbroken belts of the popular ocean, in which the revolutionary wave has risen high. The popular privileges have been elevated, in consequence, in these States, considerably above the British level; and it is very questionable whether this country will be long able to preserve its lower surface-line unaltered, when the flood is toppling at a higher line all around it. It would be at least well to be prepared for a steady setting in of the flood-tide on our shores; it would be wise—to return to the figure of Lord Jeffrey—to be casting about for some second firmament, through which a farther modicum of bulk and volume might be subtracted from the waters below, and added to the waters above.

But does there exist, we ask, a portion of these lower waters that might be so separated with safety? We think there does. The *bona fide* property qualification we have ever regarded as peculiarly valuable,—greatly more so than the mere tenant qualification. The man who inhabits as tenant a house for which he pays a yearly rental of ten pounds, may be in many cases a man well as hafted in society, and possessed of as considerable a stake in the stability of the country and the maintenance of its institutions, as the proprietor to whom the ten pounds are paid. But the *class* are by no means so safe on the average. Their stake, as a body, is considerably less; they are a greatly more fluctuating portion of the population, and more unsteady and unbalanced in their views and opinions.

There is really no comparison between the man who, in some of the close alleys of a city like Edinburgh, opens a spirit-cellar on speculation, for which he pays a yearly rent of ten pounds, and the man who, after steadily adding pound to pound during the course of half a lifetime, at length invests his little capital in a house that brings him in ten pounds per annum, or, if he be his own tenant, that saves him that sum. The ten-pound tenants and the ten-pound proprietors compose, in the aggregate, bodies of men of an essentially different status and standing; and we hold that along the scale of proprietorship the franchise might safely descend a very considerable way indeed ere it correspond with the existing level, if we may so express ourselves, on the tenant scale. We hold that the proprietor who *possesed* a house valued at *five* yearly pounds, would be on a higher, not a lower level, than the tenant who merely *occupied* a house valued at *ten* yearly pounds.

Our dread of universal, or even mere household suffrage, is derived chiefly from our long and intimate aquaintance with the classes into whose hands it would throw the political power of the country. "A poor man that oppresseth the poor," says Solomon, "is like a sweeping rain which leaveth no food." Alas! tyranny, as the wise man well knew, is not the exclusive characteristic of the wealthy and the powerful, nor is oppression the offence of a mere class. It is not the aristocracy, and they only, that are cruel and unjust: the poor can also override the natural liberties of the poor, and trample upon their rights; and it is according to our experience that there is more of this injustice and tyranny among that movement class now known as Chartists, but which we have closely studied under other names, when coming in contact with them in strikes, combinations, and political meetings, than in perhaps any other class in the country.

It has been at least our own fate in life never personally to experience the oppression of the higher ranks, but not a little of the tyranny of the lower classes, especially that of this movement class. And we derive much of our confidence in the property qualification, nor merely from the sort of ballast in the State which it furnishes, but from the fact that we never yet saw a workman who made a right use of his wages with an eye to his advancement in life, or who was in any respect a rising man, at all disposed to join in oppressing a comrade or neighbour. We have very frequently seen him made a victim of a tyrannical combination,—unmanly odds taken against him if at all formidable for native power,—but rarely, if ever, enacting the part of a tyrant himself.

June 7, 1848.

A SENSE OF OCCASION

LIKE all good newspaper editors Hugh Miller had a well-tuned sense of occasion. He never allowed a public event to slip by without using it either to provide The Witness with some lively copy or to make a point, or both. When the young Queen Victoria had her first child on 9th November 1841, Miller took the opportunity, in The Infant Prince, to strike a sour note. The palace-generated hullabaloo was fine up to a point, Miller wrote, but behind "the ringing of bells, the crackling of fireworks, and the blazing of bonfires", much of the country was in a very sorry state. He reminded his readers that life, even for Royal Princes, was short, and for many people in Victoria's Britain, "The present, in the main, is assuredly no happy time".

But different occasions elicited different responses. When the City of Edinburgh laid the foundation stone of their monument to Sir Walter Scott, Miller was there, notebook in hand, to watch the celebrations. He did not share the view that erecting a huge Gothic pinnacle on the south side of Princes Street was going too far. Scott deserved something special because, "Wherever his writings are known, a Scotsman can be no mere abstraction". But he noticed that the Edinburgh crowd jeered the pomp and finery of the Masons in the procession, and he wondered if the day was coming when "stars and garters" were given the same ribald treatment. His article on The Late Mr. Kemp is a poignant footnote; George Kemp was the amiable, talented young architect/builder who had designed the Scott Monument. One night, possibly while drunk, Kemp fell into the canal basin at Fountainbridge in Edinburgh and was drowned. Plans to bury him in the vault under the Scott monument flopped when some miserable citizen thought it unsuitable, and managed to divert the funeral to a less exalted lair.

The Centenary of the Forty-Five and The Burns Festival and Hero Worship are both Miller's reflections on what has become known as Scottish kitsch. One hundred years after Charles Stuart raised the Jacobite standard at Glenfinnan, a bedraggled little group of ersatz Jacobites gathered there in the rain to mark the day. Miller charts the decline of Jacobitism from something solid and very much alive, to "the shadow of a shade". The Burns Festival in Ayr was a larger, just as wet, but even more ludicrous event. But daft as it was, Miller thought that "deep below the ridiculous gaud and glitter, we may find occult principles of our nature at work . . . "

The Infant Prince

A Prince born to the throne of Great Britain! The firing of cannon, the ringing of bells, the crackling of fire-works, the blazing of bonfires, holiday dresses and holiday faces everywhere, all testify to the general joy.

We are reminded of a day which must have mingled with the first recollections of even the most aged of our readers, and which men in the prime of early manhood are quite old enough to remember too,—that happy fourth of June, the birthday of the good George III, on which, for two whole generations, and a little longer, there used to be such a waving of flags and flashing of gunpowder, and, notwithstanding all our wars abroad, and all our difficulties and troubles at home, so large an amount of hearty national enjoyment. Is the ninth of November to be just another day to the generations of the future? Shall flags be flaunting gaily in the sun, to welcome the birthday of the reigning monarch,—the child of our Victoria,—at a time when our tombstones shall be casting their shadows across the withered November sward of silent churchyards? and shall bonfires be blazing on the hills, as the stars twinkle out one by one from amid the deepening blue, to look down upon our graves? There is a coffin in the distance that lies in the gloomy solitude of a royal vault; and the golden tablet that rests on the lid bears a date and an age well known to Him, for his own finger hath inscribed it.

Our children are around us,—the bright eyes, and silken locks, and rosy cheeks of infancy. Is there no pleasure in saying to them, Listen to these sounds,—to that distant peal of the city bells, and that measured sullen boom of the cannon: there has been a king born, who is to be your king, though, we can trust, not ours for we are old enough to remember the birth of The Queen, his mother. But he is to be *your* king, and in happier days, we would fain hope, than those of either the present or the past. The world will not always be what it has been; misery will not be for ever the prevailing state, nor unhappiness the o'ermastering feeling, nor evil the dominant power.

It were little wonder though men should weary of the present. There are, we doubt not, some of our readers who can look back on the events of sixty years. How has the space been filled? A sullen and doubtful peace has just succeeded the disastrous, we must add unjust, war with our American brethren. It was broken by the fierce and bloody tumults of the French Revolution. Atheism and murder

stalked abroad; nation rose up against nation; Europe bristled over
with arms; and for eighteen years together, during which millions
perished by famine, fire, and the sword, manslaying was the trade of
the *civilised* and *Christian* world! Men, as little wise as their rude
ancestors, were playing at the old vulgar trick of hero-making, and
the progress of the species stood still till the disastrous game was
finished. In our own country, times of hardship and discontent
succeeded, and poor, hunger-bitten men, maddened and blinded by
their misery, snatched hold of uncouth weapons, in the vain hope of
bettering their condition by violence. The madness passed, and a
period of political heats and animosities ensued. Civil right was
regarded as but another name for national happiness. The delirium
of this second fever is over for the time. The rights have been gained;
but the poor overtoiled man who wrought sixteen hours every day
ere the struggle began, works sixteen hours still, and hunger and the
sense of hapless degradation presses upon him as sorely as ever.

The present, in the main, is assuredly no happy time. Never were
there such frightful accumulations of misery in our cities, and rarely
have the sullen murmurs of the masses evinced deeper discontent. In
our own country we have witnessed the revival of the evils of an
earlier period; superstition stalking abroad unquestioned; persecution assailing the truth; the spiritual nature, the eternal concerns of
man, made the game of quibbling lawyers impressed by no true
sense of a hereafter; consciences outraged; and the care of souls
transferred by an abuse of law to the charge of wretched hirelings. It
is well to believe there are better times in store; that the right shall
eventually prevail, whatever may be the fate of those who contend for
it in the present.

November 13th, 1841

The Scott Monument

THE foundation-stone of the metropolitan monument in memory of
Sir Walter Scott was laid with masonic honours on Saturday last. The
day was pleasant, and the pageant imposing. All business seemed
suspended for the time; the shops were shut. The one half of
Edinburgh had poured into the streets, and formed by no means the
least interesting part of the spectacle. Every window and balcony that
overlooked the procession, every house-top almost, had its crowd of

The Scott Monument in Edinburgh in the course of construction. "What has Sir Walter done for Scotland to deserve such a gorgeous monument?" Miller asked. But he concluded that, "Wherever his writings are known, a Scotsman can be no mere abstraction. . ." (Courtesy of The National Galleries of Scotland).

spectators. We marked, among the flags exhibited, the Royal
Standard of Scotland, apparently a piece of venerable antiquity, for
the field of gold had degenerated into a field of drab.

The entire pageant was such a one as Sir Walter himself could
perhaps have improved. He would not have fired so many guns in
the hollow, and the grey old castle so near: he would have found
means, too, to prevent the crowd from so nearly swallowing up the
procession. Perhaps no man had ever a finer eye for pictorial effect
than Sir Walter, whether art or nature supplied the scene. It has been
well said that he rendered Abbotsford a romance in stone and lime,
and imparted to the king's visit to Scotland (George IV in 1822) the
interest and dignity of an epic poem.

Still, however, the pageant was an imposing one, and illustrated
happily the influence of a great and original mind, whose energies
had been employed in enriching the national literature, over an
educated and intellectual people.

It is a bad matter when a country is employed in building
monuments to the memory of men chiefly remarkable for knocking
other men on the head; it is a bad matter too, when it builds
monuments to the memory of mere courtiers, of whom not much
more can be said than that when they lived they had places and
pensions to bestow, and that they bestowed them on their friends.
We cannot think so ill, however, of the homage paid to genius.

The Masonic Brethren of the several lodges mustered in great
numbers. It has been stated that more than a thousand took part in
the procession. The laugh, half in ridicule, half in good nature, with
which the crowd greeted every very gaudily dressed member, richer
in symbol and obsolete finery than his neighbour, showed that the
day had passed in which such things could produce their originally
intended effect. Will the time ever arrive in which stars and garters
will claim as little respect as broad-skirted doublets of green velvet,
surmounted with three-cornered hats tagged with silver lace?

Much, we suppose, must depend on the characters of those who
wear them, and the kind of services on which they will come to be
bestowed. An Upper House of mere diplomatists—skilful only to
overreach—imprudent enough to substitute cunning for wisdom—
ignorant enough to deem the people not merely their inferiors in
rank, but in discernment also—weak enough to believe that laws may
be enacted with no regard to the general good—wrapped up in
themselves and acquainted with the masses only through their

eavesdroppers and dependents—would bring titles and orders to a lower level in half an age, than the onward progress of intellect had brought the quaintnesses of mechanic symbol and mystery in two full centuries. We but smile at the one; we would learn to execrate the other.

What has Sir Walter done for Scotland to deserve so gorgeous a monument? Assuredly not all that he might have done; and yet he has done much—more, in some respects, than any other merely literary man the country ever produced. He has interested Europe in the national character, and in some corresponding degree in the national welfare; and this of itself is a very important matter indeed. Shakespeare seems to have been less intensely imbued with the love of country. It is quite possible for a foreigner to luxuriate over his dramas, as the Germans are said to do, without loving Englishmen any the better in consequences, or respecting them any the more. But the European celebrity of the fictions of Sir Walter must have had the inevitable effect of raising the character of his country,—its character as a country of men of large growth, morally and intellectually. Besides, it is natural to think of foreigners as mere abstractions; and hence one cause at least of the indifference with which we regard them,—an indifference which the first slight misunderstanding converts into hostility. It is something towards a more general diffusion of goodwill to be enabled to conceive of them as men with all those sympathies of human nature, on which the corresponding sympathies lay hold, warm and vigorous about them. Now in this aspect Sir Walter presented his countrymen to the world. Wherever his writings are known, a Scotsman can be no mere abstraction; and in both these respects has the poet and novelist deserved well of his country.

Within the country itself, too, his great nationality, like that of Burns, has had a decidedly favourable effect. The cosmopolism so fashionable among a certain class about the middle of the last century was but a mock virtue, and a very dangerous one. The 'citizen of the world'; if he be not a mere pretender, is a man defined by negatives. It is improper to say he loves all men alike: his is merely equally indifferent to all. Nothing can be more absurd than to oppose the love of country to the love of race. The latter exists but as a wider diffusion of the former. The Saviour, when He took to Himself a human heart, wept over the city of His fathers. Now, it is well that this spirit should be fostered, not in its harsh and exclusive, but in its human and more charitable form.

Liberty cannot long exist apart from it. The spirit of war and aggression is yet abroad: there are laws to be established, rights to be defended, invaders to be repulsed, tyrants to be deposed. And who but the patriot is equal to these things? A people cannot survive without the national spirit, except as slaves. The man who adds to the vigour of the feeling at the same time that he lessens its exclusiveness, deserves well of his country—and who can doubt that Sir Walter has done so?

The Late Mr. Kemp

THE funeral of this hapless man of genius took place yesterday, and excited a deep and very general interest, in which there mingled the natural sorrow for high talent prematurely extinguished, with the feeling of painful regret, awakened by a peculiarly melancholy end. It was numerously attended, and by many distinguished men. The several streets through which it passed were crowded by saddened spectators—in some few localities very densely; and the windows overhead were much thronged. At no place was the crowd greater, except perhaps immediately surrounding the burying ground, than at the fatal opening beside the Canal Basin, into which the unfortunate man had turned from the direct road in the darkness of the night, and had found death at its termination.

The scene of the accident is a gloomy and singularly unpleasant spot. A high wall, perforated by a low, clumsy archway, closes abruptly what the stranger might deem a thoroughfare. There is a piece of sluggish stagnant water on the one hand, thick and turbid, and somewhat resembling in form and colour a broad muddy highway, lined by low walls; not a tuft of vegetation is to be seen on its tame rectilinear sides: all is slimy and brown, with here and there dank, muddy recesses, as if for the frog and the rat; while on the damp flat above, there lie, somewhat in the style of the grouping in a Dutch painting, the rotting fragments of canal passage-boats and coal-barges, with here and there some broken-backed hulk, muddy and green, the timbers peering out through the planking, and all around heaps of the nameless lumber of a deserted boat-yard.

The low, clumsy archway is wholly occupied by a narrow branch of

George Meikle kemp, the architect/builder of the Scott Monument, who was accidentally drowned in the Union Canal in Edinburgh. To Miller's fury, a plan to bury him in the vault of the Scott Monument was thwarted at the last moment. (Courtesy of The National Galleries of Scotland).

the canal,—brown and clay-like as the main trunk, from which it strikes off at nearly right angles. It struck us forcibly, in examining the place, that in the uncertain light of midnight, the flat, dead water must have resembled an ordinary cart-road, leading through the arched opening in the direction of the unfortunate architect's dwelling; and certainly at this spot, just where he might be supposed to have stepped upon the seeming road under the fatal impression, was the body found.

It had been intended, as the funeral letters bore, to inter the body of Mr Kemp in the vault under the Scott Monument,—a structure which, erected to do honour to the genius of one illustrious Scotsman, will be long recognised as a proud trophy of the fine taste and vigorous talent of another. The arrangement was not without precedent; and had it been possible for Sir Walter to have anticipated it, we do not think it would have greatly displeased him. Had the Scott Monument been erected, like the monument of a neighbouring square, to express a perhaps nor very seemly gratitude for the services of some tenth-rate statesman, who procured places for his friends, and who did not much else, it would have been perilous to convert it into the tomb of a man of genius like poor Kemp. It would have been perilous had it been the monument of some mere *litterateur*. The *litterateur's* works would have disappeared from the public eye, while that of the hapless architect would be forever before it. And it would be thus the architect, not the *litterateur* that would be permanently remembered.

But the monument of Sir Walter was in no danger; and Sir Walter himself would have been quite aware of the fact. It would not have displeased him, that in the remote future, when all its buttresses had become lichened and grey and generation after generation had disappeared from around its base, the story would be told that the poor architect who had designed its exquisite arches and rich pinnacles in honour of the Shakespeare of Scotland, had met an untimely death when engaged on it, and had found under its floor an appropriate grave.

The intention, however, was not carried into effect. It had been intimated in the funeral letters that the burial procession should quit the humble dwelling of the architect—for a humble dwelling it is—at half past one. It had been arranged, too, that the workmen employed at the monument, one of the most respectable-looking bodies of mechanics we ever saw, should carry the corpse to the grave. They had gathered round the dwelling, a cottage at Morningside, with a wreath of ivy nodding from the wall; and the appearance of both it and them naturally suggested that the poor deceased, orginally one of themselves, though he had risen, after a long struggle, into celebrity, had not risen into affluence. Death had come too soon. He had just attained his proper position—just reached the upper edge of the table-land which his genius had given him a right to occupy, and on which a competency might be soon and honourably secured— when a cruel accident struck him down. The time specified for the burial passed—first one half-hour, and then another. The assembled group wondered at the delay. And then a gentleman from the dwelling-house came to inform them that some interdict or protest, we know not what—some, we suppose, perfectly legal document— had inhibited, at this late hour, the internment of the body in the monument, and that there was a grave in the course of being prepared for it in one of the city churchyards.

The Centenary of 'The Forty-Five'

THE General Assembly of the Free Church of Scotland held its first meeting at Inverness on Thursday the 21st ult; and on Tuesday the 19th, just two days before, a party of gentlemen and ladies, accompanied by half-a-dozen pipers, visited Glenfinnon in rather showery weather, and called their visit the "Centennial Commemoration of the Gathering of the Clans". A great reality, and the meagre ghost of what had been a great reality a hundred years ago, entered upon the stage at nearly the same place and time, but with a very different result from that which almost always takes place in the ghost scene in Hamlet. Hamlet the living,—a thing, as he himself informs us, of "too, too solid flesh",—attracts but a small share of attention compared with that excited by the unsolid spectre of Hamlet the dead; the shadow fairly eclipses the substance. The solid reality so occupied the mind of the Highlands, that it had not a thought to spare on the unsolid ghost; and so the ghost, all drooping and disconsolate, passed off the stage, unapplauded and unseen. A feather has been held to the lips of dead Jacobitism, to ascertain whether there was a breath enough left within to stir the fibres, and not a single fibre has moved.

There are curious mental phenomena connected with the history of the decay of Jacobitism in Scotland. Like the matter of decomposing bodies, it passed, at a certain stage in its progress, from the solid to the gaseous form, and found entrance in the more subtle state into a class of minds from which, in its grosser and more tangible condition, it had been excluded. We are introduced in the letters of Burns to an ancient lady, stately and solemn, and much a Jacobite, who boasted that she had the blood of the Bruce in her veins, and who conferred, in virtue of her descent, the dignity of knighthood on the poet. She proposed toasts so full of loyalty to the exiled family, that they were gross treason against the reigning one; but, notwithstanding their extremeness, the poet cordially drank to them, and, in short, seemed in every respect as zealous a Jacobite as herself.

But there was a wide difference between the Jacobitism of Burns and that of the ancient lady. Hers was of the solid, his of the gaseous cast. Her mind was of the order in which *effète* opinions and dying beliefs are cherished to the last; his of the salient order, that are the first to receive new impressions, and to take up new views. She would undoubtedly have died a Jacobite of the old grim type, that were content to forfeit land and life in the cause of a shadowy loyalty; he, on the other hand, only a few years after, incurred the suspicion and displeasure of Government, by sending a present of artillery to the French Convention, to assist in defending a people who had deposed their king, against all other kings, and the Jacobites of their own country. The Jacobite of one year, who addressed enthusiastic verses to the "revered defenders of the beauteous Stuart" and composed the "Chevaliers Lament" had become in the next the uncompromising Jacobin, who wrote "A Man's a man for a' that".

The class of true Jacobites,—the men in whom Jacobitism was a solid principle,—died with the generation that fought at Culloden, and they were succeeded by the class to whom Jacobitism, formed merely a sort of laughing gas, that agreeably excited the feelings. Their principle was ineffective as a principle of action: it was purely a thing of excited imaginations, and of feelings strung by the aspirations of romance; and died away, even when elevated to its highest pitch, in tones of sweet music, or the wild cadences of ballad poetry.

But this Jacobitism of the middle stage of decay had at least the merit of being a reflection of the real Jacobitism that had gone before. It was Jacobitism mirrored in poetry. Its legs and shoulders were not equal; it stumped about on a Jacobital leg today, and sometimes stood on a Jacobinical leg tomorrow; and, if it could do nothing more, produced at least some pretty music and some exquisite song.

The existing Jacobitism, or rather, the Jacobitism not existing, but merely supposed to exist,—a shadow of a shade,—a cripple a thousand times more lame than the Jacobitism its immediate predecessor, for it has got no legs at all, and can neither sing nor make poetry,—is rendered ridiculous by being represented as one of, not the fantasies, but the forces of the country,—as one, not of its mere night-dreams, but of its waking-day realities,—as not a phantom, but a power.

The grand mistake of *The Times* on this subject must still be fresh in the minds of our readers, as it took place little more than three years ago, during the time of her Majesty's first progress through Scotland. The Scotch Lowlanders, said this journal, were no doubt a narrow-minded, fanatical, puritanical, selfish set, all agog about non-intrusion and the independence of the Kirk; but very different was the spirit of the Highlands. There the old generous loyalty still existed entire; the long-derived devotion to hereditary claims, and the ancient implicit subjection to divine right. *The Times* has since been undeceived.

But alas for the poor Highlanders! It seems to be their destiny as a people, to give evidence of their earnest and truthful natures by endurance and suffering. Such was the evidence they had to tender of old of their devotion to the Stuarts, and such the evidence which they have to tender now of their devotion to the cause of the evangelical religion and a preached gospel. We saw the stalwart Camerons of Lochiel, whose country a century ago had been wasted by fire and sword, and themselves chased to the rocks and hills, for their loyalty to the hereditary king, again chased from the tombs of their fathers and their little holdings, to the oozy sea-beach, and there worshipping God under the tide-line; and the Grants of Strathspey,— of all our Highland clans the clan that last manifested, after the old type, its devotion to its hereditary lord, these poor clansmen, over a wide and exposed district, denied a place of shelter, have to worship in the open air. And in both cases the persecutor of the clan was its chief, anxious, apparently, that his hereditary followers should be his followers no longer. We have heard wonder expressed that a single century should be sufficient to effect in the Highland mind so great a

change as the revolution indicated by the opposite aspects of the
"Centenary of the Forty-Five" and the Inverness Assembly. We do
not see that there is much cause for wonder.
September 27th 1845

The Burns' Festival and Hero Worship

"THE Burns' Festival," writes a respected correspondent in the west,
in whose veins flow the blood of Gilbert Burns, "is already well-nigh
forgotten in Ayr." We are not at all sure that it ought to be forgotten
so soon. Could we but look just a little below the surface of the event,
with its chequered patchwork of the bizarre and the picturesque, and
its, doubtless, much genuine enthusiasm, blent with at least an equal
amount of overstrained and awkward simulation, we might possibly
discover in it a lesson not unworthy of being remembered. Deep
below the ridiculous gaud and glitter, we may find occult principles
of our nature at work in this commemorative festival,—principles
which have been active throughout every period of the history of
man.

As a piece of mere show, the Festival of Burns, like the tournament
of Lord Eglinton, was singularly unhappy. Both got sadly draggled in
the mud, and looked like bepowdered *beaus* who set out for the ball-
room in their thin shoes and silk stockings, and are overwhelmed in
a thunder-shower by the way. Serious earnest stands a ducking: mere
show and make-believe becomes ridiculous in the wet. The 92nd
Highlanders were thoroughly respectable at Waterloo, though
drenched to the skin; and we have seen from twelve to fifteen
thousand of their devout countrymen gathered together amid their
wild hills, in storm and rain, on a sacramental sabbath, without
appearing in the slightest degree contemptible.

But alas for a draggled procession or a festival first dressed up in
gum flowers and then bespattered with mud! Processions and
festivals cannot stand a wetting. Like some of the cheap stuffs of the
cotton-weaver, they want *body* for it. Their respectability is painfully
dependent on the vicissitudes of the barometer. Every shower of rain
converts itself into a jest at their expense, that turns the laugh against
them; and every flying pellet of mud becomes a practical joke.

And as the festival of Burns, got particularly wet,—wet till it
steamed and smoked like a salt-pan, and the water that streamed

downwards from its nape to its heels discharged the dye of its buckram inexpressibles on its white silk stockings and flowed over the mouth of its thin-soled pumps,—it returned to its home in the evening, looking, it must be confessed, rather ludicrous than gay. It encountered the accident of being splashed and rained upon, and so turned out a failure.

But it is well to remark that the Burns' festival had an element of actual power and significancy in it, altogether separate and apart from the lowness of its immediate origin, the staring rawness of its rude machinery, or the woeful ducking in which it made its ridiculous exit. It is significant that the mind of the country should exist in such a state in reference to the memory of the departed poet, that a few obscure men over their ale could have originated such a display. The call to celebrate by a festival the memory of Burns seems, with reference to those from whom it first proceeded, to have been a low and vulgar call; but that it should have been responded to by thousands and tens of thousands,—that town and village should have poured forth their inhabitants to the spectacle,—that eminent men from remote parts of the country should have flocked to it,—are matters by no means vulgar or low. The surface of the pageant, like its origin, seems to have been a sufficiently poor affair; but underneath that surface there must have beat a living and vigorous heart, neither poor in its emotions, nor yet uninteresting in its physiology.

We would recognise in it, first of all, the singularly powerful impression made by the character of Burns on the people of Scotland. The *man* Burns exists as a large idea in the national mind, altogether independent of his literary standing as the writer of what are pre-eminently the national songs. There was a cast of true tragic greatness about it. There was a largeness in his heart, and a force in his passions, that corresponded with the mass of his intellect. and the vigour of his genius. Burns was not merely a distinguished poet,—he was a man on a large scale; and the festival of the present month bore emphatic testimony to the fact.

But we would not choose to go and worship at this festival. There was a hollowness about the ceremony, independently of the falseness of the principles on which its ritual was framed. Of the thousands who attended, how many, would have sympathised, had they seen the light some fifty years earlier, with the *man* Robert Burns? How many of them grappled in idea at his festival with other than a mere phantom of the imagination,—a large but intangible shade, obscure and indefinable as that conjured up by the uninformed Londoner of Cromwell or Johnson?

Rather more than fifty years ago, the sinking sun shone brightly, one fine afternoon, on the stately tenements of Dumfries and threw its slant rule of light athwart the principal street of the town. There was a world of well-dressed company that evening in Dumfries; for the aristocracy of the adjacent country for twenty miles round had poured in to attend a county ball, and were fluttering in groups along the sunny side of the street, gay as butterflies. On the other side, in the shade, a solitary individual paced slowly along the pavement. Of the hundreds who fluttered past, no one took notice of him; no one seemed to recognise him. He was known to them all as the exciseman and poet, Robert Burns; but he had offended the stately Toryism of the district by the freedom of his political creed; and so, tainted by the plague of Liberalism, he lay under strict quarantine. He was shunned and neglected; for it was with the *man* Burns that these his contemporaries had to deal.

Let the reader contrast with this truly melancholy scene, the scene of his festival a fortnight since. Here are the speeches of the Earl of Eglinton and of Sir John McNeill, and here the toast of the Lord Justice-General. Let us just imagine these gentlemen, with all their high aristocratic notions about them, carried back half a century into the past, and dropped down, on the same evening to which we refer, in the main street of Dumfries. Which side, does the reader think, would they have chosen to walk upon? They find it an easy matter to deal with the phantom idea of Burns now; how would they have dealt with the man then? How are they dealing with his poorer relatives; or how with men of kindred genius, their contemporaries? Alas! a moment's glance at such matters is sufficient to show how very unreal a thing a commemorative feast may be. Reality, even in idea, becomes a sort of Ithuriel spear to test it by. The Burns' festival was but an idle show, at which players enacted their parts.

August 24th 1844

A SENSE OF HISTORY

FOR all its preoccupation with the intricate politics of the Church of Scotland and the "religious question" The Witness *was an outward-looking periodical that kept a sharp eye on world affairs. From the evidence, Hugh Miller had an acute sense of history, knew an important international event when he saw one, and was never loath to draw the political and/or strategic implications. The pages of* The Witness *were liberally peppered with shrewd, lively articles on, for example, the British government's defence strategy, the state of India, China and the Chinese, the chances of Louis Kossuth the Hungarian revolutionary, the Northwest Passage, Gibraltar, Turkey, the problems of Spain, and so on.*

Much of it was decent, straightforward reporting and editorialising, but some of the pieces had a special moral resonance. Miller's essay on the Conclusion of the War In Afghanistan *is one such. The Afghan venture (1841) was one of Britain's nineteenth century military disasters, when a British/Indian force was exterminated on the retreat from Kabul to the borders of (then) British India. To Miller it was a bleak and humiliating end to an unjust war, which he hoped had taught Britain a lesson. Any war is a "great evil" Miller argued, but a war against a semi-primitive people like the Afghans on their own territory becomes "of necessity a war of extermination".*

The Disruption *is Miller's version of the great day in Edinburgh in May 1843 when Thomas Chalmers led the 400 or so evangelicals out of the Church of Scotland into the Free Church, bringing to a head the "ten years conflict" between the Church and the British state. Miller was no pacifist (and took an amateur interest in military matters) but he was interested in the nineteenth century peace movement, and the rash of* Peace Meetings *that were being held up and down the country. In his hard-headed way he doubted the intellectual and political basis of the movement, (and describes one peace-movement pamphlet as "nice, quiet, finely-modulated twaddle, as if all its sentences had been set to the piano"). He also pointed out that, for their own reasons, the most miserable of dictators and tyrants are often keen on peace and stability. But he did deeply approve of the fact that the "dislike of war which good men have entertained in all ages is, we are happy to believe, a fast spreading dislike".*

Miller's essay on the Characteristics of the Crimean War *is a very creditable attempt to pin-point just what made the Crimean war of 1854-56 so* different *from its predecessors. Miller came to the conclusion that one of the main differences was advanced technology ("a war of the world's most pre-eminently mechanical people inthe world's pre-eminently mechanical age") but*

but that the price of that technology may be an over-reliance by industrialised men on their equipment. Miller could not "help thinking that an army of back-woodsmen of the present day, or of Scotch Highlanders marked by the prevailing traits of the last century would have fared better and suffered less". Miller points out that the Crimea was the first war fought with the press looking over the shoulders of the generals, which did nothing for the reputations of such "pinheaded martinets" as their Lordships Cardigan and Lucan. Only the humanity of "the 'lady nurses' with Miss Nightingale at their head" redeemed the whole sorry mess.

Conclusion of the War in Afghanistan

WE trust we may now look back on by far the most disastrous passage which occurs in the military history of Great Britain, as so definitively concluded, that in the future we shall be unable to trace it as still disadvantageously operative in its effects. A series of decisive victories has neutralized, to a considerable extent, the influence of the most fatal campaign in which a British army was ever engaged. But this is all. One of our poets, in placing in a strong light the extreme folly of war, describes "most Christian kings" with "honourable ruffians in their hire", wasting the nations with fire and sword, and then, when fatigued with murder and sated with blood, "setting them down just where they were before". It is quite melancholy enough that our most sanguine expectations with regard to the Afghan war should be unable to rise higher by a hair's-breadth than the satiric conception of the poet.

There are passages in all our better histories that stand out in high relief, if we may so speak, from the ground-work on which they are based. They appeal to the imagination, they fix themselves in the memory; and after they have got far enough removed into the past to enable men to survey them in all their breadth, we find them caught up and reflected in the fiction of the poet and the novelist.

But it is wonderful how comparatively slight is the effect which most of them produce at the time of their occurrence. It would seem as if the great mass of mankind had no ability of seeing them in their real character, except through the medium of some superior mind, skilful enough to portray them in their true colours and proportions.

The country has not yet been able rightly to appreciate the disasters of Afghanistan. It has been unable to bestow upon them what we shall venture to term the historic prominence. When one after one the messengers reach Job, bearing tidings of fatal disasters, in which all his children and all his domestics have perished, the ever-recurring "and I only am escaped alone to tell thee", strikes upon the ear as one of the signs of a dispensation supernatural in its character. The narrative has already prepared us for events removed beyond the reach of those common laws which regulate ordinary occurrences. Did we find such a piece of history in any of our older chronicles, we would at once set it down, on Macaulay's principle, as a ballad thrown out of its original verse into prose, and appropriated by the chronicler, in the lack of less questionable materials. But finding it in the Record of eternal truth, we view it differently; for there the supernatural is not dissociated from the true. How very striking, to find in the authentic annals of our own country a somewhat similar incident; to find the "I only am escaped alone to tell thee" in the history of a well-equipped British army of the present day! There occurs no similar incident in all our past history. British armies have capitulated not without disgrace. In the hapless American war, Cornwallis surrendered a whole army to Washington, and Burgoyne another whole army to Gates and Arnold.

The British had also their disastrous retreats. The retreat from Fontenoy was at least precipitate; and there was much suffered in Sir John Moore's retreat on Corunna. But such retreats have not been wholly without their share of glory, nor have such surrenders been synonymous with extermination. In the annals of British armies, the "I only have escaped alone to tell thee" belongs to but the retreat from Kabul. It is a terrible passage in the history of our country— terrible in all its circumstances. Some of its earlier scenes are too revolting for the imagination to call up.

It is all to humiliating to conceive of it in the character of an unprincipled conspiracy of the civilised, horribly avenged by infuriated savages. It is a quite melancholy enough object of contemplation, in even its latter stages. A wild scene of rocks and mountains darkened overhead with tempest, beneath covered deep with snow; a broken and dispirited force, struggling hopelessly through the scarce passable defiles,—here thinned by the headlong assaults of howling fanatics, insensible to fear, incapable of remorse, and thirsting for blood,—there decoyed to destruction through the promises of cruel and treacherous chiefs, devoid alike of the sense of honour and the feeling of pity; with no capacity or conduct among its

leaders; full of the frightful recollections of past massacres, hopeless
of ultimate escape; struggling, however, instinctively on amid the
unceasing ring of musketry from thicket and crag, exhibiting mile
after mile a body less dense and extended, leaving behind it a long
unbroken trail of its dead; at length wholly wasting away, like the
upward heave of a wave on a sandy beach, and but one solitary
horseman, wounded and faint with loss of blood, holding on his
perilous course, to tell the fate of all the others. And then, the long
after-season of grief and suspense among anxious and at length
despairing relations at home, around many a cheerless hearth, and in
many a darkened chamber, and the sadly frequent notice in the
obituaries of all our public journals, so significant of the disaster, and
which must have rung so heavy a knell to so many affectionate
hearts, "Killed in the Khyber Pass".

To find passages of parallel calamity in the history of at least
civilised countries, we have to ascend to the times of the Roman
empire during its period of decline and disaster, when one warlike
emperor, in battle with the Goth,

"in that Serbonian bog,
Betwixt Damieta and Mount Cassus old,
With his whole army sank;"

or when another not less warlike monarch was hopelessly overthrown
by the Persian, and died a miserable slave, exposed to every indignity
which the invention of his ungenerous and barbarous conqueror
could suggest.

Britain in this event has received a terrible lesson, which we trust
her scarce merited and surely most revolting successes in China will
not have the effect of wholly neutralizing. The Afghan war, regarded
as a war of principle, was eminently unjust; regarded as a war of
expediency, it was eminently imprudent. It seems to have originated
with men of narrow and defective genius, not over largely gifted with
the moral sense.

It is satisfactory in every point of view that Britain should be at
peace with China and the Afghans. War is an evil in all
circumstances. It is a great evil, even when just; it is a great evil even
when carried on against a people who know and respect the laws of
nations. But it is peculiarly an evil when palpably not a just war, and
when carried on against a barbarous people. The barbarism of the
enemy has but the effect of heightening its horrors, not of modifying
its injustice. It is possible for one civilised man to fight with another

and yet retain his proper character as a man notwithstanding. But the civilised man who fights with the wild beast must assume, during the combat, the character of the wild beast. He cannot afford being generous and merciful; his antagonist understands neither generosity nor mercy. The war is of necessity a war of extermination. And such is always the character of a war between wild and civilised men. It takes its tone, not from the civilisation of the one, but from the cruel savageism of the other.

December 3rd 1842

The Disruption

THE fatal die has been cast. On Thursday last the Religion of Scotland was disestablished. The day that witnessed a transaction so momentous can be a day of no slight mark in modern history. It stands between two distinct states of things,—a signal to Christendom. It holds out its sign to these latter times, that God and the world have drawn off their forces to opposite sides, and that His sore and great battle is soon to begin.

The future can alone adequately develop the more important consequences of the event. At present we shall merely attempt presenting the reader with a few brief notes of the aspect which it exhibited. The early part of Thursday had its periods of fitful cloud and sunshine, and the tall picturesque tenements of the Old Town now lay dim and indistinct in shadow, now stood prominently out in the light. There was an unusual throng and bustle in the streets at a comparatively early hour, which increased greatly as the morning wore on towards noon. We marked, in especial, several knots of Moderate clergy hurrying along to the levee, laughing and chatting with a vivacity that reminded one rather of the French than of the Scotch character, and evidently in that state of nervous excitement which, in a certain order of minds, the near approach of some very great event, indeterminate and unappreciable in its bearings, is sure always to occasion.

As the morning wore on, the crowds thickened in the streets, and the military took their places. The principles involved in the anticipated Disruption gave to many a spectator a new association with the long double line of dragoons that stretched down the High Street, as far as the eye could reach, from the venerable Church of St Giles,

famous in Scottish story, to the humbler Tron. The light flashed
fitfully on their long swords and helmets, and the light scarlet of their
uniforms contrasted strongly with the dingier vestments of the
masses, in which they seemed as if more than half engulphed. When
the sun glanced out, the eye caught something peculiarly picturesque
in the aspect of the Calton Hill, with its imposing masses of
precipices overtopped by towers and monuments, and its inter-
mingling bushes and trees now green with the soft, delicate foliage of
May.

Between its upper and under line of rock, a dense living belt of
human beings girdled it round, sweeping gradually downwards from
shoulder to base, like the sash of his order on the breast of a
nobleman. The Commissioner's procession passed, with sound of
trumpet and drum, and marked by rather more than the usual
splendour. There was much bravery and glitter,—satin and
embroidery, varnish and gold lace,—no lack, in short, of that cheap
and vulgar magnificence which can be got up to order by the tailor
and the upholsterer for carnivals and Lord Mayors' days. But it was
felt by the assembled thousands, as the pageant swept past, that the
real spectacle of the day was a spectacle of a different character.

The morning levee had been marked by an incident of a somewhat
extraordinary nature, and which history, though in these days little
disposed to mark prodigies and omens, will scarce fail to record. The
crowd in the Chamber of Presence was very great, and there was, we
believe, a considerable degree of confusion and pressure in
consequence. Suddenly,—whether brushed by some passer by,
jostled rudely aside, or merely affected by the tremor of the floor
communicated to the partitioning,—a large portrait of William the
Third, that had held its place in Holyrood for nearly a century and a
half, dropped heavily from the walls. "There," exclaimed a voice
from the crowd,—"there goes the Revolution Settlement."

For hours before the meeting of Assembly, the galleries of St
Andrew's Church, with the space behind, railed off for the
accommodation of office-bearers not members, were crowded to
suffocation, and a vast assemblage still continued to besiege the
doors. Immediately after noon, the Moderate members began to
drop in one by one, and to take their places on the Moderator's right,
while the opposite benches remained well-nigh empty. What seemed
most fitted to catch the eye of the stranger was the rosy appearance of
the men, and the rounded contour of face and feature. We were

reminded, in glancing over the benches, of a bed of full-blown piony-roses glistening after a shower; and, could one have but substituted among them the monk's frock for the modern dress-coat, and given to each crown the shaven tonsure, they would have passed admirably for a conclave of monks met to determine some weighty point of abbey-income, or right of forestry.

The benches on the left began slowly to fill, and on the entrance of every more distinguished member a burst of recognition and welcome shook the gallery. Their antagonists had been all permitted to take their places in ominous silence. The music of the pageant was heard outside; the Moderator (the Rev Dr Welsh, Professor of Church History Edinburgh University) entered, attired in his gown; and ere the appearance of the Lord High commissioner, preceded by his pages and mace-bearer, and attended by the Lord Provost, the Lord Advocate, and the Solicitor-General, the Evangelical benches had filled as densely as those of their opponents, and the cross benches, appropriated, in perilous times like the present, to a middle party careful always to pitch their principles below the suffering point, were also fully occupied.

Never before was there seen so crowded a General Assembly; the number of members had been increased beyond all precedent by the double returns; and almost every member was in his place. The Moderator opened the proceedings by deeply impressive prayer; but though the silence within was complete, a Babel of tumultuary sounds outside, and at the closed doors, expressive of the intense anxiety of the excluded multitude, had the effect of rendering him scarcely audible in the more distant parts of the building. There stood beside the chair, though on opposite sides, the meet representatives of the belligerent parties. On the right we marked Principal McFarlan of Glasgow,—the man, in these altered times, who could recommend his students to organise themselves into political clubs, but dissuade them from forming missionary societies. On his left stood Thomas Chalmers, the man through whose indomitable energy and Christian zeal two hundred churches were added to the Establishment in a little more than ten years. Science, like religion, had its representatives on the Moderator's right and left. On the one side we saw *Moderate* science personified in Dr Anderson of Newburgh,—a dabbler in geology, who found a fish in the Old Red Sandstone, and described it as a beetle; we saw science *not Moderate,* on the other side, represented by Sir David Brewster.

The Moderator rose and addressed the House in a few impressive sentences. There had been an infringement, he said, on the Constitution of the Church,—an infringement so great, that they could not constitute its General Assembly withut a violation of the union between Church and State, as now authoritatively defined and declared. He was therefore compelled, he added, to protest against proceeding further; and, unfolding a document which he held in his hand, he read, in a slow and emphatic manner, the protest of the Church.

For the first few seconds, the extreme anxiety to hear defeated its object,—the universal hush, hush, occasioned considerably more noise than it allayed; but the momentary confusion was succeeded by the most unbroken silence; and the reader went on till the impressive close of the document, when he flung it down on the table of the House, and solemnly departed. He was followed, at a pace's distance, by Dr Chalmers; Dr Gordon and Dr Patrick MacFarlan immediately succeeded; and then the numerous sitters on the thickly occupied benches behind filed after them, in a long unbroken line, which for several minutes together continued to thread the passage to the eastern door, till at length only a blank space remained. As the well-known faces and forms of some of the ablest and most eminent men that ever adorned the Church of Scotland glided along in the current, to disappear from the courts of the State institution for ever, there rose a cheer from the galleries, and an impatient cry of "Out, out", from the ministers and elders not members of Assembly, now engaged in sallying forth, to join with them, from the railed area behind. The cheers subsided, choaked in not a few instances by tears. The occasion was by far too solemn for the commoner manifestations of either censure or approval; it excited feelings that lay too deep for expression. There was a marked peculiarity in the appearance of their opponents,—a blank, restless, pivot-like turning of head from the fast emptying benches to one another's faces; but they uttered no word,—not even in whispers. At length, when the last of the withdrawing party had disappeared, there ran from bench to bench a hurried, broken whispering,—"How many?"—"How many?"—"A hundred and fifty?" "No;" "Yes;" "Four hundred?" "No;"—and then for a moment all was still again. The scene that followed we deemed one of the most striking of the day.

The empty vacated benches stretched away from the Moderator's seat in the centre of the building, to the distant wall. There suddenly glided into the front rows a small party of men whom no one knew,—obscure, mediocre, blighted-looking men, that, contrasted with the well-known forms of our Chalmerses and Gordons, Candlishes and Cunninghams, McFarlans, Brewsters and Dunlops, reminded one of the thin and blasted corn-ears of Pharoah's vision, and, like them too, seemed typical of a time of famine and destitution. Who are these? was the general query; but no one seemed to know. At length the significant whisper ran along the house, "The Forty". There was a grin of mingled contempt and compassion visible on many a broad Moderate face, and a too audible titter shook the gallery. There seemed a degree of incongruity in the sight that partook highly of the ludicrous. For our own part, we were so carried away by a vagrant association, and so missed Ali Baba, the oil kettle, and the forty jars, as to forget for a time that at the doors of these unfortunate men lies the ruin of the Scottish establishment. The aspect of the Assembly sank, when it had in some degree recovered itself, into that expression of tame and flat commonplace, which it must be henceforth content to bear, until roused, happily, into short-lived activity, by the sharp paroxysms of approaching destruction.

A spectacle equally impressive with that exhibited by the ministers and elders of the Free Church, as they winded in long procession to their place of meeting, there to constitute their independent Assembly, Edinburgh has certainly not witnessed since those times of the Covenant when Johnston of Warriston unrolled the solemn parchment in the churchyard of the Greyfriars, and the assembled thousands, from the peer to the peasant, adhibited their names. The procession, with Dr Chalmers, and the Moderator in his robes and cap of office, at its head, extended, three in depth, for a full quarter of a mile. The Lord Provost of the city rode on before.

Rather more than four hundred were ministers of the church: all the others were elders. Be it remembered, that the number of ministers ejected from their charges at the Restoration, and who maintained the struggle in behalf of Presbytery during the long persecution of twenty-eight years mounted in all to but three hundred and seventy-six; but then, as now, the religious principles which they maintained were those of the country. They were principles that had laid fast hold of the national mind, and the fires of persecution served only to render their impress ineradicable. Is it not strange how utterly the great lessons of history have failed to impress the mean and wretched rulers of our country in this the day of their visitation?

May 20th, 1843

The Peace Meetings

THERE is nothing positively new in what may be termed the main or central idea of the existing Peace Associations, viz, adjustment of national differences by arbitration, not arms. The true novelty presented lies in the fact that an idea restricted in the past to but single minds should now be operative in the minds of thousands.

The reader may find in the works of Rousseau a treatise, in which the expedient of a great European Court of Arbitration for national differences is elaborately developed. We question, indeed, whether any member of the Peace Societies of the present day has presented to his fellows, or the public generally, the master idea of these institutions in so artistic and plausible a form as that in which it was submitted to the world by Rousseau considerably more than eighty years ago.

Nations can, of course, only act through their Governments; and of the European Governments in the days of Rousseau, the greater number were arbitrary in their constitution. He had no other materials of which to form his General Arbitration Court. Of the nineteen European States in his list of Arbiters, twelve were despotic, and the larger half of the remainder nearly so; and yet in order to secure the blessing of peace, he had to lay it down as a fundamental rule, that each State should be maintained by all the others in its internal rights and powers, and that its territories, at the time of the union, should be guaranteed to it entire. On other principles no union of goverments could have taken place. To put down war was the object of his proposed confederation,—internal as certainly as foreign war.

Rousseau's project, if practicable, would have secured peace, but it would have also, of necessity, arrested progress. It would have cursed the world with a torpid, unwholesome quiet, a thousand times less friendly to the best interests of humanity than that mingled state of alternate peace and war under which, with all its disadvantages, the human species have been slowly rising in the scale of intelligence, and securing for themselves constitutional rights and equal laws. Nor were there wanting men among the rulers of the world shrewd enough to see that such was the real character of the scheme; and it was with rulers, not subjects, that that attempt originated to which we have referred, to convert it from an idea into a fact.

A fierce and long protracted European war had just come to a close,—when three great monarchs met at Paris to originate a Peace Society on nearly the principles of Rousseau. These were Alexander of Russia, Francis of Austria, and Frederick William of Prussia. The document which formed the basis of the confederation was published; and it was found, as might, indeed, be expected from most Christian princes, to be of a greatly higher tone than that which marked the project of Rousseau. Most of the European princes became members of this magnificent Peace Society. What, asks the reader, was the name borne by this eminently good and truly Christian Peace Society? Its name was the Holy Alliance,—a name that now stinks in the nostril; and it was in effect a foul and detestable conspiracy against the progress of nations and the best interests of the human species. But such, of necessity, must be the nature and character of every Peace Association of which the members are Governments, if a majority of these be despotic. And if the members of a Peace Association *be not* Goverments, they can of course possess no powers of arbitration.

But, though we can thus promise ourselves no *direct* results from the Peace Societies of the times, their *indirect* results may be very important. That dislike of war which good men have entertained in all ages is, we are happy to believe, a fast-spreading dislike. It was formally entertained by units and tens; it is now cherished by thousands and tens of thousands. And, of course, the more the feeling grows in any country which, like France, Britain, and America, possesses a representative Government, the less chance will there be of these nations entering rashly into war. France and the United States have always had their senseless war parties. It is of importance, therefore, that they should possess also their balancing peace parties, even should these be well-nigh as senseless as the others. Again, in our own country, war is always the interest of a class largely represented in both Houses of Parliament. It is of great importance that they also should be kept in check, and their influence neutralized, by a party hostile to war on principle as they are favourable to it from interest. We repose very considerable confidence in the common sense of the British people, and so have no fear that an irrational peace party should so increase in the country as to put in peril the national independence; and, not fearing this, we must hail as good and advantageous any revolution in that opinion in which all power is founded, which bids fair to render more rare than formerly those profitless exhibitions of national warfare.

November 10th, 1849

Characteristics of the Crimean War

THE war now happily concluded was characterized by some very remarkable features. It was on the part of Britain the war of a highly civilised country, in a pre-eminently mechanical, and, with all its faults, singularly humane age,—in an age, too, remarkable for the diffusion of its literature; and hence certain conspicuous traits which belonged to none of the other wars in which our country had been previously engaged. Never before did such completely equipped fleets and armies quit our shores. The navies with which we covered the Black Sea and the Baltic were not at all what they would have been had the war lasted for one other campaign, but they mightily exceeded anything of the kind that Britain or the world had ever seen before. The fleets of Copenhagen, Trafalgar, and the Nile would have cut but a sorry figure beside them, and there was more of the *materiel* of war concentrated on that one siege of Sebastopol than on any half-dozen other sieges recorded in British history.

In all that mechanical art could accomplish, the late war with Russia was by far the most considerable in which our country was ever engaged. It was, in respect of *materiel,* a war of the world's pre-eminently mechanical people in the world's pre-eminently mechanical age. With this strong leading feature, however, there mingled another, equally marked, in which the element was weakness, not strength. The men who beat all the world in heading pins are unable often to do anything else; for usually, in proportion as mechanical skill becomes intense, does it also become narrow; and the history of the two campaigns before Sebastopol brought out very strikingly a certain helplessness on the part of the British army, part of which at least must be attributed to this cause.

It is surely a remarkable fact, that in an army never more than seven miles removed from the base line of its operations, the distress suffered was so great, that nearly *five* times the number of men sank under it than perished in battle. There was no want among them of pinheading and pinheaded martinets. The errors of officers such as Lucan and Cardigan are understood to be all on the side of severity; but in heading their pin, they wholly exhaust their art; and under their surveillance and direction a great army became a small one, with thesea covered b a British fleet only a few miles away. So far as the statistics of the British portion of this greatest of sieges have yet been ascertained, rather more than *three* thousand men perished in battle by the shot or steel of the enemy, or afterwards of their wounds, and rather more than *fifteen* thousand men of privation and disease.

As for the poor soldiers themselves, they could do but little in even more favourable circumstances under the pinheading martinets; and yet at least such of them as were drawn from the more thoroughly artificial districts of the country, must, we suspect, have fared all the worse in consequence of that sub-division of labour which has so mightily improved the mechanical standing of Britain in the aggregate, and so restricted and lowered the general ability in individuals. We cannot help thinking that an army of backwoodsmen of the present day, or of Scotch Highlanders marked by the prevailing traits of the last century, would have fared better and suffered less.

Another remarkable feature of the war arose out of the singularly ready and wonderfully diffused literature of the day. Like those self-registering machines that keep a strict account of their own workings, it seemed to be engaged, as it went on, in writing, stage after stage, its own history. The acting never got a single day ahead of the writing, and never a single week ahead of the publishing; and, in consequence, the whole civilised world became the interested witnesses of what was going on. The war became a great game at chess, with a critical public looking over the shoulders of the players.

It was a peculiar feature, too, that the public *should* have been so critical. As the literature of a people becomes old, it weakens in the power of originating, and strengthens in the power of criticising. Reviews and critiques become the master efforts of a learned and ingenious people, whose literature has passed its full blow; and the criticism extends always, in countries in which the press is free from the productions of men who write in their closets, to the actings of men who conduct the political business of the country, or who direct its fleets and armies. And with regard to them also it may be safely affirmed, that the critical ability overshoots and excels the originating ability.

There seems to have been no remarkably good generalship manifested by Britain in the Crimea: all the leading generalship appears, on the contrary, to have been very mediocre generalship indeed. The common men and subordinate officers did their duty nobly; and there have been such splendid examples of skilful generalship in fourth and fifth-rate commands—commands such as that of Sir Colin Campbell and Sir George Brown—that it has been not unfrequently asked, whether we had in reality the "right men in the right places", and whether there might not, after all, have been generalship enough in the Crimea had it been but rightly arranged.

But the leading generalship was certainly *not* brilliant. The criticism upon it, on the other hand, has been singularly so. The ages of Marlborough and Wellington did not produce a tithe of the brilliant military criticism which has appeared in England in newspapers, magazines, and reviews during the last two years. And yet it is possible that, had the very cleverest of these critics been appointed to the chief command, he would have got on as ill as any of his predecessors. In truth, the power of originating and the power of criticising are essentially different powers in the worlds both of thought and of action. Talent accumulates the materials of criticism from the experience of the past; and thus, as the world gets older, the critical ability grows, and becomes at length formidably complete;— whereas the power of originating, or, what is the same thing, of acting wisely, and on the spur of the moment, in new and untried circumstances, is an incommunicable faculty, which genius, and genius only, can possess. And genius is as rare now as it ever was. Any man of talent can be converted, by dint of study and painstaking, into a good military critic; but a Wellington or a Napoleon had as certainly to be born what they were, as a Dante or a Milton.

But by far the most pleasing feature of the war—of at least the part taken in it by Britain—is to be found in that humanity, the best evidence of a civilization truly Christian, which has characterized it in all its stages. Generous regard for the safety and respect for the feelings of a brave enemy, when conquered, have marked our countrymen for centuries. But we owe it to the peculiar philanthropy of the time, that, in the midst of much official neglect, our own sick and wounded soldiers have been cared for after a fashion in which British soldiers were never cared for before. The 'lady nurses', with Miss Nightingale at their head, imparted its most distinctive character to the war.

June 14th 1856

A SENSE OF EVIL

THERE is, however, an irrational, apocalyptic strand in Miller's work which gives off a strong sense of evil. It surfaces at the oddest times and for the oddest reasons, and was probably the other side of the religious coin. David Masson, who knew Miller and sketched one of the best pen-portraits of him, says that while Miller's Free Church associates admired and trusted him, they could never control "nor adequately comprehend" him. Masson believed there was a "demonic element" to Miller's genius, and that he trailed with him "a belief in ghostly influences, in mysterious agencies of the air, earth and water, always operating and sometimes revealing themselves". This made Miller wary of strangers, Masson claims: "you might be the devil, or one of his gentlemen of darkness, for all he knew, and so while he is talking to you, what are his fingers doing? Playing with the triggers of two loaded pistols! A whirr of the brain, a momentary hallucination, even a mechanical mistake, and God knows what might happen!"

A Vision of the Railroad *is Hugh Miller at his most odd. Written in 1841 it is a strange, dream-like piece which conjures up a picture of Edinburgh and the surrounding countryside desolate and in ruins after what seems to have been a series of religious and/or revolutionary wars. The landscape in Miller's* Vision *is littered with skeletons, burned villages, broken railway lines, rusting engines, derelict churches, and huge stone crucifixes, whose arms were used as gibbets, and under which lie "the tattered remains of a surplice dabbled in blood". Incredibly, what seems to have provoked Miller into this visonary ecstasy, were the plans of the Scottish railway companies to run their trains on a* Sunday. *Exactly* how *such a Sabbath-breaking venture would lead to the collapse of civilisation, Miller does not explain, and the essay puzzled even Thomas Chalmers who was heard to growl "Writing* A Vision of the Railroad *when we want money".*

Annus Mirabilis *is Miller's account of 1848, the great year of revolution in Europe, which shook the established order to its roots, and which threatened, in Miller's view, to let loose the "old Babylonish beast" of Roman Catholicism, and its executioner "the monster of atheistic liberalism".* The Bone-Cave of Eigg *is evil at first hand. Miller finds himself crawling about the bone-littered darkness of* Uamh Fhraing *(the cave of Francis) on the Island of Eigg, the scene of a piece of sixteenth-century, inter-clan nastiness, when the McDonalds of Eigg—men, women and children—were smoked to death in the cave by a war party of McLeods from Skye. Ever the scientist, Miller doubted whether it was the smoke that killed the wretched McDonalds but the huge fire at the mouth of the cave which "would draw out the oxygen within as its proper food, till at length*

all would be exhausted; and life would go out for the want of it, like the flame of
a candle under an upturned jar". Of all the ferocious creatures he had seen
traces of in the rocks, Miller writes, none were "so maliciously mischievous as
man".

A Vision of the Railroad

DARK night it was, and the storm had burst out. But it was pleasant,
when I had reached my little cottage, to pile high the fire on the
hearth, and to hear the blast roaring outside, and shaking the
window-boards, as if some rude hand were striving to unfasten them.
I lighted my little heap of moss fir on the projecting stone that serves
the poor Highlander for at once lamp and candlestick, and bent me
over your fourth page, to scan the Sabbath returns of a Scottish
railroad. But my rugged journey and the beating of the storm had
induced a degree of lassitude; the wind outside, too, had forced back
the smoke, until it had filled with a drowsy, umbery atmosphere, the
whole of my dingy little apartment: I fell fast asleep.

The scene changed, and I found myself still engaged in my late
journey, coming down over the hill, just as the sun was setting red
and lightless through the haze behind the dark Atlantic. The dreary
prospect on which I had looked so shortly before was restored in all
its features: there was the blank, leaden-coloured sea, that seemed to
mix all around with the blank, leaden-coloured sky; the moors
spread out around me, brown and barren, and studded with rock
and stone; the fogs, as they crept downwards, were lowering the
overtopping screen of hills behind to one dead level.

Through the landscape, otherwise so dingy and sombre, there ran
one long line of somewhat brighter hue: it was a long line of breakers
tumbling against the coast far as the eye could reach, and that
seemed interposed as a sort of selvage between the blank, leaden sea,
and the deep, melancholy russet of the land. Through one of those
changes so common in dreams, the continuous line of surf seemed,
as I looked, to alter its character. It winded no longer round
headland and bay, but stretched out through the centre of the
landscape, straight as an extended cord, and the bright white
saddened down to the fainter hue of decaying vegetation.

The entire landscape underwent a change. Under the gloomy sky
of a stormy evening, I could mark on the one hand the dark blue of

the Pentlands, and on the other the lower slopes of Corstorphine. Arthur's Seat rose dim in the distance behind; and in front, the pastoral valley of Wester Lothian stretched away mile beyond mile, with its long rectilinear mound running through the midst,—from where I stood beside one of the massier viaducts that rose an hundred feet overhead, till where the huge bulk seemed diminished to a slender thread on the far edge of the horizon.

It seemed as if years had passed—many years. I had an indistinct recollection of scenes of terror and of suffering, of the shouts of maddened multitudes engaged in frightful warfare, of the cries of famishing women and children, of streets and lanes flooded with blood, of raging flames enwrapping whole villages in terrible ruin, of the flashing of arms and the roaring of artillery; but all was dimness and confusion. The recollection was that of a dream remembered in a dream. The solemn text was in my mind "Voices, and thunders, and lightnings, and a great earthquake" and I now felt as if the convulstion was over, and that its ruins lay scattered around me.

The railway, I said, is keeping its Sabbaths. All around was solitary, as in the wastes of Skye. The long rectilinear mound seemed shaggy with gorse and thorn, that rose against the sides and intertwisted their prickly branches atop. The sloe-thorn, and the furze, and the bramble choked up the rails. The fox rustled in the brake; and where his track had opened up a way through the fern, I could see the red and corroded bars stretching idly across. There was a viaduct beside me: the flawed and shattered masonry had exchanged its raw hues for a crust of lichens; one of the taller piers undermined by the stream, had drawn two of the arches along with it, and lay adown the water-course a shapeless mass of ruin o'ermasted by flags and rushes. A huge ivy, that had taken root under a neighbouring pier, threw up its long pendulous shoots over the summit.

I ascended to the top. Half-buried in furze and sloe-thorn, there rested on the rails what had once been a train of carriages; the engine ahead lay scattered in fragments, the effect of some disastrous explosion, and damp, and mould, and rottenness, had done their work on the vehicles behind. Some had already fallen to pieces, so that their places could be no longer traced in the thicket that had grown up around them; others stood comparatively entire, but their bleached and shrivelled panels rattled to the wind, and the mushroom and the fungus sprouted from between their joints. The scene bore all too palpably the marks of violence and bloodshed. There was an open space in front, where the shattered fragments of the engine lay scattered; and here the rails had been torn up by violence, and there stretched across, breast-high, a rudely piled rampart of stone. A human skeleton lay atop, whitened by the winds; there was a broken pike beside it; and, stuck fast in the naked skull, which had rolled to the bottom of the rampart, the rusty fragment of a sword.

The space behind resembled the floor of a charnel-house— bindwood and ground-ivy lay matted over heaps of bones; and on the top of the hugest heap of all, a skull seemed as if grinning at the sky from amid the tattered fragments of a cap of liberty. Bones lay thick around the shattered vehicles; a trail of skeletons dotted the descending bank, and stretched far into a neighbouring field; and from amid the green rankness that shot up around them, I could see soiled and tattered patches of the British scarlet. A little further on there was another wide gap in the rails. I marked beside the ruins of a neighbouring hovel, a huge pile of rusty bars, and there lay inside the fragment of an uncouth cannon marred in the casting.

I wandered on in unhappiness, oppressed by that feeling of terror and disconsolateness so peculiar to one's more frightful dreams. The country seemed everywhere a desert. The fields were roughened with tufts of furze and broom; hedgerows had shot up into lines of stunted trees, with wide gaps interposed; cottage and manor-house had alike sunk into ruins; here the windows still retained their shattered frames, and the roof-tree lay rotting amid the dank vegetation of the floor; yonder the blackness of fire had left its mark, and there remained but reddened and mouldering stone. Wild animals and doleful creatures had everywhere increased. The toad puffed out his freckled sides on hearths whose fires had been long extinguished, the fox rustled among bushes, the masterless dog howled from the thicket, the hawk screamed shrill and sharp as it fluttered overhead.

I passed what had been once the policies of a titled proprietor. The trees lay rotting and blackened among the damp grass—all except one huge giant of the forest, that, girdled by the axe half a man's height from the ground, and scorched by fire, stretched out its long dead arms toward the sky. In the midst of this wilderness of desolation lay broken masses, widely scattered, of what had been once the mansion-house. A shapeless hollow, half filled with stagnant water, occupied its immediate site; and the earth was all around torn up, as if battered with cannon. The building had too obviously owed its destruction to the irresistible force of gunpowder.

There was a parish church on the neighbouring eminence, and it, too, was roofless and a ruin. Alas! I exclaimed, as I drew aside the rank stalks of nightshade and hemlock that hedged up the breach in the wall through which I passed into the interior—alas! have the churches of Scotland also perished? The inscription of a mutilated tombstone that lay outside caught my eye, and I paused for a moment's space in the gap to peruse it. It was an old memorial of the times of the Covenant, and the legend was more than half defaced. I succeeded in deciphering merely a few half sentences—"killing-time", "faithful martyr", "bloody prelates", and beneath there was a fragmentary portion of the solemn text, "How long, O Lord, holy and true, dost Thou not judge and avenge our blood?"

I stepped into the interior; the scattered remains of an altar rested against the eastern gable. There was a crackling as of broken glass under my feet, and stooping down, I picked up a richly-stained fragment; it bore a portion of that much-revered sign, the pelican giving her young to eat of her own flesh and blood—the sign which Puseyism and Popery equally agree in regarding as adequately expressive of their doctrine of the real presence, and which our Scottish Episcopalians have so recently adopted as the characteristic vignette of their service-book. The toad and the newt had crept over it, and it had borrowed a new tint of brilliancy from the slime of the snail.

Destruction had run riot along the walls of this parish church. There were carvings chipped and mutilated, as if in sport, less apparently with the intention of defacing, than rendering them contemptible and grotesque. A huge cross of stone had been reared over the altar, and both the top and one of the arms had been struck away, and from the surviving arm there dangled a noose. The cross had been transformed into a gibbet. Nor were there darker indications wanting. In a recess set apart as a cabinet for relics, there were human bones all too fresh to belong to a remote antiquity; and in a niche under the gibbet lay the tattered remains of a surplice dabbled in blood. I stood amid the ruins, and felt a sense of fear and horror creeping over me: the air darkened under the scowl of the coming tempest and the closing night, and the wind shrieked more mournfully amid the shattered and dismantled walls.

There came another change over my dream. I found myself wandering in darkness, I knew not whither, among bushes and broken ground; there was the roar of a large stream in my ear, and the savage howl of the storm. I retain a confused, imperfect recollection of a light streaming upon broken water—of a hard struggle in a deep ford—and of at length sharing in the repose and safety of a cottage, solitary and humble almost as my own. The vision again strengthened, and I found myself seated beside a fire and engaged with a few grave and serious men in singing the evening psalm, with which they closed for the time their services of social devotion.

"The period of trial wears fast away," said one of the number, when all was over—a grey-haired, patriarchal looking old man— "The period of trial is well-nigh over, the storms of our long winter are past, and we have survived them all. Patience! a little more patience, and we shall see the glorious spring-time of the world begin! The vial is at length exhausted."

Annus Mirabilis

THE year now at its close has been beyond comparison more remarkable. In the earlier twelvemonth, no real change took place in the existing state of things. Its striking events resembled merely the phenomena of a mid-winter storm in Greenland, where, over a frozen ocean, moveless in the hurricane as a floor of rock or of iron, the hail beats, and the thick whirling snows descend, and, high above head, the flashing of aurora borealis lend their many-coloured hues of mystery to the horrors of the tempest. Its transactions, picturesque rather than important, wholly failed to affect the framework of society. That floor of ice which sealed down the wide ocean of opinion retained all its mid-winter solidity, and furnished foundations as firm as before for the old despotic monarchies and the blood-stained persecuting churches.

But how immensely different the events of the year now at an end! Its tempests have been, not those of a Greenland winter, but of a Greenland spring: the depths of society have been stirred to the dark bottom, where all slimy and monstrous things lie hid, and, under the irresistible upheavings of the ground-swell, the ice has broken up; and amid the wide weltering of a stormy sea, cumbered with the broken ruins of ancient tyrannies, civil and ecclesiastical, the eye can scarce rest upon a single spot on which to base a better order of things. The "foundations are removed". A time of great trouble has come suddenly upon the kingdoms of Europe—a time of "famines, and pestilences, and fearful sights, and great signs from heaven"; "signs in the sun, and in the moon, and in the stars; and on the earth distress of nations, with perplexity; the sea and the waves roaring."

A twelvemonth has not yet passed since history seemed to want incident. Time and Destiny watched as statue-like sentinels in a quiet hall, walled round by the old rigid conventionalities, and human sagacity failed to see aught beyond them; the present so resembled the past, that it seemed over-boldness to anticipate a different complexion for the future. But amid the unbreathing stillness, the appointed hour arrived. The rigid marble curtain of the old conventionalities was struck asunder by the iron mace of Destiny; and the silence was straightway broken by a roar as if of many waters, by the wrathful shouts of armed millions—the thunderings of cannons blent with the rattle of musketry—the wild shrieks of dismay and suffering—the wailings of sorrow and terror—the shouts of triumph and exultation—the despairing cry of sinking dynasties, and the crash of falling thrones. And with what strange rapidity the visions have since flitted along the opened chasm!

A royal proclamation forbids in Paris a political banquet; four short days elapse, and France is proclaimed a Republic, and Louis Phillipe and his Ministers have fled. Britain at once recognises the Provisional Government; but what are the great despotisms of the Continent to do? Six days more pass, and the Canton of Neufchatel declares itself independent of Prussia. In a few days after, the Duke of Saxe-Coburg Gotha grants to his subjects a representative constitution, freedom of the press, and trial by jury; the King of Hanover has also to yield, and the King of Bavaria abdicates.

But still the flame spreads. There is a successful insurrection at Vienna, the very stronghold of despotism in Central Europe; and the Prime Minister, Metternich, the grim personification of the old policy, is compelled to resign. Then follows an equally successful insurrection at Berlin; Milan, Vicenza, and Padua are also in open insurrection. Venice is proclaimed a Republic. Holstein declares itself independent of Denmark, Hungary of Austria, Sicily of Naples. Prague and Cracow have also their formidable outbreaks. Austria and Prussia proclaim new constitutions. Secondary revolutionary

movements in both Paris and Vienna are put down by the military.
There are bloody battles fought between the Austrians and the
Piedmontese on the one hand, and the Germans and the Danes on
the other; and, in a state of profound peace, the people of a British
port hear from their shores the boom of the hostile cannon. The
Emperor of Austria abdicates his throne, the Pope flees his
dominions, and a nephew of Napoleon Bonaparte is elected
President of France.

We regard the old state of things as gone forever. The foundations
have broken up on which the ancient despotisms were founded. It
would seem as if "the stone cut out without hands" has fallen during
the past year on the feet of the great image, and ground down into
worthless rubbish the "iron, the clay, the brass, the silver, and the
gold". And "the wind", though not yet risen to its height, seems fast
rising which will sweep them all away "like the chaff of the summer
thrashing-floor"; so that "there shall be no place found for them".

But while we can entertain no hope for the old decrepit
despotisms, we cannot see in the infidel liberalism—alike unwise and
immoral—by which they are in the course of being supplanted, other
than a disorganising element, out of which no settled order of things
can possibly arise. It takes the character, not of a reforming principle
destined to bless, but of an instrument of punishment, with which
vengeance is to be taken for the crimes and errors of the past; and, so
far at least, a time when we need expect to witness but the struggles
of the two principles—the old and the new—as they act and react
against each other, stronger and weaker by turns, as they disgust and
alienate by their atrocities in their hour of power, such of the more
moderate classes as had taken part with them in their hour of
weakness. It is the grand error of our leading statesmen, that they fail
to appreciate the real character of the crisis, and would fain deal with
the consequent existing difficulties in that petty style of diplomatic
manoeuvre with which it was their wont to meet the comparatively
light demands of the past. It would seem as if we had arrived at a
stage in the world's history in which statesmanship after this style is
to be tolerated no longer.

There are two wild beasts, like those which Daniel saw in vision,
contending together in fierce warfare, —the old Babylonish beast,
horrid with the blood of saints, and its cruel executioner—the
monster of Atheistic Liberalism; but Christ has identified His cause
with neither. No reprieve from the prince awaits the condemned

culprit; and with the disreputable and savage executioner he will hold no intercourse. Destruction, from which there is no escape, awaits equally on both.

December 30th 1848

The Bone-Cave of Eigg

MY friend the minister stopped short. "There," he said, pointing to the hollow, "you will find such a bone-cave as you never saw before. Within that opening there lie the remains of an entire race, palpably destroyed, as geologists in so many other cases are content merely to imagine, by one great catastrophe. That is the famous cave of Francis *(Uamh Fhraing)*, in which the whole people of Eigg were smoked to death by the McLeods."

We struck a light, and, worming ourselves through the narrow entrance, gained the interior,—a true rock gallery, vastly more roomy and lofty than one could have anticipated from the mean vestibule placed in front of it. Its extreme length we found to be two hundred and sixty feet; its extreme breadth twenty-seven feet; its height, where the roof rises highest, from eighteen to twenty feet. The floor is blocked up with accumulations of bulky decaying masses, that have dropped from above; and it is covered over its entire area by a stratum of earthy rubbish, which has fallen from the sides and ceiling in such abundance that it covers up the straw beds of the perished islanders, which still exist beneath as a brown mouldering felt, to the depth of from five to eight inches. Never yet was tragedy enacted on a gloomier theatre. An uncertain twilight glimmers gray at the entrance, from the narrow vestibule; but all within, for full two hundred feet, is black as with Egyptian darkness. As we passed onward with our one feeble light, along the dark mouldering walls, and roof which absorbed every straggling ray that reached them, and over the dingy floor, roppy and damp, the place called to recollection that hall in Roman story, hung and carpeted with black, into which Domitian once thrust his senate in a frolic, to read their own names on the coffin-lids placed against the wall. The darkness seemed to press upon us from every side, as if it were a dense jetty fluid, out of which our light had scooped a pailful or two, and that was rushing in to supply the vacuum; and the only objects we saw distinctly visible were each other's heads and faces, and the lighter parts of our dress.

The floor, for about a hundred feet inwards from the narrow vestibule, resembles that of a charnel-house. At almost every step we come upon heaps of human bones, grouped together, as the Psalmist so graphically describes, "as when one cutteth and cleaveth wood upon the earth". They are of brownish, earthy hue, here and there tinged with green; the skulls, with the exception of a few broken fragments have disappeared; for travellers in the Hebrides have of late years been numerous and curious; and many a museum —that at Abbotsford among the rest—exhibits, in a grinning skull, its memorial of the Massacre at Eigg. We find, too, further marks of visitors in the single bones separated from the heaps and scattered over the area; but enough still remains to show, in the general disposition of the remains, that the hapless islanders died under the walls in families, each little group separated by a few feet from the others. Here and there the remains of a detached skeleton may be seen, as if some robust islander, restless in his agony, had stalked out into the middle space ere he fell; but the social arrangement is the general one.

And beneath every heap we find, at the depth, as has been said, of a few inches, the remains of the straw-bed upon which the family had lain, largely mixed with the smaller bones of the human frame, ribs and vertebrae, and hand and feet bones; occasionally, too, with fragments of unglazed pottery, and various other implements of a rude housewifery. The minister found for me, under one family heap, the pieces of a half-burned, unglazed earthen jar, with a narrow mouth, that, like the sepulchral urns of our ancient tumuli, had been moulded by the hand without the assistance of the potter's wheel; and to one of the fragments there stuck a minute pellet of gray hair. From under another heap he disinterred the handle-stave of a child's wooden porringer (bicker), perforated by a hole still bearing the mark of the chord that had hung it to the wall; and beside the stave lay a few of the larger, less destructible bones of the child, with what for a time puzzled us both not a little,—one of the grinders of a horse. Certain it was, no horse could have got there to have dropped a tooth,—a foal of a week old could not have pressed itself through the opening; and how the single grinder, evidently no recent introduction into the cave, could have got mixed up in the straw with the human bones, seemed an enigma somewhat of the class to which the reel in the bottle belongs. I found in Edinburgh an unexpected commentator on the mystery, in the person of my little boy,—an experimental philosopher in his second year. I had spread out on the floor the curiosities of Eigg,—among the rest the relics of the cave, including the pieces of earthen jar and the fragments of the porringer; but the horse's tooth seemed to be the only real curiosity among them in the eyes of little Bill. He laid instant hold of it; and, appropriating it as a toy, continued playing with it till he fell asleep. I have now little doubt that it was first brought into the cave by the poor child amid whose mouldering remains Mr Swanson found it. The little pellet of gray hair spoke of feeble old age involved in this wholesale massacre with the vigorous manhood of the island; and here was a story of unsuspecting infancy amusing itself on the eve of destruction with its toys. Alas for man! God's image must have been sadly defaced in the murderers of the poor inoffensive children of Eigg, ere they could have heard their feeble wailings, raised, no doubt, when the stifling atmosphere within began first to thicken, and yet ruthlessly persist in their work of indiscriminate destruction.

I also found a few teeth: they were sticking fast in a fragment of jaw; and, taking it for granted, as I suppose I may, that the dentology of the murderous McLeods outside the cave must have very much resembled that of the murdered McDonalds within, very harmless-looking teeth they were for being those of an aimal so maliciously mischievous as man. I have found in the Old Red Sandstone the strong-based tusks of the semi-reptile Holoptychius; I have chiselled out of the limestone of the Coal Measures the sharp, dagger-like incisors of the Megalichthys; I have picked up in the Lias and Oolite the cruel spikes of the crocodile and the Ichthyosaurus; I have seen the trenchant saw-edged teeth of the gigantic Cestracions and Squalidae that had been disinterred from the Chalk and the London Clay; and I have felt, as I examined them, that there could be no possibility of mistake regarding the nature of creatures to which they had belonged; —they were teeth made for hacking, tearing, mangling,—for amputating limbs at a bite, and laying open bulky bodies with a crunch: but I could find no evidence in the human jaw, with its three inoffensive-looking grinders, that the animal it had belonged to—far more ruthless and cruel than reptile-fish, crocodiles, or sharks,—was of such a nature that it could destroy creatures of even its own kind by hundreds at a time, when not in the least incited by hunger, and with no ultimate intention of eating them. Man must surely have become an immensely worse animal than his teeth show him to have been designed for: his teeth give no evidence regarding his real character. Who, for instance, could gather from the dentology of the McLeods the passage in their history to which the cave of Francis bears evidence?

A SENSE OF WONDER

OF all the characteristics that made up Hugh Miller's complex personality, none was more powerful than his sense of sheer wonder at the intricacy, beauty, and endless variety of the world around him. He possessed a stunning ability to convey something of that pure delight in his accounts of the animals, plants, fossils and stones he found. Time after time he exhorts his readers to try to capture that excitement for themselves, and in The Old Red Sandstone he urges them to "Learn to make use of your eyes. The commonest things are worth looking at, even stones and weeds and the most familiar animals."

It was that quality of wonder that informed Miller's first serious piece of writing, his Letters On The Herring Industry, which brought him to the attention of the literati of the North of Scotland. In the course of the five Letters, Miller contrives to put together a solid picture of the problems and economics of the herring industry, while at the same time studding it with some ravishing descriptive passages. "The heavens were glowing with stars," he writes of his night on the Guillam bank, "and the sea from the smoothness of the surface appeared a second sky, as bright and starry as the other, but with this difference that all its stars appeared comets." The breaking of the shoals of herring on the surface Miller describes as "a continual twinkling . . . . like a blue robe sprinkled with silver". And on the quayside at Cromarty "the dance of commerce" went on to the music of "the rolling of casks, the rattling of carts, and the confused hum of a thousand voices".

In the extract from The Old Red Sandstone (his first, and probably most important book), he describes his first days as an apprentice stonemason in the sandstone quarries of the Black Isle, and his astonishment at the riches he found among the rocks. "In the course of the first day's employment I picked up a nodular mass of blue limestone, and laid it open by a strike of the hammer. Wonderful to relate, it contained inside a beautifully finished piece of sculpture — one of the volutes, apparently, of an Ionic Capital . . . . Was there another such curiosity in the whole world?"

Letters On The Herring Industry IV

SIR,— In the latter end of August 1819, I went out to the fishing then prosecuted on Guilliam in a Cromarty boat. The evening was remarkably pleasant. A low breeze from the west scarcely ruffled the surface of the frith, which was varied in every direction by unequal stripes and patches of a dead calmness. The bay of Cromarty, burnished by the rays of the declining sun until it glowed like a sheet of molten fire, lay behind, winding in all its beauty beneath purple hills and jutting headlands; while before stretched the wide extent of the Moray Frith speckled with fleets of boats which had lately left their ports, and were now all sailing in one direction. The point to which they were bound was the bank of Guilliam, which, seen from betwixt the Sutors, seemed to verge on the faint blue line of the horizon; and the fleets which had already arrived on it had, to the naked eye, the appearance of a little rough-edged cloud resting on the water. As we advanced, this cloud of boats grew larger and darker; and soon after sunset, when the bank was scarcely a mile distant, it assumed the appearance of a thick leafless wood covering a low brown island.

The tide, before we left the shore, had risen high on the beach, and was now beginning to recede. Aware of this, we lowered sail several hundred yards to the south of the fishing ground; and after determining the point from whence the course of the current would drift us direct over the bank, we took down the mast, cleared the hinder part of the boat, and began to cast out the nets. Before the Inlaw appeared in the line of the Gaelic Chapel, (the landmark by which the southernmost extremity of Guilliam is ascertained,) the whole drift was thrown overboard and made fast to the swing. Night came on. The sky assumed a dead and leaden hue. A low dull mist roughened the outline of the distant hills, and in some places blotted them out from the landscape. The faint breeze that had hitherto scarcely been felt now roughened the water, which was of a dark blue colour, approaching to black. The sounds which predominated were in unison with the scene. The almost measured dash of the waves against the sides of the boat and the faint rustle of the breeze were incessant; while the low dull moan of the surf breaking on the distant beach and the short sudden cry of an aquatic fowl of the diving species, occasionally mingled with the sweet though rather monotonous notes of a Gaelic song. "It's ane o' the Gairloch fishermen," said our skipper; "puir folk, they're aye singin' an' thinkin' o' the Hielands."

Our boat, as the tides were not powerful, drifted slowly over the bank. The buoys stretched out from the bows in an unbroken line.

Some of the Inhabitants of the nineteenth century fishertown of Cromarty. (Courtesy of the National Museum of Antiquities of Scotland)

There was no sign of fish, and the boatmen, after spreading the sail over the beams, laid themselves down on it. The scene was at the time so new to me, and, though of a somewhat melancholy cast, so pleasing that I stayed up. A singular appearance attracted my notice. "How," said I to one of the boatmen, who a moment before had made me an offer of his greatcoat,—"how do you account for that calm silvery spot on the water, which moves at such a rate in the line of our drift?" He started up. A moment after he called on the others to rise, and then replied: "That moving speck of calm water covers a shoal of herrings. If it advances a hundred yards farther in that direction, we shall have some employment for you."

This piece of information made me regard the little patch, which, from the light it caught, and the blackness of the surrounding water, seemed a bright opening in a dark sky, with considerable interest. It moved onward with increased velocity. It came in contact with the line of the drift, and three of the buoys immediately sunk. A few minutes were suffered to elapse, and we then commenced hauling. The two strongest of the crew, as is usual, were stationed at the cork, the two others at the ground baulk. My assistance, which I readily tendered, was pronounced unnecessary, so I hung over the gunwale watching the nets as they approached the side of the boat.

The three first, from the phosphoric light of the water, appeared as if bursting into flames of a pale green colour. The fourth was still brighter, and glittered through the waves while it was yet several fathoms away, reminding me of an intensely bright sheet of the aurora borealis. As it approached the side, the pale green of the phosphoric matter appeared as if mingled with large flakes of snow. It contained a body of fish. "A white horse! a white horse!" exclaimed one of the men at the cork baulk; "lend us a haul." I immediately sprung aft, laid hold on the rope, and commenced hauling. In somewhat less than half an hour we had all the nets on board, and rather more than twelve barrels of herrings.

The night had now become so dark, that we could scarcely discern the boats which lay within gunshot of our own; and we had no means of ascertaining the position of the bank except by sounding. The lead was cast, and soon after the nets shot a second time. The skipper's bottle was next produced, and a dram of whisky sent round in a tin measure containing nearly a gill. We then folded down the sail, which had been rolled up to make way for the herrings, and were soon fast asleep.

Ten years have elapsed since I laid myself down on this couch, and I was not then so accustomed to a rough bed as I am now, when I can look back on my wanderings as a journeyman mason over a considerable part of both the Lowlands and Highlands of Scotland. About midnight I awoke quite chill, and all over sore with the hard beams and sharp rivets of the boat. Well, thought I, this is the tax I pay for my curiosity. I rose and crept softly over the sail to the bows, where I stood, and where, in the singular beauty of the scene, which was of character as different from that I had lately witnessed as is possible to conceive, I soon lost all sense of every feeling that was not pleasure.

The breeze had died into a perfect calm. The heavens were glowing with stars, and the sea, from the smoothness of the surface, appeared a second sky, as bright and starry as the other, but with this difference, that all its stars appeared comets. There seemed no line of division at the horizon, which rendered the illusion more striking. The distant hills appeared a chain of dark thundery clouds sleeping in the heavens. In short, the scene was one of the strangest ever witnessed; and the thoughts and imaginations which it suggested were of a character as singular. I looked at the boat as it

appeared in the dim light of midnight, a dark irregularly-shaped
mass; I gazed on the sky of stars above, and the sky of comets below,
and imagined myself in the centre of space, far removed from the
earth and every other world,—the solitary inhabitant of a planetary
fragment. This illusion, too romantic to be lasting, was dissipated by
an incident which convinced me that I had not yet left the world. A
crew of south-shore fishermen, either by accident or design, had
shot their nets right across those of another boat, and, in
disentangling them, a quarrel ensued. Our boat lay more than half a
mile from the scene of contention, but I could hear without being
particularly attentive that on the one side there were terrible threats
of violence immediate and bloody, and on the other, threats of the
still more terrible pains and penalties of the law. In a few minutes,
however, the entangled nets were freed, and the roar of altercation
gradually sunk into a silence as dead as that which had preceded it.

An hour before sunrise, I was somewhat disheartened to find the
view on every side bounded by a dense low bank of fog, which hung
over the water, while the central firmament remained blue and
cloudless. The neighbouring boats appeared through the mist huge
misshapen things, manned by giants. We commenced hauling, and
found in one of the nets a small rock cod and a half-starved whiting,
which proved the whole of our draught. I was informed by the
fishermen, that even when the shoal is thickest on the Guilliam, so
close does it keep by the bank, that not a solitary herring is to be
caught a gunshot from the edge on either side.

We rowed up to the other boats, few of whom had been more
successful in their last haul than ourselves, and none equally so in
their first. The mist prevented us from ascertaining, by known
landmarks, the position of the bank, which we at length discovered
in a manner that displayed much of the peculiar art of the
fisherman. The depth of the water, and the nature of the bottom,
showed us that it lay to the south. A faint tremulous heave of the
sea, which was still calm, was the only remaining vestige of the gale
which had blown from the west in the early part of the night, and
this heave, together with the current, which at this stage of the flood
runs in a south-western direction, served as our compass. We next
premised how far our boat had drifted down the frith with the ebb-
tide, and how far she had been carried back by the flood. We then
turned her bows in the line of the current, and in rather less than
half an hour were, as the lead informed us, on the eastern extremity

of Guilliam, where we shot our nets for the third time.

Soon after sunrise the mist began to dissipate, and the surface of the water to appear for miles around roughened as if by a smart breeze, though there was not the slightest breath of wind at the time. "How do you account for that appearance," said I to one of the fishermen. "Ah, lad, that is by no means so favourable a token as the one you asked me to explain last night. I had as lief to see the *Bhodry-more*." "Why, what does it betoken? and what is the *Bhodry-more?*" "It betokens the shoal have spawned, and will shortly leave the frith; for when the fish are sick and weighty they never rise to the surface in that way;—but have you never heard of the *Bhodry-more?*" I replied in the negative. "Well, but you shall." "Nay," said another of the crew, "leave that for our return; do you not see the herrings playing by thousands round our nets, and not one of the buoys sinking in the water? There is not a single fish swimming so low as the upper baulk of our drift. Shall we not shorten the buoy-ropes, and take off the sinkers?" This did not meet the approbation of the others, one of who, took up a stone, and flung it in the middle of the shoal. The fish immediately disappeared from the surface for several fathoms round. "Ah, there they go," he exclaimed, "if they go but low enough;—four years ago I startled thirty barrels of light fish into my drift just by throwing a stone among them."

The whole frith at this time, so far as the eye could reach, appeared crowded with herrings; and its surface was so broken by them as to remind one of the pool of a waterfall. They leaped by millions a few inches into the air, and sunk with a hollow plumping noise, somewhat resembling the dull rippling sound of a sudden breeze; while to the eye there was a continual twinkling, which, while it mocked every effort that attempted to examine in detail, showed to the less curious glance like a blue robe sprinkled with silver. But it is not by such comparisons that so singular a scene is to be described so as to be felt. It was one of those which, through the living myriad of creation, testify of the infinite Creator.

About noon we hauled for the third and last time, and found nearly eight barrels of fish. I observed when hauling that the natural heat of the herring is scarcely less than that of quadrupeds or birds; that when alive its sides are shaded by a beautiful crimson colour which it loses when dead; and that when newly brought out of the water, it utters a sharp faint cry somewhat resembling that of a mouse. We had now about twenty barrels on board. The *easterly har*,

The north of Scotland herring fishery. Miller decribes the herring season in Cromarty as "an exciting scene that combined the bustle of the workshop with the confusion of the crowded fair". (Courtesy of the National Museum of Antiquities of Scotland).

a sea-breeze so called by fishermen, which in the Moray Frith, during the summer months and the first month of autumn, commonly comes on after ten o'clock A.M., and fails at four o'clock P.M., had now set in. We hoisted our mast and sail and soon were scudding right before it.

The story of the *Bhodry-more*, which I demanded of the skipper as soon as we had trimmed our sail, proved interesting in no common degree, and was linked with a great many others. The *Bhodry-more*, is an active, mischievous fish of the whale species, which has been known to attack and even founder boats. About eight years ago, a very large one passed the town of Cromarty through the middle of the bay, and was seen by many of the townsfolk leaping out of the water in the manner of a salmon, fully to the height of the boat's mast. It appeared about thirty feet in length. This animal may almost be regarded as the mermaid of modern times: for the fishermen deem it to have full a much of the demon as of the fish.

There have been instances of its pursuing a boat under sail for many miles, and even of its leaping over it from side to side. It appears, however, that its habits and appetites are unlike those of the shark; and that the annoyance which it gives the fisherman is out of no desire of making him his prey, but from its predilection for amusement. It seldom meddles with a boat when at anchor, but pursues one under sail, as a kitten would a rolling ball of yarn. The large physalus whale is comparatively a dull, sluggish animal; occasionally, however, it evinces a partiality for the amusement of the *Bhodry-more*.

Our skipper said, that when on the Caithness coast, a few years before, an enormous fish of the species kept direct in the wake of his boat for more than a mile, frequently rising so near the stern as to be within reach of the boat-hook. He described the expression of its large goggle eyes as at once frightening and amusing; and so graphic was his narrative that I could almost paint the animal stretching out for more than sixty feet behind the boat, with its black marble-looking skin and cliff-like fins. He at length grew tired of its gambols, and with a sharp fragment of rock struck it between the eyes. It sunk with a sudden plunge, and did not rise for ten minutes after, when it appeared a full mile a-stern.

This narrative was but the first of I know not how many, of a similar cast, which presented to my imagination the *Bhodry-more* whale and hun-fish in every possible point of view. The latter, a voracious formidable animal of the shark species, frequently makes great havoc among the tackle with which cod and haddock are caught. Like the shark, it throws itself on its back when in the act of seizing its prey. The fishermen frequently see it lying motionless, its white belly glittering through the water, a few fathoms from the boat's side, employed in stripping off every fish from their hooks as the line is drawn over it. This formidable animal is from six to ten feet in length, and formed like the common shark.

One of the boatmen's stories, though somewhat in the Munchausen style, I shall take the liberty of relating. Two Cromarty men, many years ago, were employed on a fine calm day in angling coal-fish and rock-cod, with rods and hand-lines. Their little skiff rode to a large oblong stone, which served for an anchor, nearly opposite a rocky spire termed the chapel, three miles south of Shandwick. Suddenly the stone was raised from the bottom with a jerk, and the boat began to move. "What can this mean," exclaimed the elder of the men, pulling on his rod, "we have surely broken loose, but who could have thought that there ran such a current here." The other, a young daring fellow, John Clark by name, remarked in reply, that the apparent course of the skiff was directly contrary to that of the current. The motion, which was at first gentle, increased to a frightful velocity; the rope a-head was straitened until the very stem cracked; and the sea rose upon either bows in a furrow that nearly overtopped the gunwhale. "Old man," said the young fellow, "didst thou ever see the like o' that!" "Guid save us, boy," said the other, "cut, cut the swing." "Na, na, bide a wee first, I manna skaith the rape: didst thou ever see the like o' that!" In a few minutes, according to the story, they were dragged in this manner nearly two miles, when the motion ceased as suddenly as it had begun, and the skiff rode to the swing as before.

The scenes exhibited on the shores of Cromarty, during the busy season of the fishing, afford nearly as much scope for description, though of a different character, as those in which the occupation of the fishermen mingle with the sublime scenes of the Moray Frith. But this description I will not attempt. Your readers must have already anticipated it. If not, let them picture to themselves the shores of a seaport town crowded with human figures, and its harbour with boats and vessels of trade. Let them imagine the bustle of the workshop combining with the confusion of the crowded fair! You, Mr Editor, who have seen Holbein's Dance of Death, would perhaps not question the soundness of the imagination that would body forth so busy a scene as the dance of commerce. Sailors, fishermen, curers, mechanics, all engaged, lead up the ball amid heaps of fish that glitter to the sun, tiers of casks and pyramids of salt. Hark to the music! It is a wild combination of irregular sounds,—the hammering of mechanics, the rolling of casks, the rattling of carts, and the confused hum of a thousand voices.—I am, sir, your obedient servant, M.

29th August 1829

The Old Red Sandstone

IT was twenty years last February since I set out, a little before sunrise, to make my first acquaintance with a life of labour and restraint; and I have rarely had a heavier heart than on that

morning. I was but a slim, loose-jointed boy at the time, fond of the
pretty intangibilities of romance, and of dreaming when broad
awake; and, woeful change! I was now going to work at what Burns
has instanced, in his "Twa Dogs", as one of the most disagreeable of
all employments,—to work in a quarry. Bating the passing uneasiness
occasioned by a few gloomy anticipations, the portion of my life
which had already gone by had been happy beyond the common lot.
I had been a wanderer among rocks and woods, a reader of curious
books when I could get them, a gleaner of old traditionary stories;
and now I was going to exchange all my day-dreams, and all my
amusements, for the kind of life in which men toil every day that they
may be enabled to eat, and eat every day that they may be enabled to
toil!

The quarry in which I wrought lay on the southern shore of a
noble inland bay, or frith rather, with a little clear stream on the one
side, and a thick fir wood on the other. It had been opened in the
Old Red Sandstone of the district, and was overtopped by a huge
bank of diluvial clay, which rose over it in some places to the height
of nearly thirty feet, and which at this time was rent and shivered,
wherever it presented an open front to the weather, by a recent frost.
A heap of loose fragments, which had fallen from above, blocked up
the face of the quarry and my first employment was to clear them
away. The friction of the shovel soon blistered my hands, but the
pain was by no means very severe, and I wrought hard and willingly,
that I might see how the huge strata below, which presented so firm
and unbroken a frontage, were to be torn up and removed.

Picks, and wedges, and levers, were applied by my brother workmen; and, simple and rude as I had been accustomed to regard these
implements, I found I had much to learn in the way of using them.
They all proved inefficient, however, and the workmen had to bore
into one of the inferior strata, and employ gunpowder. The process
was new to me, and I deemed it a highly amusing one: it had the
merit, too, of being attended with some such degree of danger as a
boating or rock excursion, and had thus an interest independent of
its novelty. We had a few capital shots: the fragments flew in every
direction; and an immense mass of the diluvium came toppling
down, bearing with it two dead birds, that in a recent storm had crept
into one of the deeper fissures, to die in the shelter. I felt a new
interest in examining them. The one was a pretty cock goldfinch,
with its hood of vermilion, and its wings inlaid with the gold to which

One of the Hill/Adamson calotypes of Miller himself. In his essay on The Calotype *he describes himself in the third person as a "bonneted mechanic . . . resting on a piece of grotesque sculpture . . . . one half of his face is in deep shade, the other in strong light". (Courtesy of the National Galleries of Scotland).*

it owes its name, as unsoiled and smooth as if it had been preserved for a museum. The other, a somewhat rarer bird, of the woodpecker tribe, was variegated with light blue and a grayish yellow.

The gunpowder had loosened a large mass in one of the inferior strata, and our first employment, on resuming our labours, was to raise it from its bed. I assisted the other workmen in placing it on edge, and was much struck by the appearance of the platform on which it had rested. The entire surface was ridged and furrowed like a bank of sand that had been left by the tide an hour before. I could trace every bend and curvature, every cross-hollow and counter ridge, of the corresponding phenomena; for the resemblance was half-resemblance,—it was the thing itself; and I had observed it a hundred and a hundred times, when sailing my little schooner in the shallows left by the ebb. But what had become of the waves that had thus fretted the solid rock, or of what element had they been composed? I felt as completely at fault as Robinson Crusoe did on his discovering the print of the man's foot in the sand.

The evening furnished me with still further cause of wonder. We raised another block in a different part of the quarry, and found that the area of a circular depression in the stratum below was broken and flawed in every direction, as if it had been the bottom of a pool recently dried up, which had shrunk and split in the hardening. Several large stones came rolling down from the diluvium in the course of the afternoon. They were of different qualities from the sandstone below, and from one another; and, what was more wonderful still, they were all rounded and water-worn, as if they had been tossed about in the sea or the bed of a river for hundreds of years. There could not, surely, be a more conclusive proof that the bank which had enclosed them so long could not have been created on the rock on which it rested. No work-man ever manufactures a half-worn article, and the stones were all half-worn! And if not the bank, why then the sandstone underneath? I was lost in conjecture, and found I had food enough for thought that evening, without once thinking of the unhappiness of a life of labour.

In the course of the first day's employment I picked up a nodular mass of blue limestone, and laid it open by a stroke of the hammer. Wonderful to relate, it contained inside a beautifully finished piece of sculpture,—one of the volutes apparently, of an Ionic capital; and not the far-famed walnut of the fairy tale, had I broken the shell and found the little dog lying within, could have surprised me more.

Was there another such curiosity in the whole world? I broke open a few other nodules of similar appearance,—for they lay pretty thickly on the shore,—and found that there might. In one of these there were what seemed to be the scales of fishes, and the impressions of a few minute bivalves, prettily striated; in the centre of another there was actually a piece of decayed wood. Of all Nature's riddles, these seemed to me to be at once the most interesting and the most difficult to expound. I treasured them carefully up, and was told by one of the workmen to whom I showed them, that there was a part of the shore about two miles further to the west where curiously-shaped stones, somewhat like the heads of boarding-pikes, were occasionally picked up; and that in his father's days the country people called them thunderbolts, and deemed them of sovereign efficacy in curing bewitched cattle. Our employer, on quitting the quarry for the building on which we were to be engaged, gave all the workmen a half-holiday. I employed it in visiting the place where the thunderbolts had fallen so thickly, and found it a richer scene of wonder than I could have fancied in even my dreams.

What first attracted my notice was a detached group of low-lying skerries, wholly different in form and colour from the sandstone cliffs above, or the primary rocks a little farther to the west. I found them composed of thin strata of limestone, alternating with thicker beds of a black slaty substance which, as I ascertained in the course of the evening, burns with a powerful flame, and emits a strong bituminous odour. The layers into which the beds readily separate are hardly an eighth part of an inch in thickness, and yet on every layer there are the impressions of thousands.and tens of thousands of the various fossils peculiar to the Lias.

We may turn over these wonderful leaves one after another, like the leaves of a herbarium, and find the pictorial records of a former creation in every page: scallops, and gryphites, and ammonites, of almost every variety peculiar to the formation, and at least some eight or ten varieties of belemnite; twigs of wood, leaves of plants, cones of an extinct species of pine, bits of charcoal, and the scales of fishes; and, as if to render their pictorial appearance more striking, though the leaves of this interesting volume are of a deep black, most of the impressions are of a chalky whiteness. I was lost in admiration and astonishment, and found my very imagination paralysed by an assemblage of wonders that seemed to out-rival the fantastic and the extravagant even in its wildest conceptions.

But Miller's sense of wonder was not confined to the works of his God. Many of the works of his fellow-creatures impressed him no end, and like many (and perhaps most) intelligent Victorians, Miller was something of a technology buff. In The Locomative Age *he wonders at the huge and startling growth of the railway network, and comes to the (MacLuhanesque) conclusion that this massive growth in communications technology will have unlooked for effects on the British people. The fact that the London newspapers could now appear on the streets of Edinburgh on the same day that they appeared in London, he predicted, would make the population better informed, but politically more volatile. The railways would shunt ideas into the countryside, and make townspeople take an interest in the country as somewhere to relax. But the effect, he thought, would be to "make the nation, if we may so express ourselves, all town".*

In The Calotype *he sees, and welcomes, a new technology that will revolutionise art; an important innovation (much practised by Miller's friends, David Octavius Hill and Robert Adamson) that offers "truth itself" in the place of the paltry versions offered by minor limners. In his* Parting Impressions of the Great Exhibitions *of 1851, Miller was taken by Paxton's great Crystal Palace, but he makes the point that architectural historians have been making ever since; that the glass and cast iron structure was "simply an extension of the first glass frame that covered the first few delicate flowers", that it was impressive for its "largeness" and not its greatness, and was almost infinitely extendible. He also thought that the British had better take a hard look at what was on display from the US, Europe and the rest of the civilised world, "seeing that to undervalue a competitor or opponent is one of the most certain ways possible to secure defeat".*

The Locomotive Age

OF all the ages which the world ever saw, the present is peculiarly the age of peregrination and locomotion. There have been more journeys undertaken within the confines of Great Britain during a single week of the present year, than during any single month of the year 1827, or during any twelvemonth of the early half of the last century. The stage coach and travelling-waggon interest was never a very great one in Britain; whereas its railway interest is at once one of the most important commercial interests in the kingdom, and the most influential in not only its Lower, but in also its Upper House,— strong enough of itself to carry elections outside the walls of Parliament, and in some instances to leave Ministers in a minority within. There are single evening trains on the Edinburgh and Glasgow Railway, that carry as many passengers as formed only ten years ago the average complement for a week of the stage coaches that plied between the two cities.

Even into recesses of the country into which railways themselves will never be carried, do they discharge a tide of visitors unprecedented in former times. We have been told by a friend who visited, a few weeks since, one of the most romantic localities of the Western Highlands, that he found each evening the inns crammed to the door, and not only no beds, but scarce sitting room and shelter procurable by the travellers who were luckless enough to come late. Every new bit of railway, though but a mere branch some two or three miles in extent, adds to the general current of locomotion in the country, as every little branch stream serves to increase the bulk and the volume of the river into which it falls.

Those social arrangements of the day, too, through which the members of Friendly and Temperance Societies several hundred strong take an airing together in pleasure trips to Glasgow and the land of Burns, or to Berwick, and even to London,—all for half price, with time to see the lions,—form peculiarly a new feature of the age. Never before was there a time, in any country, in which some five or six hundred working men could set out on a fine morning in their Sunday attire, and, after travelling a hundred miles together, and seeing sights and visiting aquaintances, return unfatigued in the evening.

Now, it is scarce possible that all this locomotion can exist as a new element in the country, without producing marked effects; and it is natural enough to ask what these effects are likely to be. It must operate to a certain extent on the popular mind. The prophet speaks of a time when "many shall run to and fro, and knowledge shall be increased." It is indisputably an effect of "running to and fro" to increase knowledge. A country no sooner gets roads even than it begins to change its character: old local prejudices, that have lain in its quieter recesses undisturbed for centuries, like rust amid the wheels and pinions of an unwrought engine, begin to wear off and fall away, as minds are brought in contact to brighten up and sharpen each other, and the general machine gets into motion. And the more thorough and extensive the working of the engine, of course the more thorough and extensive the change. Rapid and frequent intercourse has also an assimilating effect. It stirs, agitates, mixes up the general mass, and, like those great currents of the ocean that equalize the temperature of the waters over vast areas, very various in their climate, renders it all of one kind and quality.

Under the old state of things, there used to exist great differences between town and country. In towns, the stirring, sharpening process went on; while in villages and the country, mind lay in an inert, quiescent condition, covered over by the rust of centuries. We need scarce remind the reader, that in the earlier ages of Christianity, Pagan and villager were synonymous terms; or that at the Reformation in our own country, all the large towns had declared for the Reformed doctrines, while Popery still remained strong in the Highlands and on the Borders, and in not a few of the more retired Lowland districts besides. Indeed, there is properly no national Popery in Scotland at the present day,—for that of our large towns is Irish, not Scotch Popery,—save in remote and stagnant recesses of the country, such as Barra and the Long Island, Lochaber and Arisaig, with some of the fishing villages of Banffshire and Aberdeen,—places unvisited of old by the stirring influences.

But this disposition on the part of towns to receive new impressions and beliefs has not been operative always, on the right side. The impious superficialities of Paine were popular in our cities at a time when they had scarce any hold of the rural districts; and it is chiefly among our own town mechanics, not among the ploughmen and farmers of the country, that the superficialities of Combe are regarded as philosophic in the present day. Now, the wonderfully accelerated locomotion and the widely developed travelling dis-position of the age, must, as we have said, have the effect of greatly assimilating town and country. It will make the nation, if we may so express ourselves, all town, by spreading over its wide area that motion, friction, collision of mind, which in the old state of things was restricted to the crowded neighbourhoods which cities compose.

It is truly wonderful how space and distance have been annihilated during the last few years, and the entire inhabitants of the country brought into close contact. Through an arrangement entered into during the last three weeks, the Edinburgh newspapers can now present their town readers with the London news at as early an hour as the London newspapers themselves. *The Witness,* for instance, is delivered to its Edinburgh readers on the mornings of Wednesday and Saturday,—the London *Times* and *Morning Chronicle* of Tuesday and Friday at the same time; and as, from a recent acceleration of the trains, the English papers come into town during the night, when the reading public is asleep, and the printers and editors of the Edinburgh papers are awake in their behalf, *The Witness* and its fellows are thus enabled to transfer to their columns the latest intelligence of these London journals, and to submit it to their readers at as early an hour. Simple as the fact may seem, it would have been deemed a very inexplicable one only ten years ago.

One important effect of the greatly increased locomotion of the country is palpably beginning to tell. The popular intellect is not led to cogitate more deeply in consequence,—rather the reverse, we fear; but it is led, if we may so speak, to *cogitate faster*. A larger amount of idea passes through the public mind in a given time than at any former period; and hence a quickening of that cycle in which it is the tendency of human thought to revolve. As we had elsewhere occasion to remark of late, "we are not only travelling, but also, as a people, living fast; and see revolutions which were formerly the slow work of ages, matured in a few brief seasons." And the "living fast," in this sense, is in no inconsiderable degree a direct consequence of the "travelling fast."

The process of saturating the public mind was formerly, from the lack of ready communication, a tedious one; and, just as in the processes of a dye-house, one stage of saturation had to be completed, however slow the rate of progress, ere another could commence. The action and re-action followed each other at a snail's pace, and centuries passed away ere the cycle revolved. Its revolutions for the future bid fair to be comprised within comparatively narrow limits; but we question whether what may be gained in point of time may not be lost in energy of movement.

Now, during the times of the earlier cycle, especially in our own country, such was the comparative slowness of the revolution, that men could be consistently engaged from early, vigorous youth, until their heads had become grey, and their step short and feeble, in one stage of process of the change. The partizan contemporaries of the political martyrs, though many of them, no doubt, softened as they got old, were the assertors of democratical principles all their days; while their extremer opponents were, on the other hand, as consistently Tory. And hence a certain degree of strength and earnestness in their contendings. There promises to be considerably less of strength in the political feelings of the present day. The cycle revolves ere they have time to gather headway. How many minds in this country in the present age must be conscious of having themselves moved in the cycle, in at least a modified sense, since the first heats of the Reform Bill began! They have been in perfect sincerity keen Reformers, zealous Conservatives, and, if we may venture to coin a word for the occasion, cool *Indifferentists,* by turn and in succession; and in this last state not a few of them remain.

There are, however, certain important social questions that can be adjusted on only the political arena, which bid fair, we trust, greatly to gather strength through the newly formed locomotive habits of the country. There are certain interests of town and country, hitherto regarded as distinct, which the quickened intercourse will serve to render common. It will give the town, for instance, an interest in the abolition of the game laws, which, under the old state of things, it could scarce have possessed; and a very direct interest, too, in keeping the country open to its people,—Scotland to the Scotch,— against the narrow appropriating spirit of the Dukes of Leeds and of Athole. The opening up of the railways will serve to militate very directly against the shutting up of the Grampians and Glen Tilt, by rendering the rights and interest of the countryman regarding these localities,—with many a green loan and pleasant footpath besides,— those of the townsman also. The newly acquired locomotive habits will have the effect of bringing, on such questions, the whole popular forces into the field, and of ultimately insuring victory to the rights of the combined many over the usurpations of the privileged few.

And the country, as if to pay back the benefits thus conferred, will we trust, have its freshening, *realizing* effect on the town. There will in consequence be less Cockneyism than hitherto in the empire,—by the way, a thing not at all confined to London, but which grows up in all large cities, begotten between a conceit which appropriates to one's-self the greatness and splendour of one's place of habitation, and an acquaintance with words dissociated from a knowledge of things. The country has always a wholesome developing influence on the town mind. Its many striking objects, at once pleasing and novel, set the observing powers,—the knowing faculties, as the Phrenologists would say,—fairly a-working; and it is the natural effect of these to communicate motion to the entire intellect.

We are particularly pleased with those railway pleasure excursions of working men, especially when united with Temperance-Association principles, which are becoming so prominent in the general locomotion of the time, and of which one sees the frequent advertisements staring from post and pillar as one walks the streets. To such of our readers as know what it is to toil day after day for months and years at some laborious employment, we need scarce refer to that weariness of customary exertion which grows upon the mind, and at length presses upon it like a load.

Now, it does gratify us to see the working man taking his *secular Sabbaths,* not as a matter of necessity, but of choice, and spending them rationally in exploring new scenes, and in filling his mind with fresh images. The taste, confined to proper limits, and its appropriate working-day portions of time, is an eminently wholesome one, and, united to habits of temperance and providence, might do much to lighten and abridge, and some degree supplant, those joyless resting-times in which the wheels of trade are clogged by the deteriorated accumulations of over-production, and the curse of labour is suspended in its action by a greatly heavier and more crushing one,—the curse of an utter *want* of labour.

We have referred to that quickening of the cycle of opinion which it is the tendency of a rapid and widely-spread intercourse of thought to induce. Now, prophecy everywhere represents the ultimate struggle between the powers of good and evil as short and sharp; and we are mistaken if there may not be seen in this still accelerating motion of the wheel a predisposition in the nature of things to such a result. Alas, that there should be so little progress in the spread of those vital truths which alone can steady its movements, and prevent it from scattering around, as its sole gifts to the country, fruitless revolution, inconsistency, and indifference!

The Calotype

THERE are some two or three slight advantages which real merit has, that ficticious merit has not; among the rest, an especial advantage, which, we think, should recommend it to at least the quieter members of society—the advantage of being unobtrusive and modest. It presses itself much less on public notice than its vagabond antagonist, and makes much less noise; it walks, for a time at least, as if slippered in felt, and leaves the lieges quite at freedom to take notice of it or no, as they may feel inclined. It is content, in its infancy, to thrive in silence. It does not squall in the nursery, to the disturbance of the whole house, like "the major roaring for his

porridge". What, for instance, could be quieter or more modest, in
its first stages than the invention of James Watt?

There are few lovers of art who have looked on the figures or
landscapes of a camera obscura without forming the wish that,
among the hidden secrets of matter, some means might be
discovered for fixing and rendering them permanent. If nature could
be made her own limner, if by some magic art the reflection could be
fixed upon the mirror, could the picture be other than true? But the
wish must have seemed an idle one. Could aught seem less probable
than that the forms of the external world should be made to convert
the pencils of light which they emit into real *bona fide* pencils, and
commence taking their own likenesses? Improbable as the thing may
have seemed, however, there were powers in nature of potency
enough to effect it, and the newly discovered art of the photographer
is simply the art of employing these. The figures and landscapes of
the camera obscura can now be fixed and rendered permanent,—not
yet in all their various shades of colour, but in a style scarcely less
striking, and to which the limner, as if by anticipation, has already
had recourse.

The connoisseur unacquainted with the results of the recent
discovery, would decide, if shown a set of photographic impressions,
that he had before him the carefully finished drawings in sepia of
some great master. The stronger lights, as in sketches done in this
colour, present merely the white ground of the paper; a tinge of soft
warm brown indicates the lights of lower tone; a deeper and still
deeper tinge succeeds, shading by scarce perceptible degrees through
all the various gradations, until the darker shades concentrate into an
opaque and dingy umber, that almost rivals black in its intensity. We
have at the present moment before us—and very wonderful things
they certainly are—drawings on which a human pencil was never
employed. They are strangely suggestive of the capabilities of the art.
Here, for instance, is a scene in George Street,—part of the
pavement; and a line of buildings, from the stately erection at the
corner of Hanover Street, with its proud Corinthian columns and
rich cornice, to Melville's monument and the houses which form the
eastern side of St. Andrew Square. St. Andrew's Church rises in the
middle distance. The drawing is truth itself; but there are cases in
which mere truth might be no great merit: were the truth restricted
here to the proportions of the architecture, there could be nothing
gained by surveying the originals. In this little brown drawing,

A Hill/Adamson calotype of some of the Free Church dignitaries, including the moderator Thomas Chalmers. Miller was quick to notice that the definition of the centre of the picture was better than the definition at the edge, and came to the conclusion that there was nothing subjective about this phenomenon (as had been supposed) but that it was determined by "laws that relate not to the mind, but to the eye." (Courtesy of The National Galleries of Scotland).

however, the truth is truth according to the rules of lineal perspective, unerringly deduced; and from a set of similar drawings, this art of perspective, so important to the artist—which has been so variously taught, and in which so many masters have failed—could be more surely acquired than by any other means. One result of the discovery of the calotype will be, we doubt not, the production of completer treatises on perspective than have yet been given to the world.

Another very curious result will be, in all probablity, a new mode of design for the purposes of the engraver, especially for all the illustrations of books. For a large class of works the labours of the artist bid fair to be restricted to the composition of *tableaux vivants,* which it will be the part of the photographer to fix, and then transfer to the engraver. To persons of artistical skill at a distance, the suggestion may appear somewhat wild. Such of our readers, however, as have seen the joint productions of Mr. Hill and Mr. Adamson in this department, will, we are convinced, not deem it wild in the least. Compared with the mediocre prints of nine-tenths of the illustrated works now issuing from the press, these productions serve admirably to show how immense the distance between nature and her less skilful imitators. There is a truth, breadth, and power about them which we find in only the highest walks of art, and not often even in these.

We have placed a head of Dr Chalmers taken in this way beside one of the most powerful prints of him yet given to the public, and find from the contrast that the latter, with all its power, is but a mere approximation. There is a *skinniness* about the lips which is not true to nature; the chin is not brought strongly enough out; the shade beneath the under lip is too broad and too flat; the nose droops, and lacks the firm-set appearance so characteristic of the original; and while the breadth of the forehead is exaggerated, there is scarce justice done to its height. We decide at once in favour of the calotype—it is truth itself; and yet, while the design of the print—a mere approximation as it is—must have cost a man of genius much pains and study, the drawing in brown beside it was but the work of a few seconds: the eye of an accomplished artist determined the attitude of the original, and the light reflected from the form and features accomplished the rest. Were that sketch in brown to be sent to a skilful engraver, he would render it the groundwork of by far the most faithful print which the public has yet seen. And how

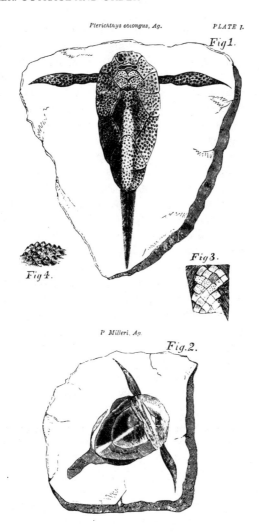

Pterichthys oblongus, Ag.

PLATE I.

Fig 1.

Fig 4.

Fig 3.

P. Milleri, Ag.

Fig. 2.

One of the products of Miller's work among the Old Red Sandstone quarries of Cromarty. Pterichthys Milleri, *or Miller's Winged Fish (classified as such by the great Swiss palaeontologist Louis Agassiz). Miller describes the moment he first came across the fossilised creature: "there, on a ground of light-coloured limestone, lay the effigy of a creature fashioned apparently out of jet, with a body covered with plates, two powerful-looking arms articulated at the shoulders, a head as entirely lost in the trunk as that of the ray or the sun-fish, and a long angular tail. My first-formed idea regarding it was, that I had discovered a connecting link between the tortoise and the fish. . . . "*

interesting to have bound up with the writings of this distinguished
divine, not a mere print in which there might be deviations from the
truth, but the calotype drawing itself! In some future book sale,
copies of the *Astronomical Discourses* with calotype heads of the author
prefixed, may be found to bear very high prices indeed. An
autograph of Shakespeare has been sold of late for considerably
more than an hundred guineas. What price would some early edition
of his works bear, with his likeness in calotype fronting the title?

We have two well-marked drawings before us, in which we
recognise the capabilities of the art for producing pictures of
composition. They are *tableaux vivants* transferred by the calotype. In
the one a bonneted mechanic rests over his mallet on a tombstone—
his one arm bared above his elbow; the other wrapped up in the
well-indicated shirt folds, and resting on a piece of grotesque
sculpture. There is a powerful sun; the somewhat rigid folds in the
dress of coarse stuff are well marked; one half the face is in deep
shade, the other in strong light; the churchyard wall throws a broad
shadow behind, while in the foreground there is a gracefully
chequered breadth of intermingled dark and light in the form of a
mass of rank grass and foliage. Had an old thin man of striking figure
and features been selected, and some study-worn scholar introduced
in front of him, the result would have been a design ready for the
engraver when employed in illustrating the *Old Mortality* of Sir Walter.
The other drawing presents a *tableaux vivant* on a larger scale, and of a
much deeper interest. It forms one of the groups taken under the eye
of Mr Hill, as materials for the composition of his historic picture. In
the centre Dr. Chalmers sits on the Moderator's chair, and there are
grouped around him, as on the platform, some eighteen or twenty of
the better known members of the Church, clerical and lay. Nothing
can be more admirable than the truthfulness and ease of the figures.
Wilkie, in his representations of a crowd, excelled introducing heads,
and hands, and faces, and parts of faces into the interstices behind,—
one of the greatest difficulties with which the artist can grapple. Here,
however, is the difficulty surmounted—surmounted, too, as if to bear
testimony to the genius of the departed—in the style of Wilkie. We
may add further, that the great massiveness of the head of Chalmers,
compared with the many fine heads around him, is admirably
brought out in the drawing.

In glancing over these photographic sketches, one cannot avoid
being struck by the silent but impressive eulogium which nature

pronounces, through their agency, on the works of the more eminent
masters. There is much in seeing nature truthfully, and in registering
what are in reality her prominent markings. Artists of a lower order
are continually falling into mere mannerisms—pecularities of style
that belong not to nature, but to themselves, just because, contended
with acquirement they cease seeing nature. In order to avoid these
mannerisms, there is an eye of fresh observation required—that
ability of continuous attention to surrounding phenomena which
only superior men possess; and doubtless to this eye of fresh
observation, this ability of continuous attention, the masters owed
much of their truth and their power. How very truthfully and
perseveringly some of them saw, is well illustrated by these
photographic drawings. Here, for instance, is a portrait exactly after
the manner of Raeburn. There is the same broad freedom of touch;
no nice miniature stipplings, as if laid in by the point of a needle—no
sharp-edged strokes; all is solid, massy, broad; more distinct at a
distance than when viewed near at hand. The arrangement of the
lights and shadows seems rather the result of happy haste, in which
half the effect was produced by design, half by accident, than of great
labour and care; and yet how exquisitely true the general aspect!
Every stroke tells, and serves, as in the portraits of Raeburn, to do
more than relieve the features: it serves also to indicate the prevailing
mood and predominant power to the mind.

The subject is so suggestive of thought at the present stage, that it
would be no easy matter to exhaust it; and it will, we have no doubt,
be still more suggestive of thought by and by; but we are encroaching
on our limits and must restrain ourselves, therefore, to the indication
of just one of the trains of thought which it has served to originate.
Many of our readers must be acquainted with Dr. Thomas Brown's
theory of attention,—"a state of mind," says the philosopher, "which
has been understood to imply the exercise of a peculiar intellectual
power, but which, in the case of attention to objects of sense, appears
to be nothing more than the co-existence of desire with the
perception of the object to which we are said to attend". He proceeds
to instance how, in a landscape in which the incurious gaze may *see*
many objects without *looking* at or knowing them, a mere desire to
know brings out into distinctness every object in succession on which
the desire fixes. "It is as if everything before had been but the
doubtful colouring of enchantment, which had disappeared, and left
us the few prominent realities on which we gaze; or rather as if some

instant enchantment, obedient to our wishes, had dissolved every reality beside, and brought closer to our sight the few objects we desired to see."

Now, in the transcript of the larger *tableau vivant* before us—that which represents Dr. Chalmers seated among his friends on the Moderator's chair—we find an exemplification sufficiently striking of the laws on which this seemingly mysterious power depends. They are purely structural laws and relate not to the mind, but to the eye,—not to the province of the metaphysician, but to that of the professor of optics. The lens of the camera obscura transmits the figures to the prepared paper, on quite the same principle on which in vision the crystalline lens conveys them to the retina. In the centre of the field in both cases there is much distinctness, while all around its circumference the images are indistinct and dim. We have but to fix the eye on some object directly in front of us, and then attempt, without removing it, to ascertain the forms of objects at some distance on both sides, in order to convince ourselves that the field of distinct vision is a very limited field indeed. And in this transcript of the larger *tableau vivant* we find exactly the same phenomena. The central figures come all within the distinct field. Not so, however, the figures on both sides. They are dim and indistinct; the shades dilute into the lights, and the outlines are obscure.

How striking a comment on the theory of Brown! We see his mysterious power resolved in that drawing into a simple matter of light and shade, arranged in accordance with certain optical laws. The clear central space in which the figures are so distinct, corresponds to the central space in the retina; it is the attention-point of the picture, if we may so speak. In the eye this attention-point is brought to bear, through a simple effort of the will, on the object to be examined; and the rest of the process, so pleasingly, but at the same time so darkly, described by the philosopher, is the work of the eye itself.

Parting Impressions Of The Great Exhibition

THE exhibition closed upon Saturday last; and one of the most marvellous and instructive sights which the world ever saw now survives only as a great recollection,—as a lesson unique in the history of the species, which has been fairly given, but which, upon the same scale at least, we need scarce hope to see repeated. I spent the greater part of last week amid its long withdrawing aisles and galleries; and, without specially concentrating myself on any one set of objects, artistic or mechanical, set my thoughts loose among the whole, to see whether they could not glean up for future use a few general impressions, better suited to remain with me than any mere recollections of the particular and the minute. The memory lays fast hold of the sum total in an important calculation, and retains it; but of all the intermediate sums employed in the work of reduction or summation it takes no hold whatsoever; and so, in most minds, on a somewhat similar principle, general results are remembered, while the multitudinous items from which they are derived fade into dimness and are forgotten.

Like every other visitor, I was first impressed by the great building which spanned over the whole, having ample room in its vast areas for at once the productions of a world and the population of a great city. I was one of a hundred and eight thousand persons who at once stood under its roof; nor, save at a few points, was the pressure inconveniently great. And yet this greatest of buildings did not impress me as great. In one point at least, where the airy transept raises its transparent arch seventy feet over the floor, and the sunlight from above sported freely amid the foliage of the imprisoned trees and on the play of crystal fountains, it struck me as eminently beautiful; but the idea which it conveyed everywhere else was simply one of *largeness*,—not of greatness.

Two or three centuries ago, some lover of flowers and shrubs bethought him of shielding his more delicate plants from the severity of the climate by a small glass-frame, consisting of a few panes. In course of time, the idea embodied in the frame expanded into a moderate-sized hot-house, then into a green-house of considerably larger size, then into a tall palm-house; and, last of all, an ingenious gardener, bred among groves of exotics protected by huge erections of glass and iron, and familiar with the necessity of adding to the size of a case as the objects which it had to contain multiplied or were enlarged, bethought him of expanding the idea yet further into the Crystal Palace of the Exhibition. And such seems to be the history and lineage of perhaps the largest of all buildings: it is simply an expansion of the first glass-frame that covered the first few delicate flowers transplanted from a warmer to a colder climate; and, notwithstanding its imposing proportions, is as much a mere *case* as it was. And were its size to be doubled,—if, instead of containing two hundred miles of sash-bars and nine hundred thousand superficial feet of glass, it were stretched out so as to contain four hundred miles of bars and eighteen hundred thousand feet of glass,—it would be of course a larger building than it is, but not a greater.

Once fairly entered within the edifice, the objects first singled out by the eye were a few noble statues, such as the Greek Slave and the Amazon and Tiger; nor was it until these works of genius were scanned that the humbler works of mere talent and art succeeded in forcing themselves on the attention. And yet these last served to show much more definitely the actual stage of progress at which the nations that produced them had arrived, than the higher order of works. When genius is the artist, the goal is soon reached; whereas talent labours slowly. I found, however, that in works of genius, as certainly as of talent, what may be properly termed the civilized nations of the world march abreast of each other in nearly the same line,—not serially in file; and it is one of the advantages of the exhibition that it should teach this lesson. The United States of America, France, Austria, Northern Germany, Denmark, Italy and Sardinia, England and Scotland, are all labouring in nearly the same arts, artistic and mechanical, and producing nearly the same results. Their inhabitants are intellectually of like stature, and similarly trained,—a fact which national pride, schooled in the Exhibition, will now scarce venture to deny, and which, we are disposed to think, the English people will be much the better for knowing; seeing that to undervalue a competitor or opponent is one of the most certain ways possible to secure defeat, and to form a correct estimate of him one of the most effectual means of avoiding it.

It is now more than three thousand years since the patriach Job compared the short life of man to the swift and brief flight of a weaver's shuttle. Judging from what appears in the Exhibition, it seems not improbable that weavers' shuttles, and this simple art of painting by light without the aid of chemistry, may have been spread all over the world at the dispersal of mankind from before the great tower. And it seemed quite curious enough to reflect, that in this world's other great building the nations should have assembled for the first time, to show whether and to what extent they had been improving the talent, or whether, like a few of the barbarous tribes, they had not sunk into utter degradation, and buried it in the earth.

One of the next things that struck, in the general survey, was the tendency of all the merely ornamental ideas presented in the Exhibition to arrange themselves in the mind, irrespective of the dates of their production, into modern and ancient. In one sense, *new* and *true*, *old* and *false*, are evidently convertible terms. A false idea in art always becomes old; while a true idea lives on, and bears about it the freshness of youth. I was much struck, in the mediaeval department of the Exhibition,—a department which we owe to Puseyism,—by the large amount of the false in art which this superstititon has been the means of calling back from its grave. The Gothic architecture is true,—but the Gothic sculpture and the Gothic painting are both false; and Puseyism has, with the nonsense and false doctrine of the middle ages, been restoring both the false painting and the false sculpture. The grotesque figures gaudily stained into glass, or grimly fretted into stone, harmonized well with tall candles of bees' wax and cotton wick,—to light which is worship,—and with snug little cages of metal, into which priests put their god when they have made him out of a little dried batter. We are told that James VII strove hard to convert his somewhat unscrupulous favourite, the semi-infidel Sheffield, to Popery. "Your Majesty must excuse me," said the courtier: "I have at length come to believe that God made man which is something; but I cannot believe that man, to be quits with his Maker, turns round and discharges the obligation by making God." In such a display of human faculty as the Great Exhibition, the strangely expressed feeling of Sheffield must surely have come upon many a visitor of the mediaeval department.

Popery, however, had, I found, one grand advantage over Puseyism in its use of art. With Puseyism all was restoration from a barbarous age, that possessed only one true artistic idea, among many false ones; whereas Popery, on the other hand, had availed itself of art in all its stages; and so all its artistic ideas were the best and truest of their respective ages. When a Michael Angelo appeared, it forthwith adopted the sculpture of Michael Angelo; when a Raphael appeared, it forthwith adopted the paintings of a Raphael. Instead of perpetuating an obsolete fashion in its trinkets and jewels, it set its Benvenuto Cellini to model and set them anew; nay, in Italy, surrounded by noble fragments of the old classic architecture, it broke off its associations with the Gothic, and erected its fairest temples in the old Vitruvian symmetry, under the eyes of a Palladio.

This great difference between the two churches was most instructively shown in the portion of the Exhibition devoted to the display of stained glass. The English contributions, manufactured for the Puseyite market, abounded in ugly saints and idiotical virgins, flaming in tasteless combinations of gaudy colour; whereas in much of the stained glass contributed by the Popish countries of the Continent the style is exquisitely Raphaelesque.
October 15 1851

BUT perhaps Hugh Miller was at his most dazzling when he fused his expertise and his literary cunning to his powerful imagination to evoke the remote past. "Shoals of Caphalasides, *with their broad arrow-like head, and their slender angular bodies feathered with fins, sweep past like clouds of cross-bow bolts in an ancient battle" he writes in the* Old Red Sandstone, *conjuring up a picture of the Coal Measures near Edinburgh. "We see the distant gleam of scales, but the forms are indistinct and dim; we can merely ascertain that the fins are elevated by spines of various shape and pattern; that some of the coats glitter with enamel; and that others—the sharks of this ancient period—bristle over with minute thorny points. A huge crustacean of uncouth proportion stalks over the weedy bottom, or burrows in the hollows of the bank."*

It was a technique Miller used time after time, and which he developed in his later work (and especially in the lectures he gave to the Philosophical Institution in Edinburgh, which Lydia later published as The Sketchbook of Popular Geology). *In the last lecture in* The Sketchbook *he draws a picture of an even earlier period, "A solitary hell without suffering or sin" when there is little other than a ". . dark atmosphere of steam and vapour which for age after age conceals the face of the sun, and through which the light of the moon or star never penetrates; oceans of thermal water, heated in a thousand centres to the boiling point; low, half-molten islands, dim through the fog, and scarce more fixed than the waves themselves, that heave and tremble under the impulsions of the igneous agencies; roaring geysers that ever and anon throw up their intermittent jets of boiling fluid, vapour, and thick steam from these tremulous lands; and, in the dim outskirts of the scene, the red gleam of fire, shot forth from the yawning cracks and deep chasms, and that bears aloft fragments of molten rocks and clouds of ashes."*

In an earlier lecture it was the Oolite, he "called up", the time of the great reptiles. The scene is northeast Sutherland where it joins Caithness and, "The calm stillness of the air makes itself faintly audible in the drowsy hum of insects; there is a gorgeous light-poised dragon-fly darting hither and thither through the *minuter gnat-like groups: it settles for a moment on one of the lesser ferns, and a small insectivorous creature, scarcely larger than a rat, issues noiselessly from its hole, and creeps stealthily towards it. But there is the whirr of wings heard overhead, and lo! a monster descends and the little mammal starts back into its hole. 'Tis a winged dragon of the Oolite, a carnivorous reptile, keen of eye and sharp of tooth, and that to the head and jaws of the crocodile adds the neck of a bird, the tail of an ordinary mammal, and that floats through the air on leathern wings resembling those of the great vampire bat. We have seen, in the minute, rat-like creature, one of the two known mammals of this vast land of the Oolite,—the insect-eating*Ampitherium*; and in the flying reptile, one of its strangely-organized* Pterodactyls". *Miller goes on to describe the gargantuan herbivorous* Iguanadon *"with no desire to attack and no necessity to defend", the short bulky body and "swan-like neck" of the* Plesiosaurus, *and the immense eye of the* Ichthyosaurus *which the fish-lizard used to ". . examine microscopically, or to explore as a telescope!" A bizarre universe of "Reptiles, reptiles, reptiles,—flying, swimming, waddling, walking" a succession of marvels "strange beyond even the conceptions of the poet . . ."*

Miller's evocations of the geological past seem to have held his audience open-mouthed. And he returned to the device in his last book The Testimony of the Rocks *in which he explains the biblical metaphor of the* Mosaic Vision of Creation *where each of the seven days of creation "is made the representative of myriads". By the morning of the sixth day "Cattle and beasts of the field graze upon the plains; the thick-skinned rhinoceros wallows in the marshes; the squat hippopotamus rustles among the reeds, or plunges sullenly into the river; great herds of elephants seek their food among the young herbiage of the woods; while animals of a fiercer nature,—the lion, the leopard and the bear,—harbour in deep caves till evening, or lie in wait for their prey amid tangled thickets, or beneath some broken bank."*

One of the best of Miller's reconstructions of geological time is contained in his Second Lecture on Geology *where he describes how the familiar topography of Scotland changed through the age of the great glacier to historic times. It is a masterly run of words, Miller's descriptive powers and imagination at their best. Gigantic ice-bergs are floating over what is now Edinburgh, on a blue sunny day, and ". . . the light, polarised by a thousand cross-reflections, sports amid the planes and facets, the fissures and pinnacles, in all the rainbow gorgeousness of the prismatic hues" a tranquility which is replaced by "black tempest" when ". . . the grounded masses, moved by the violence of the aroused winds, grate heavily along the bottom; and while the whole heavens are foul with sleet and snow rack, and the driving masses clash in rude collision, till all beneath is one wide stunning roar . . .". As a piece of earth-science Miller's reconstruction is very dubious, as a piece of imaginative writing it is superb.*

Lectures on Geology: Lecture Second

LET US attempt calling up the features of our country in one continuous landscape, as they appeared at the commencement of the glacial period, just as the paroxysm of depression had come on, and bold headland and steep iron-bound islet had begun slowly to settle into the sea.

The general outline is that of Scotland, though harsher and more rugged than now, for it lacks the softening integument of the subsoil. Yonder are the Grampians, and yonder the Cheviots, and, deeply indenting the shores, yonder are the well-known estuaries and bays,—the firths of Forth, Tay, and Moray, and the long withdrawing lakes, of Loch Katrine, and Loch Awe, and Loch Maree, and the far-gleaming waters of the deep Caledonian Valley, the Ness, and the Oich, and the Lochy. But though the summer sun looks down upon the scene, the snow-line descends beneath the top of even our second-class mountains; and the tall beetling Ben Nevis, and graceful Ben Lomond, and the broad-based Ben Muich Dhui, glitter in the sunshine, in their coats of dazzling white, from their summits half-way down to their bases.

There are extended forests of the native fir on the lower plains, mingled with the slimmer forms of a more richly-tinted foliage of the spruce pine. On the upper grounds, thickets of stunted willows and straggling belts of diminutive birches skirt the ravines and water courses, and yellow mosses and grey lichens form the staple covering of the humbler hill-sides and the moors. But the distinctive feature of the country is its glaciers. Fed by the perpetual snows of the upper heights, the deeper valleys among the mountains have their rigid ice rivers, that in the narrower firths and lochs of the western and northern coasts shoot far out, mole-like, into the tide. And, lo! along the shores, in sounds and bays never yet ploughed by the keel of voyager, vast groups of ice-bergs, that gleam white to the sun like the sails of distant fleets, lie moveless in the calm, or drift slowly along in rippling tideways.

Nor is the land without its inhabitants, though man has not yet appeared. The colossal elephant, not naked and dingy of coat like his congener of the tropics, but shaggy, with long red hair, browses among the woods. There is a strong-limbed rhinoceros wallowing in yonder swamp, and a herd of reindeer cropping the moss high on the hillside beyond. The moose is basking on that half-tide skerry; and a wolf, swept seawards by the current, howls loud in terror from yonder drifting ice-floe. We have looked abroad on our future country in the period of the first local glaciers, ere the submergence of the land.

Ages pass, and usher in the succeeding period of the boulder-clay. The prospect, no longer that of a continuous land, presents us with a wintry archipelago of islands, broken into three groups by two deep ocean-sounds,—the ocean sound of the Great Caledonian Valley, and that of the broader but shallower valley which stretches across the island from the Clyde to the Forth. We stand full in front of one of these vast ocean rivers,—the southern one. There are snow-enwrapped islets on either side. Can yonder thickly-set cluster be the half-submerged Pentlands? and yonder pair of islets, connected by a low flat neck, the eastern and western Lomonds? and yonder half-tide rock, blackened with algae, and around which a shoal of porpoises are gambolling, the summit of Arthur Seat? The wide sound, now a rich agricultural valley, is here studded by its fleets of tall ice-bergs,—there cumbered by its level fields of drift ice.

Nature sports wantonly amid every variety of form; and the motion of the great floating masses, cast into shapes with which we associate moveless solidity, adds to the magical effect of the scene. Here a flat-roofed temple, surrounded by colonnades of hoar and wasted columns, comes drifting past; there a cathedral, furnished with towers and spire, strikes heavily against the rocky bottom, many fathoms beneath, and its nodding pinnacles stoop at every blow. Yonder, already fast aground, there rests a ponderous castle, with its curtained towers, its arched gateway, and its multitudinous turrets, reflected on the calm surface beneath; and pyramids and obelisks, buttressed ramparts, and embrasured watch towers, with shapes still more fantastic,—those of ships, and trees, and brute and human forms,—crowd the retiring vista beyond.

There is a scarce less marked variety of colour. The intense white of the field-ice, thinly covered with snow, and glittering without shade in the declining sun, dazzles the eye. The taller ice-bergs gleam in hues of more softened radiance,—here of an emerald green, there of a sapphire blue, yonder of a paly marble grey; the light, polarized by a thousand cross reflections, sports amid the planes and facets, the fissures and pinnacles, in all the rainbow gorgeousness of the prismatic hues. And bright over all rise on the distant horizon the detached mountain-tops, now catching a flush of crimson and gold from the setting luminary.

But the sun sinks, and the clouds gather, and the night comes on black with tempest; and the grounded masses, moved by the violence of the aroused winds, grate heavily along the bottom; and while the whole heavens are foul with sleet and snow-rack, and the driving masses clash in rude collision, till all beneath is one wide stunning roar, the tortured sea boils and dashes around them, turbid with the comminuted débris of the fretted rocks below.

The vision belongs to an early age of the boulder-clay: it changes to a later time; and the same sea spreads out as before, laden by what seem the same drifting ice-floes. But the lower hills, buried in the profound depths of ocean, are no longer visible; the Lammermuirs have disappeared, and the slopes of Braid and Duddingston, and we can only determine their place by the huger icebergs that lie stranded and motionless on their peaks; while the lesser masses drift on to the east. Moons wax and wane, and tides rise and fall; and still the deep current of the gulf-stream flows ever from the west, traversing the wide Atlantic, like some vast river winding through an enormous extent of meadow; and, in eddying over the submerged land, it arranges behind the buried eminences, in its own easterly line, many a long trail of gravel and débris, to form the Crag and Tail phenomenon of future geologists.

As we extend our view, we may mark, far in the west, where the arctic current, dotted white with its ice-mountains and floes, impinges on the gulf stream; and where, sinking from its chill density to a lower stratum of sea, it gives up its burden to the lighter and more tepid tide. A thick fog hangs over the junction, where the warmer waters of the west and south encounter the chill icy air of the north; and steaming forth into the bleak atmosphere like a seething caldron, the cloud, when the west wind blows, fills with its thick grey reek the recesses of the half-foundered land, and obscures the prospect.

Anon there is another change in the dream. The long period of submergence is past; the country is again rising; and, under a climate still ungenial and severe, the glaciers lengthen out seawards, as the land broadens and extends, till the northern and western Highlands seem manacled in ice. Even the lower hill-tops exhibit an alpine vegetation, beautiful, though somewhat meagre; while in the firths and bays, the remote ancestors of many of our existing shells that thrive in the higher latitudes, still mix, as at an earlier period, with shells whose living representatives are now to be sought on the coast of northern Scandinavia and Greenland.

Ages pass; the land rises slowly over the deep, terrace above terace; the thermal line moves gradually to the north; the line of perpetual snow ascends beyond the mountain summits; the temperature increases; the ice disappears; the semi-arctic plants creep up the hill-sides to be supplanted on the plains by the leafy denizens of happier climates; and at length, under skies such as now look down upon us, and on nearly the existing breadth of land, the human period begins. The half-naked hunter, armed with his hatchet or lance of stone, pursues the roe or the wild ox through woods, that, though comparatively but of yesterday, already present appearances of a hoary antiquity; or, when the winter snows gather around his dwelling, does battle at its beleaguered door threshold with the hungry wolf or the bear.

The last great geologic change takes place; the coast line is suddenly elevated; and the country presents a new front to the sea. And on the widened platform, when yet other ages have come and gone, the historic period commences, and the light of a classical literature falls for the first time on the incidents of Scottish story, and on the bold features of Scottish character.

It is said that modern science is adverse to the exercise and development of the imaginative faculty. But is it really so? Are visions such as those in which we have been indulging less richly charged with that poetic pabulum on which fancy feeds and grows strong, than those ancient tales of enchantment and *faery* which beguiled of old, in solitary homesteads, the long winter nights. Because science flourishes, must poesy decline? The complaint serves but to betray the weakness of the class who urge it. True, in an age like the present,—considerably more scientific than poetical,—science substitutes for the smaller poetry of fiction, the great poetry of truth; and as there is a more general interest felt in new revelations of what God has wrought, than in exhibitions of what the humbler order of poets have half-borrowed, half-invented, the disappointed dreamers complain that the 'material laws' of science have pushed them from their place. As well might the Arab who prided himself upon the beauty of some white tent which he had reared in some green oasis of the desert, complain of the dull tools of Belzoni's labourers, when engaged in clearing from the sands the front of some august temple of the ancient time. It is not the tools, it might be well said to the complainer, that are competing with your neat little tent; it is the sublime edifice, hitherto covered up, which the tools are laying bare.

Nor is it the material laws, we may, on the same principle, say to the poets of the querulous cast, that are overbearing your little inventions and making them seem small; but those sublime works and wonderful actings of the Creator which they unveil, and bring into comparison with yours. But from His works, and His actings have the masters of the lyre ever derived their choicest materials; and whenever a truly great poet arises,—one that will add a profound intellect to a powerful imagination,—he will find science not his enemy but an obsequious caterer and a devoted friend. He will find sermons in stones, and more of the suggestive and the sublime in a few broken scaurs of clay, a few fragmentary shells, and a few green reaches of the old coast line, than versifiers of the ordinary calibre in their once fresh gems and flowers,—in sublime ocean, the broad earth, or the blue firmament and all its stars.

MILLER'S short essays on The Cuttle Fish, *the* Caves of Cromarty *and the* Recent Types of Fossils *are fragments, sketches from a collection to which he gave only a working title* (Tours Through the Northern Counties of Scotland) *but which he planned to craft into his* maximum opus *on* The Geology of Scotland. *The work, of course, was never finished, but the sketches give an insight into the way Miller worked, the value he placed on using his eyes, and his ability to convert chance happenings (like the arrival of a cuttlefish at his feet one morning) into work that was interesting, informative, and often very beautiful. Miller's description of the cuttle-fish inspired Sir David Brewster to send him an account of his own work on the optics of the cuttle-fish eye. It was a brief mathematical explanation (Brewster was the man who invented stereoscopic photographic viewers) but he ended on the Millerian note: "When the lenses (of the cuttle-fish eye) become indurated, they often exhibit the most beautiful internal reflections, and I have often thought of having them set as brooches."*

Cuttle-fish

THE day was extremely calm; I heard a peculiar sound,—a *squelch*, if I may employ such a word; and *there*, a few yards away, was a loligo (cuttle fish) nearly two feet in length, high and dry upon the pebbles. I laid hold of it by the sheath or sack; and the loligo, in turn, laid hold of the pebbles, just as I have seen a boy, when borne off against his will by a stronger than himself, grasping fast to projecting door-posts and furniture. The pebbles were hard, smooth, and heavy, but the creature raised them with ease, by twining its flexible arms around them, and then forming a vacuum in each of its suckers.

I subjected one of my hands to its grasp, and it seized fast hold; but though the suckers were still employed, it employed them on a different principle. Around the circular rim of each there is a fringe of minute thorns, hooked somewhat like those of the wild rose. In fastening on the hard smooth pebbles, these were overtopped by a fleshy membrane, much in the manner that the cushions of a cat's paw overtop its claws, when the animal is in a state of tranquillity; and, by means of the projecting membrane, the hollow inside was rendered air-tight and the vacuum completed; but in dealing with the hand, a soft substance, the thorns were laid bare, like the claws of the cat when stretched out in anger, and at least a thousand minute prickles were fixed in the skin at once. They failed to penetrate it, for they were short, and individually not strong, but acting together and by hundreds, they took at least a very firm hold.

What follows the reader may deem barbarous; but the men who gulp down at a sitting half a hundred live oysters to gratify their taste will surely forgive me the destruction of a single mollusc to gratify my curiosity. I cut open the sack of the creature with a sharp penknife, and laid bare the viscera. What a sight for Harvey when prosecuting, in the earlier stages, his grand discovery of the circulation! *There*, in the centre, was the *yellow* muscular heart propelling into the transparent tubular arteries the *yellow* blood. Beat —beat—beat; I could see the whole as in a glass model; and all I lacked were the powers of vision nice enough to enable me to detect the fluid passing through the minuter arterial branches, and then returning by the veins to the two other hearts of the creature; for, strange to say, it is furnished with three. There is the yellow heart in the centre, and lying altogether detached from it, two other darker-coloured hearts at the sides!

I cut a little deeper. *There* was the gizzard-like stomach, filled with fragments of minute mussel and crab shells; and *there*, inserted in the spongy, conical, yellowish-coloured liver, and somewhat resembling in form a Florence flask, the ink-bag distended, with its deep dark *sepia*,—the identical pigment sold under that name in our colour shops, and so extensively used in landscape drawing by the limner. I once saw a pool of water within the chamber of a salmon-wear, darkened by this substance almost to the consistence of ink. Where the bottom was laid dry, some fifteen or twenty cuttle-fish lay dead, some of them green, some blue, some yellow; for it is one of the characteristics of the creature that, in passing into a state of decomposition, it assumes a succession of brilliant colours; but at one of the sides of the chamber, where there was a shallow pool, six or eight individuals, the sole survivors of the shoal, still retained their original pink tint, freckled with red, and went darting about in panic terror within their narrow confines, emitting ink at almost every dart, until the whole pool became a deep solution of *sepia*. But I digress.

I next laid open the huge eyes of the stranded cuttle-fish. They were curious organs,—more simple in their structure than those of any quadruped, or even any fish, with which I am acquainted, but well adapted, I doubt not, for the purpose of seeing. A camera-obscura may be described as consisting of two parts,—a lens in front, and a darkened chamber behind; but in both the brute and human eye we find a third part added: there is a lens in the middle, a darkened chamber behind, and a lighted chamber, or rather vestibule, in front. But this lighted vestibule—the cornea—is wanting in the eye of the cuttle-fish. The lens is placed in front, and the darkened chamber behind; the construction of the organ is that of a common camera-obscura, without aught additional. I found something worthy of remark, too, in the peculiar style in which the chamber is darkened. In the higher animals it may be described as a chamber hung with black velvet; the *pigmentum nigrum* which covers it is of the deepest black: but in the cuttle-fish it is a chamber hung with velvet, not of black, but of a dark purple hue; the *pigmentum negrum* is of a purplish-red colour. There is something curious in marking this, as it were first, departure from an invariable condition of eyes of the more perfect structure, and in them tracing the peculiarity downwards through almost every shade of colour, to the emerald-like eye-specks of the pecten, and the still more rudimental *red* eye-specks of the star-fish.

After examining the eyes, I next laid open, in all its lengths, from the neck to the point of the sack, the dorsal bone of the creature,—its internal shell I should rather say, for bone it has none. The form of the shell in this species is that of a feather equally developed in the web on both sides. It gives rigidity to the body, and furnishes the muscles with a fulcrum; and we find it composed, like all other shells, of a mixture of animal matter and carbonate of lime. In some of the genera it is much more complicated and rigid than in that to which the *strollach* belongs, consisting, instead of one, of numerous plates, and in form somewhat resembling a flat shallop with its cargo rising over the gunwale, or one of the valves of a pearl mussell occupied by the animal.

Is my description of this curious creature too lengthy? The young geologist who sets himself to study the fossils of the Oolitic and Cretaceous systems would be all the better for knowing a great deal more regarding it than I have told him here. He will discover that at least one-half the molluscous remains of these deposits, their belemnites, amonites, nautili, nummulites, baculites, hamites, lituites, turrilites, and scaphites, belonged to the great natural class— singularly rich in its extinct orders and genera, though comparatively poor in its existing ones—which we find represented by the cuttle-fish.

Caves of Cromarty, or the Art of Seeing Over the Art of Theorizing.

WE swept downwards through the noble opening of the Cromarty Firth, and landed under the southern Sutor, on a piece of rocky beach, overhung by a gloomy semicircular range of precipices. The terminal points of the range stand so far out into the sea, as to render inaccessible, save by boat, or at the fall of ebb in stream tides, the piece of crescent-shaped beach within. Each of the two promontories is occupied by a cave in which the sea at flood stands ten or twelve feet over the gravel bottom, and there are three other caves in the semi-circle, into which the tide has not entered since it fell back from the old coast line. The larger and deeper of the three caves in the semicircular inflection is mainly that which we had landed to explore.

It runs a hundred and fifty feet into the granitic rock, in the line of a fault that seems first to have opened some eight or ten feet, and then, leaning back, to have closed its sides atop, forming in this way a long angular hollow. It has borne for centuries the name of the *Doocot* (i.e. Dove-cot) *Cave*, and has been from time immemorial a haunt of pigeons. We approach the opening: there is a rank vegetation springing up in front, where the precipice beetles over, and a small stream comes pattering in detached drops like those of a thunder-shower; and we see luxuriating under it, in vast abundance, the hot, bitter, fleshy-leaved scurvy-grass, of which Cook made such large use, in his voyages, as an anti-scorbutic.

The floor is damp and mouldy; the green ropy sides, which rise some five-and-twenty feet ere they close, are thickly furrowed by ridges of stalactites, that become purer and whiter as we retire from the light and the vegetative influences, and present in the deeper recesses of the cave, the hue of statuary marble. The last vegetable that appears is a minute delicate moss, about half an inch in length, which slants outwards to the light on the prominences of the sides, and overlies myriads of similar sprigs of moss, long since converted into stone, but which, faithful in death to the ruling law of their lives, still point, like the others, to the free air and sunshine. A few steps further, and evening has deepened into twilight. We still advance; and twilight gives place to a gloom dusky as that of midnight. We grope on, till the rock closes before us; and, turning round, see the blue waves of the firth through the long, dark vista, as if we viewed them through the tube of some immense telescope.

We strike a light. The roof and sides are crusted with white stalactites, that depend from the one like icicles from the eaves of a roof in a severe frost, and stand out from the other in pure, semi-transparent ridges, that resemble the folds of a piece of white drapery dropped from the roof; while the floor below has its rough pavement of stalagmite, that stands up, wherever the drops descend, in rounded prominences, like the bases of columns. Here, however, is a puzzle to exercise our ingenuity. Some of the minuter stalactites of the roof, after descending perpendicularly, or at least nearly so, for a few inches, turn up again, and form a hook, to which one may suspend one's watch by the ring; while there are others that form a loop, attached to the roof at both ends. Pray, how could the descending drop have returned upwards to form the hook, or what attractive power could have drawn the two drops together, to compose the elliptical curve of the loop? The problem is not quite a simple one. It is sufficiently hard at least, as it has to deal with only half-ounces of rock, to inculcate caution on the theorists who profess to deal with whole continents of similar material.

Let us examine somewhat narrowly. Dark as the recess is, and though vegetation fails fully fifty feet nearer the entrance than where we now stand, the place is not without its inhabitants. We see among the dewy damps of the roof the glistening threads of some minute spider, stretching in lines or descending in loops. And just look here. Along this loop there runs a single drop. Observe how it descends, with but a slight inclination, for about two inches or so, and then turns round for about three quarters of an inch more; observe further, that along this other loop there trickle two drops, one on each side; that, as a consequence of the balance which they form the one against the other, their descent has a much greater sweep; and that, uniting in the centre, they fall together. We have found the solution of our riddle, and received one proof more of the superiority of the simple art of seeing over the ingenious art of theorizing.

Recent Types of Fossils

AN imagination curious to re-erect and restore finds assistance of no uninteresting kind among the pools and beneath the bunches of sea-weed which we find scattered, at the fall of the tide, over the surface of the Navidale deposits. One very minute pool of seawater, scarcely thrice the size of a common washing basin, and scarcely half a foot in depth, furnished me with recent types of well-nigh all the fossils that lay embedded for several feet arund it; though there were few places in the bed where these lay more thickly.

Three beautiful sea anemones,—two of crimson, and the third of a greenish-buff colour,—stretched out their sentient petals along the sides; and the minute currents around them showed that they were all employed in their proper trade of winnowing the water for its animalcular contents, working that they might live. One of the three had fixed its crimson base on the white surface of a fossil corral; the pentagonal cavities, out of reach of which a creature of resembling form had once stretched its slim body and still minuter petals, to agitate the water with similar currents, were lying open around it.

In another corner of the pool a sea-urchin was slowly dragging himself up the slope, with all his red fleshy hawsers that could be brought to bear, and all his nearer handspokes hard strained in the work. His progress resembled that of the famous Russian boulder, transported for so many miles to make a pedestal for the statue of Peter the Great; with this difference, however, that here it was the boulder itself that was plying the handspokes and tightening the ropes. And lo! from the plane over which he moved there projected the remains of creatures of similar type;—the rock was strewed with fossil handspokes, greater in bulk than his, and somewhat diverse in form, but whose general identity of character it was impossible to mistake. The spines of echini, fretted with lines of projections somewhat in the style of the pinnacles of a Gothic building, lie as thickly in this deposit as in any deposit of the Chalk itself. The pool had its zoophytes of the arborescent form,—the rock its flustra; the pool had its cluster of minute muscles,—the rock its scallops and ostrea; the pool had its buccinidae,—the rock its numerous whorls scallops and ostrea; of some nameless turreted shell; the pool had its cluster of serpulae,—the serpulae lay so thick in the rock, as to compose, in some layers, no inconsiderable proportion of its substance.

IT WAS not until 1845, when he was 43 years old and approaching the height of his powers, that Hugh Miller set foot over the border into England. Semiexhausted by the twice-weekly grind of The Witness, *and still plagued by the silicosis in his lungs, Miller set off on an eight-week sojourn among the English in a depressing wet autumn, "ungenial and lowering" which was marked with "fields deeply tinged with brown" and "large tracts of diseased potatoes". But the result was a book (published in 1847) called* First Impressions of England and its People *a subdued, low-key account of the landscape, geology, agriculture, industries and cities of England, and the political, religious, and social mores of the English.*

Although Miller's wanderings in England took in Stratford and London, his passionate curiosity about the geology of England (and about the haunts of his favourite poets Shenstone and Cowper) took Miller well off the beaten track. After Newcastle, Manchester and York, he spent some of his time in the distinctly unglamorous surroundings of the West Midlands, in towns like Wolverhampton, Dudley, Stourbridge, and Hales Owen. In the course of describing (in considerable detail) the New Red Sandstone, the Coal Measures and the salt deposits and limestone of the West Midlands, Miller produces, almost incidentally, some handsome Victorian cameos; the nail-making girls of Hales Owen, the limestone quarriers of Aymestry, inn landladies and their families, Dudley coal miners, and simply the variety of English he met on the road, in country pubs, on coaches, or on the 'penny-a-mile' trains.

First Impressions, *like most of Miller's work, is closely observed, solid, and laced with descriptive passages of real beauty. He describes a late-night coach ride from Stourbridge to Hales Owen: "The Hales Owen road runs for the greater part of the way within the southern edge of the Dudley coal field, and, lying high, commands a downward view of its multitudinous workings for many miles. It presented from the coach-top this evening, a greatly more magnificent prospect than by day. The dark space—a nether firmament, for its gray wasteful desolation had disappeared with the vanished daylight—was spangled bright by innumerable furnaces, twinkling and star-like in the distance, but flaring like comets in the foreground. We could hear the roaring of the nearer fires; here a tall chimney or massy engine peered doubtfully out, in dusky umber from amid the blackness; while the heavens above glowed in the reflected light, a blood red."*

Inevitably perhaps, all the way through First Impressions, *Miller compares the English to the Scots, and has many a sour word to say about his compatriots. While contending that the Scots are, on average, sharper and more intellectually-curious than the English, he decides they lack the Englishman's solid independence, and simple moral courage. And while endowed with physical nerve (and even recklessness) he finds the Scots painfully lacking in the political will to defend their own interests. They are "calculating, cautious, timid. The man ready in one sort of quarrel to lay down his life, is not at all prepared in another to sacrifice his livelihood." Where an Englishman ". . would peril his livelihood any day in behalf of a stile that had existed in the time of his grandfather" the country-living Scots ". . in those rural districts in which land is of most value find themselves shut out of their country."*

On his way back to the north, Miller found Birmingham in the throes of its annual fair. "There were double rows of booths along the streets, a full half-mile in length,—ginger-bread booths, and carraway and barley-sugar booths, and nut and apple booths, and booths rich in halfpenny dolls and penny trumpets, and booths not particularly rich in anything, that seemed to have been run up on speculation. There were shows too, of every possible variety of attraction—shows of fat boys, and large ladies, and little men and great serpents, and wise poneys; and shows of British disaster in India, and of British successes in China; mad-cap minded merry-andrews, who lived on their wits, nor wished for more; agile tumblers, glittering in tinsel; swings, revolvers and roundabouts; and an old, original Punch in all his glory. But what formed by far the best part of the exhibitions were the round, ruddy, unthinking faces of the country-bred English, that had poured into the town to stare, wonder, purchase and be happy."

First Impressions of England and Its People

THE town of Dudley has been built half on the Silurian deposit, half
on the coal-field, and is flanked on the one side by pleasant fields,
traversed by quiet green lanes, and on the other by ruinous coal-
workings and heaps of rubbish. But as the townspeople are not "lie-
wasters", we find, in at least the neighbourhood of the houses, the
rubbish-heaps intersected with innumerable rude fences, and
covered by a rank vegetation. The mechanics of the place have
cultivated without levelling them, so that for acres together they
present the phenomenon of a cockling sea of gardens,—a rural Bay
of Biscay agitated by the ground swell—with rows of cabbages and
beds of carrots riding on the tops of huge waves, and gooseberry and
currant bushes sheltering in deep troughs and hollows. I marked, as
I passed through the streets, several significant traits of the mining
town: one of the signboards, bearing the figure of a brawny, half-
naked man, armed with a short pick, and coiled up like an Andrea
Ferrara broadsword in a peck basket, indicates the inn of the "Jolly
Miner"; the hardware shops exhibit in their windows rows of Davy's
safety-lamps, and vast piles of mining tools; and the footways show
their sprinkling of rugged-looking men, attired in short jackets and
trousers of undyed plaiding, sorely besmutted by the soil of an
underground occupation. In some instances, the lamp still sticking in
the cap, and the dazzled expression of countenance, as if the eye had
not yet accommodated itself to the light, indicate the close proximity
of the subterranean workings.

I dropped into a respectable-looking tavern to order a chop and a
glass of ale, and mark, meanwhile, whether it was such a place as I
might convert into a home for a few days with any reasonable
prospect of comfort. But I found it by much too favourite a resort of
the miners, and that, whether they agreed or disputed, they were a
noisy generation over their ale. The landlady, a kindly, portly dame,
considerably turned of fifty, was a Scotchwoman, a native of Airdrie,
who had long ago married an Englishman in her own country, and
had now been settled in Dudley for more than thirty years. My
northern accent seemed to bespeak her favour; and taking it for
granted that I had come into England in quest of employment, but

had not yet been successful in procuring any, she began to speak comfort to my dejection, by assuring me that *our* countryfolk in that part of the world were much respected, and rose always, if they had but character, into places of trust. I had borne with me, on my homely suit of russet, palpable marks of my labours at Sedgely and the Wren's Nest, and looked, I daresay, rather geological than genteel. Character and scholarship, said the landlady, drawing her inference, were just everything in that neighbourhood. Most of the Scotch people who came the way, however poor, had both: and so, while the Irish always remained drudges, and were regarded with great jealousy by the labouring English, the Scotch became overseers and book-keepers, sometimes even partners in lucrative works, and were usually well liked and looked up to. I could fain have taken up my abode at the friendly Scotchwoman's; but the miners in a neighbouring apartment were becoming every moment more noisy; and when they began to strike the table with their fists till the glasses danced and rung, I got up, and, taking leave of my countrywoman, sallied into the street.

After sauntering about the town for half an hour, I found in one of the lanes a small temperance coffee-house, with an air of quiet sobriety about it that at once recommended it to my favour. Finding that most of the customers of the place went into the kitchen to luxuriate over their coffee in front of the fire, I too went into the kitchen, and took my seat in a long wooden settle, with tall upright back and arms, that stretched along the side of the apartment, on the clean red tiles. The English are by much a franker people than the Scotch—less curious to know who the stranger may be who addresses them, and more ready to tell what they themselves are, and what they are doing and thinking; and I soon found I could get as much conversation as I wished. The landlady's youngest son, a smart little fellow in his ninth year, was, I discovered, a stern tee-totaller. He had been shortly before at a temperance meeting, and had been set up to make a speech, in which he had acquitted himself to the admiration of all. He had been a tee-totaller for about nine years, he said, and his father was a tee-totaller too, and his mother, and brothers and sisters, were all tee-totallers; and he knew men, he added, who, before taking the pledge, had worn ragged clothes and shoes without soles, who, on becoming tee-totallers, had improved into gentlemen.

He was now engaged in making a second speech, which was, however, like a good many other second speeches produced in such circumstances, very much an echo of the first; and every one who dropped in this evening, whether to visit the landlady and her daughters, or to drink coffee, was sure to question little Samuel regarding the progress of his speech. To some of the querists Samuel replied with great deference and respect; to some with no deference or respect at all. Condition or appearance seemed to exert as little influence over the mind of the magnanimous speech-maker as over that of the eccentric clergyman in Mr Fitzadam's *World*, who paid to robust health the honour so usually paid to rank and title, and looked down as contemptuously on a broken constitution as most other people do on dilapidated means. But Samuel had quite a different standard of excellence from that of the eccentric clergyman. He had, I found, no respect save for pledged tee-totalism; and no words to bestow on drinkers of strong drink, however moderate in their potations. All mankind consisted, with Samuel, of but two classes—drunkards and tee-totallers. Two young ladies—daughters of the supervisor of the district—came in and asked him how he was getting on with his speech; but Samuel deigned them no reply. "You were rude to the young ladies, Samuel," said his mother when they had quitted the room; "why did you not give them an answer to their question?" "They drink," replied the laconic Samuel. "Drink!" exclaimed his mother—"Drink!—the young ladies." "Yes, drink," reiterated Samuel, "they have not taken the pledge."

I found a curious incident which had just occurred in the neighbourhood, forming the main topic of conversation—exactly such a story as Crabbe would have chosen for the basis of a descriptive poem. A leaden pipe had been stolen a few evenings before from one of the town's churches: it was a long, ponderous piece of metal; and the thieves, instead of carrying, had dragged it along, leaving behind them, as they went, a significant trail on grass and gravel, which had been traced on the morrow by the sexton to the house of an elderly couple, in what, for their condition, were deemed snug circumstances, and who, for full thirty years, had borne a fair character in the place. There lived with them two grown-up sons, and they also bore fair characters. A brief search, however, revealed part of the missing lead; a still further search laid open a vast mine of purloined moveables of every description. Every tile in the back court, every square yard in the garden, every board in the house-floor, covered its stolen article;—kitchen utensils and fire-irons, smiths' and miners' tools, sets of weights from the market-place, pieces of hardware goods from the shops, garden railings, sewerage grates, house-spouts—all sorts of things useful and useless to the purloiners—some of them missed but yesterday, some of them abstracted years before—were found heaped up together in this strange jay's nest.

Two-thirds of the people of Dudley had gone out to mark the progress of discovery; and as the police furrowed the garden, or trenched up the floor, there were few among the numerous spectators who were not able to detect in the mass some piece of their own property. I saw the seventh cart-load brought this evening to the police-office; and every fresh visitor to the coffee house carried with him the intelligence of further discoveries. The unhappy old man, who had become so sudden a bankrupt in reputation when no one had doubted his solvency, and the two sons whom he had trained so ill, had been sent off to Gloucester jail the evening before, to abide their trial at the ensuing assizes. I was reminded by the incident of an occurrence which took place some time in the last age, in a rural district in the far north. A parish smith had lived and died with an unsuspected character, and the population of half the country-side gathered to his funeral. There had been, however, a vast deal of petty pilfering in his time. Plough and harrow irons were continually disappearing from the fields and steadings of the farmers, his nearer neighbours. Not a piece of hen-mounting or trace-chain, not a cart-axle or wheel-rim was secure. But no one had ever thought of implicating the smith. Directly opposite his door there stood a wall of loose uncemented stones, against which a party of the farmers who had come to the burial were leaning until the corpse should be brought out. The coffin was already in the passage; the farmers were raising their shoulders from the wall to take their places beside it; in ten minutes more the smith would have been put under the ground with a fair character; when, lo! the frail masonry behind suddenly gave way; the clank of metal was heard to mingle with the dull rumble of the stones; and there, amid the rubbish, palpable as the coffin on the opposite side of the road, lay, in a scattered heap, the stolen implements so mysteriously abstracted from the farmers. The awe-struck men must have buried the poor smith with feelings which bore reference to both worlds, and which a poet such as Wordsworth would perhaps know how to describe.

My landlady's eldest son, a lad of nineteen, indulged a strong predeliction for music, which, shortly prior to the date of my visit, had received some encouragement in his appointment as organist in one of the town churches. At a considerable expense of patient ingenuity he had fitted up an old spinet, until it awoke into life, the identical instrument it had been a century before. He had succeeded too, in acquiring no imperfect mastery over it; and so, by a series of chances all very much out of the reach of calculation, I, who till now had never seen but dead spinets—rickety things of chopped wainscot lying in waste garrets from the days of the grandmothers and great-grandmothers of genteel families—was enabled to cultivate acquaintance with the capabilities of a resuscitated spinet, vocal, and all alive. It gave me the idea, when at its best, of a box full of Jew's harps, all twanging away at the full extent of their compass, and to the best of their ability. The spirit of the musician, however, made such amends for the defects of his instrument, that his evening performances, carried on when his labours for the day had closed, were exceedingly popular in the neighbourhood. The rude miner paused under the windows to listen; and groups of visitors, mostly young girls, came dropping in every night to enjoy the fresh melodies brought out of the old musty spinet.

With little Samuel, the speech-maker, I succeeded in forming a friendship of the superlative type; though, strange to relate, it must be to this day a profound mystery to Samuel whether his *fidus Achates,* the Scotchman, be a drinker of strong drink, or a tee-totaller. Alas for even tee-totalized human nature when placed in trying circumstances! Samuel and I had a good many cups of coffee together, and several glasses of *Sampson*, a palatable Dudley beverage, compounded of eggs, milk and spicery; and, as on these occasions a few well-directed coppers enabled him to drive hard bargains with his mother for his share of the tipple, he was content to convert on my behalf the all-important question of the pledge into a mootpoint of no particular concernment. I unfortunately left Dudley ere he had an opportunity presented him of delivering his second speech. But he entertained, he assured me, no fears for the result. It was well known in the place, he said, that he was to speak at the first temperance meeting; there were large expectations formed so the audience could not be otherwise than very numerous and attentive; and he was quite satisfied he had something worth while to give them. My friend Samuel bore a good deal of healthy precocity about him. It would be, of course, consummately absurd to found aught on a single instance; but it has been so often remarked that English children of the lively type develop into cleverness earlier than the Scotch, that the observation has, in all likelihood, some foundation in reality. I find too, from the experiments of Professor Forbes of Edinburgh, that the English lad in his sixteenth, seventeenth, and eighteenth years possesses more bodily strength than the Scot of the same years and standing, and that it is not until their nineteenth year that the young men of both countries meet on a footing of equality. And it seems not irrational to infer that the earlier development of body in the case of the embryo Englishman should be accompanied by a corresponding development of mind also—that his school exercises should be better than those of the contemporary Scot, and his amateur verse rather more charged with meaning, and more smoothly rounded. *(1847)*

BIBLIOGRAPHY

Works by Hugh Miller

Poems written in the Leisure Hours of a Journeyman Mason; Inverness, 1829.

Letters on the Herring Industry; Inverness Courier pamphlet, 1829.

Scenes and Legends of the North of Scotland; Edinburgh, 1835.

Letter from one of the Scotch People to the Right Honourable Brougham and Vaux; Edinburgh, 1839.

The Whiggism of the Old School; Edinburgh 1839.

Memoir of William Forsyth; London, 1839.

The Old Red Sandstone or, New Walks in an Old Field; Edinburgh, 1841.

First Impressions of England and its People; Edinburgh, 1847.

Footprints of the Creator or, the Asterolepsis of Stromness; London, 1849.

The Sites Bill and the Toleration Laws; Edinburgh, 1848.

Geology of the Bass Rock (in M'Crie's *History of the Bass Rock*); Edinburgh, 1848.

Thoughts on Education; Edinburgh, 1850.

My Schools and Schoolmasters or, the Story of My Education; Edinburgh, 1854.

The Fossiliferous Deposits of Scotland; Edinburgh, 1854.

Geology versus Astronomy or, the Conditions and the Periods; being a view of the Modifying Effects of Geological Discovery on the Old Astronomic Inferences respecting the Plurality of Inhabited Worlds; Glasgow, 1855.

The Testimony of the Rocks or, Geology in its bearing on the Two Theologies, Natural and Revealed; Edinburgh, 1857.

The Cruise of the Betsey or, a Summer Ramble among the Fossiliferous Deposits of the Highlands; with Rambles of a Geologist, or Ten Thousand Miles over the Fossiliferous Deposits of Scotland; Edinburgh, 1858.

Sketch Book of Popular Geology; Edinburgh, 1859.

Essays (reprinted from *The Witness*); Edited by Peter Baynes; Edinburgh, 1862.

Tales and Sketches; Edited by Lydia Miller; Edinburgh, 1863.

Edinburgh and Its Neighbourhood; Edited by Lydia Miller; Edinburgh, 1864.

Complete Works of Hugh Miller; Edinburgh and London, 1871-1876.

The Headship of Christ and the Rights of the Christian People; Edinburgh, 1889.

Biography and Criticism

Labour and Triumph; The life and times of Hugh Miller; T.N. Brown; London and Glasgow, 1859.

The Life and Writings of Hugh Miller; W. Bingham; New York, 1858.

The Life and Letters of Hugh Miller; Peter Bayne; Two vols; London, 1871.

Hugh Miller (in 'Famous Scots' series); W.K. Leask; Edinburgh and London, 1896.

The Centenary of Hugh Miller; Archibald Geikie et al; Glasgow 1902.

Hugh Miller, A Critical Study; W.M. Mackenzie; London, 1905.

Memories of Two Cities, Edinburgh and Aberdeen; David Masson; Edinburgh and London, 1911.

Hugh Miller The Cromarty Stonemason; Charles D. Waterston/ National Trust for Scotland; Edinburgh, 1966.

Rosie, George.
  Hugh Miller, outrage and order : a
biography and selected writings / by
George Rosie ; with an introduction by
Neal Ascherson. -- Edinburgh :
Mainstream Pub., [1981]
  236 p. : ill., ports. ; 23 cm.
  Bibliography: p. [235]-236.
  ISBN 0-906391-17-2

  1. Miller, Hugh, 1802-1856.
2. Geologists--Scotland--Biography.
3. Geology--Addresses, essays,
lectures. 4. Natural history--
Addresses, essays, lectures.
I. Miller, Hugh, 1802-1856.